Hands-On Full Stack Development with Go

Build full stack web applications with Go, React, Gin, and GopherJS

Mina Andrawos

BIRMINGHAM - MUMBAI

Hands-On Full Stack Development with Go

Commissioning Editor: Aaron Lazar
Acquisition Editor: Shahnish Khan
Content Development Editor: Zeeyan Pinheiro
Technical Editor: Sabaah Navlekar
Copy Editor: Safis Editing
Project Coordinator: Vaidehi Sawant
Proofreader: Safis Editing
Indexer: Tejal Daruwale Soni
Graphics: Alishon Mendonsa
Production Coordinator: Jyoti Chauhan

First published: March 2019

Production reference: 1260319

Published by Packt Publishing Ltd.
Livery Place
35 Livery Street
Birmingham
B3 2PB, UK.

ISBN 978-1-78913-075-1

www.packtpub.com

For Nabil, Mervat, Catherine, and Fady.
Thanks to all of my family for their amazing support and continuous encouragement.

– Mina Andrawos

`mapt.io`

Mapt is an online digital library that gives you full access to over 5,000 books and videos, as well as industry leading tools to help you plan your personal development and advance your career. For more information, please visit our website.

Why subscribe?

- Spend less time learning and more time coding with practical eBooks and Videos from over 4,000 industry professionals

- Improve your learning with Skill Plans built especially for you

- Get a free eBook or video every month

- Mapt is fully searchable

- Copy and paste, print, and bookmark content

Packt.com

Did you know that Packt offers eBook versions of every book published, with PDF and ePub files available? You can upgrade to the eBook version at `www.packt.com` and as a print book customer, you are entitled to a discount on the eBook copy. Get in touch with us at `customercare@packtpub.com` for more details.

At `www.packt.com`, you can also read a collection of free technical articles, sign up for a range of free newsletters, and receive exclusive discounts and offers on Packt books and eBooks.

Contributors

About the author

Mina Andrawos is an experienced engineer who has acquired deep experience in Go from using it personally and professionally. He regularly authors articles and tutorials about the language, and also shares Go's open source projects. He has written numerous Go applications with varying degrees of complexity. Other than Go, he has skills in Java, C#, Python, and C++. Besides software development, he has working experience of scrum mastering, sales engineering, and software product management.

About the reviewer

Pankaj Khairnar is a founder and CEO of Scalent Infotech Pvt. Ltd. (a Golang-specialized development company.) In his career of over 12 years, he has developed many highly scalable platforms for various domains such as digital advertising, the Internet of Things (IoT), and e-commerce. Pankaj always likes to explore and implement new cutting-edge technologies.

> *I would like to thank Anant Haral for helping by re-reviewing all the chapters and testing all the examples again.*

Packt is searching for authors like you

If you're interested in becoming an author for Packt, please visit `authors.packtpub.com` and apply today. We have worked with thousands of developers and tech professionals, just like you, to help them share their insight with the global tech community. You can make a general application, apply for a specific hot topic that we are recruiting an author for, or submit your own idea.

Table of Contents

Section 2: The Frontend

Preface

The Go programming language has been rapidly adopted by developers for building web applications. With its impressive performance and ease of development, Go enjoys the support of a wide variety of open source frameworks for building scalable and high-performance web services and applications. This book is a comprehensive guide that covers all aspects of full stack development with Go. As you progress through the book, you'll gradually build an online musical instrument store application from scratch.

This clearly written, example-rich book begins with a practical exposure to Go development, by covering Go's building blocks, as well as Go's powerful concurrency features. We'll then explore the popular React framework, and work on building the frontend of our application with it. From there, you will build RESTful Web APIs utilizing the Gin framework, which is a very powerful and popular Go framework for Web APIs. After that, we will dive deeper into important software backend concepts, such as connecting to the database using an **object-relational mapping (ORM)**, designing routes for your services, securing your services, and even charging credit cards using the popular Stripe API. We will also cover how to test and benchmark your applications efficiently in a production environment. In the concluding chapters, we will cover isomorphic development in pure Go by learning about GopherJS.

By the end of the book, you will be confident in taking on full stack web applications in Go.

Who this book is for

This book will appeal to developers who are planning to start building functional full stack web applications in Go. Basic knowledge of the Go language and JavaScript is expected. Some knowledge of HTML and CSS is also expected. The book targets web developers who are looking to move to the Go language.

What this book covers

Chapter 1, *Welcome to Full Stack Go*, provides an introduction to the topics covered in the book, as well as an overview of the architecture of the application that will be built throughout the book. This chapter also provides us with a glimpse of what to expect from the book.

Chapter 2, *Building Blocks of the Go Language,* introduces us to the building blocks of the Go language, and how to utilize them to build simple applications. It starts by covering Go's syntax for variables, conditional statements, loops, and functions. From there, it covers how to construct data structures in Go, and how to attach methods to them. It then concludes by focusing on learning how to write interfaces that can describe the behaviors of our program.

Chapter 3, *Go Concurrency,* covers the concurrency features of the Go language. It covers Go's concurrency primitives, such as goroutines, channels, and select statements, and then moves to cover some important concepts for productive concurrent software, such as locks, and wait groups.

Chapter 4, *Frontend with React.js,* covers the building blocks of the extremely popular React.js framework. It starts by taking a look at React components, which are the foundation for the React framework. From there, it covers props for passing data to components. And finally, it describes handling state and using developer tools.

Chapter 5, *Building a Frontend for GoMusic,* builds our GoMusic frontend with the knowledge gained from the previous chapter. It builds the React components needed for the GoMusic store, and makes use of React's developer tools to troubleshoot the frontend. The majority of the frontend code will be covered in this chapter.

Chapter 6, *RESTful Web APIs in Go with the Gin Framework,* introduces you to RESTful Web APIs and the Gin framework. It then goes ahead and dives into the key building blocks of Gin, and explains how to start writing Web APIs with it. It also covers how to do HTTP request routing and how to group HTTP request routes in Gin.

Chapter 7, *Advanced Web Go Applications with Gin and React,* discusses more advanced topics regarding the Gin web framework and our backend Web APIs. It covers important practical topics such as how to extend functionality by using middleware, how to achieve user authentication, how to attach logs, and how to add validations to our model bindings. It also covers the concept of ORMs, and how to connect our Web API backend to a MySQL database through a Go ORM. At the end, it will cover some of the remaining React code, then we will discuss how to connect the React app to our Go backend. The chapter also covers how to build and deploy a React application to production.

Chapter 8, *Testing and Benchmarking Your Web API,* discusses how to test and benchmark the Go application. It will help us to learn about the types and methods that can be used with the testing package to create unit tests that can be integrated with the code. It will then focus on learning how to benchmark our code to inspect its performance.

`Chapter 9`, *Introduction to Isomorphic Go with GopherJS*, covers GopherJS, which is a very popular open source project that helps to transpile Go's code into JavaScript, which in effect allows us to write frontend code in Go. If you are looking to write your frontend in Go instead of JavaScript, GopherJS is the way to do it. This chapter will discuss the basics of GopherJS, then cover some examples and use cases. We will also discuss how to combine GopherJS with React.js, by building a simple React application in GopherJS.

`Chapter 10`, *Where to Go from Here?* provides suggestions for where to continue the learning journey from here. It talks about cloud-native architectures, containers, and mobile app development using React Native.

To get the most out of this book

The best way to get the most benefit out of this book is to follow the chapters one by one. Try to practice the code examples along with the chapters. Most chapters contain a section that outlines the tools and software required for the code in the chapter to work. The code for each chapter will be available on GitHub.

Download the example code files

You can download the example code files for this book from your account at `www.packt.com`. If you purchased this book elsewhere, you can visit `www.packt.com/support` and register to have the files emailed directly to you.

You can download the code files by following these steps:

1. Log in or register at `www.packt.com`.
2. Select the **SUPPORT** tab.
3. Click on **Code Downloads & Errata**.
4. Enter the name of the book in the **Search** box and follow the onscreen instructions.

Once the file is downloaded, please make sure that you unzip or extract the folder using the latest version of:

- WinRAR/7-Zip for Windows
- Zipeg/iZip/UnRarX for Mac
- 7-Zip/PeaZip for Linux

The code bundle for the book is also hosted on GitHub at `https://github.com/PacktPublishing/Hands-On-Full-Stack-Development-with-Go`. In case there's an update to the code, it will be updated on the existing GitHub repository.

We also have other code bundles from our rich catalog of books and videos available at `https://github.com/PacktPublishing/`. Check them out!

Download the color images

We also provide a PDF file that has color images of the screenshots/diagrams used in this book. You can download it here: `https://www.packtpub.com/sites/default/files/downloads/9781789130751_ColorImages.pdf`.

Conventions used

There are a number of text conventions used throughout this book.

`CodeInText`: Indicates code words in text, database table names, folder names, filenames, file extensions, path names, dummy URLs, user input, and Twitter handles. Here is an example: "We'll also cover some concepts that are specific to Go, such as slice, `panic`, and `defer`."

A block of code is set as follows:

```
package mypackage
```

When we wish to draw your attention to a particular part of a code block, the relevant lines or items are set in bold:

```
type Student struct{
    Person
    studentId int
}

func (s Student) GetStudentID()int{
    return s.studentId
}
```

Any command-line input or output is written as follows:

```
go install
```

Bold: Indicates a new term, an important word, or words that you see onscreen. For example, words in menus or dialog boxes appear in the text like this. Here is an example: "This is called **type inference**, since you infer the variable type from the provided value."

 Warnings or important notes appear like this.

 Tips and tricks appear like this.

Get in touch

Feedback from our readers is always welcome.

General feedback: If you have questions about any aspect of this book, mention the book title in the subject of your message and email us at customercare@packtpub.com.

Errata: Although we have taken every care to ensure the accuracy of our content, mistakes do happen. If you have found a mistake in this book, we would be grateful if you would report this to us. Please visit www.packt.com/submit-errata, selecting your book, clicking on the Errata Submission Form link, and entering the details.

Piracy: If you come across any illegal copies of our works in any form on the Internet, we would be grateful if you would provide us with the location address or website name. Please contact us at copyright@packt.com with a link to the material.

If you are interested in becoming an author: If there is a topic that you have expertise in and you are interested in either writing or contributing to a book, please visit authors.packtpub.com.

Reviews

Please leave a review. Once you have read and used this book, why not leave a review on the site that you purchased it from? Potential readers can then see and use your unbiased opinion to make purchase decisions, we at Packt can understand what you think about our products, and our authors can see your feedback on their book. Thank you!

For more information about Packt, please visit packt.com.

Section 1: The Go Language

The objective of this section is to introduce the reader to the Go language. In this section of the book, the reader will gain practical knowledge of how to build effective software in Go.

This section consists of the following chapters:

Welcome to Full Stack Go 1

This book is the result of an effort to provide you, the reader, with a very practical and concise learning tool for building full stack web applications in Go. Learning how to build full stack web applications in a powerful language such as Go can be a very valuable skill, as it allows you to write fully functional and scalable applications on your own. Go is known in the industry for both its performance and relative ease of use. This ensures that your applications can sustain growing data loads and expanding users, without suffering from scalability issues too early.

Full stack developers are the main drivers behind software startups; this is because of their ability to build products both quickly and efficiently from scratch. They are also typically the key members or the **subject-matter experts** (**SMEs**) in large corporations, as they help architect software systems, from the user interface down to the backend code. Even as an individual developer, learning full stack web programming can help you build your product ideas quickly, over a weekend or two.

In this chapter, we will cover the following topics:

- What is full stack development?
- What will we build?
- The outline of this book

What is full stack development?

Before we take any further steps, we first need to answer a simple question; what does it really mean to be a full stack developer? A **full stack developer** can be defined as a software engineer who has the skill to work on both the frontend and the backend of an application.

The frontend of a web application is basically anything related to the user interface of the application. For web applications, the technologies that are needed to build the user interface are HTML, CSS, and JavaScript. In production environments, an application can support different types of frontends, depending on the device by which the user is viewing the web application. For example, a frontend on a mobile smartphone may need different rules to accommodate the limited screen size of the device, compared to a screen size of a large desktop monitor.

In order to make the application perform the tasks it is expected to do, the backend of a web application consists of all the software layers that need to communicate with the frontend of the application. The backend includes the database layers, the security layer, the user request-handling layer, all the API layers, and more. The backend of a web application can be written in any mature programming language. We will obviously be using Go as our backend language for this book.

What will we build?

Throughout this book, we will build a full stack web application from scratch. The application will be called GoMusic; it's a store for musical instruments written in React.js and Go. The following screenshot demonstrates how the main page will look:

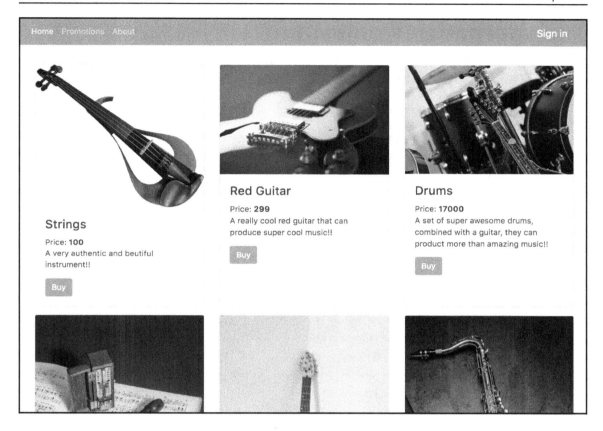

Users will be able to browse the musical instruments in the store, buy what they like with their credit cards, and log in to their accounts to see their existing orders.

Let's take a look at the architecture of the application that we are going to build in this book.

The application architecture

Our application architecture will be relatively straightforward—we will use the extremely popular React.js framework for our frontend code, and then we will use the powerful Gin framework for our backend code. Gin comes with a wide array of useful packages that we will be using to build our web application. We will also make use of the **Go object-relational mapping (GORM)** package, which is one of the most popular **object-relational mapping (ORM)** layers in the Go language:

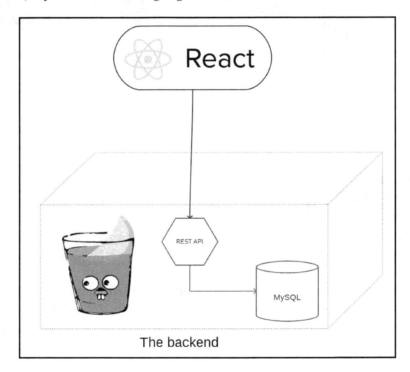

We'll build our application piece by piece, starting from the frontend, and then moving to the backend. We will cover some very important concepts in the world of modern web applications, such as reactive UIs, RESTful APIs, security, ORMs, credit card handling, testing, benchmarking, and more.

As we cover these different topics, we'll cover the majority of the code involved in building the application.

In the next section, we'll take a tour to discover the outline of this book, and what each chapter will cover.

The outline of this book

This book will cover numerous practical topics to help you acquire the deep skills necessary for a full stack developer:

- In Chapter 2, *Go's Building Blocks,* and Chapter 3, *Go Concurrency,* we will take a deep and a practical tour into the Go language. You will learn about some of the key features of the language, as well as some of its popular design patterns.
- In Chapter 4, *Frontend with React.js,* and Chapter 5, *Building a Frontend for GoMusic,* we will cover how to build beautiful and responsive frontend applications using the React.js framework. This is also where we'll start building our GoMusic web application. We will cover React's building blocks, design patterns, best practices, and more. The majority of the frontend code of the book project will be covered in Chapter 4, *Frontend with React.js,* and Chapter 5, *Building a Frontend for GoMusic;* however, we won't cover every single line of JavaScript code, so as not to lose focus. All the code will be available in the GitHub repository for this book.
- In Chapter 6, *RESTful Web APIs in Go with the Gin Framework,* and Chapter 7, *Advanced Web Go Applications with Gin and React,* we will start building our backend code using the Gin framework. We will cover RESTful APIs, ORMs, secure web connections, and more.
- In Chapter 8, *Testing and Benchmarking Your Web API,* we will learn how to test and benchmark our Go code using Go's testing package, and the best practices in the industry.
- In Chapter 9, *Introduction to Isomorphic Go with GopherJS,* we will go through a crash course in isomorphic Go programming. Isomorphic Go programming is the practice of using Go for both the frontend and the backend. This is possible through the GopherJS framework. Chapter 9, *Introduction to Isomorphic Go with GopherJS,* is a standalone chapter, as it doesn't attempt to rebuild the GoMusic app using Isomorphic Go. However, the chapter covers how to build a React application in Isomorphic Go.
- In Chapter 10, *Where to Go from Here?* we will touch some topics that the reader should pursue in order to expand their knowledge beyond the scope of this book.

Let's get started with the learning journey!

Building Blocks of the Go Language 2

Welcome to the first chapter of our journey, where we will learn about full stack development in Go. This chapter is dedicated to readers who are not yet familiar with Go. If you are already proficient in the Go language, you can skip this chapter. We'll cover the basic building blocks that form the foundation of the Go language, which will be covered in a brief but practical manner. Then, we'll show you the Go syntax for basic programming constructs like functions and loops. We'll also cover some concepts that are specific to Go like slice, `panic`, and `defer`. This chapter assumes that you have some familiarity with programming concepts in general (like variables, functions, loops, and conditional statements). This chapter also assumes that you have some familiarity with Terminals, and command lines, as well as the concept of environmental variables.

A very good resource to learn about the Go language from scratch can be found at `tour.golang.org`.

In this chapter, we'll cover the following topics:

- Basic concepts—packages, variables, data types, and pointers
- Functions and closures
- Conditional statements and loops
- `panic`, `recover`, and `defer`
- Go data structures
- Go interfaces

Technical requirements

To follow along with this chapter, you can do either of the following:

- Go to `play.golang.org`, which will allow you to run or test your code online
- Download the Go programming language, along with a compatible IDE

If you haven't downloaded Go yet, you can download the Go language by going to `https://golang.org/dl/`, downloading the Go flavor for your operating system, and then installing it.

For the local IDE, I prefer Visual Studio Code (`https://code.visualstudio.com`), along with its popular Go plugin (`https://code.visualstudio.com/docs/languages/go`).

Go's playground

The Go playground is a fairly popular website, which allows the Go community to test Go code samples online. The website can be found at `play.golang.org`. Whenever you would like to quickly test a simple piece of Go code, visit the website and run your code.

Setting up Go's workspace

For you to write Go code on your computer, you need to set up a Go workspace. A Go workspace is a folder where you will write your Go code. Setting up a Go workspace is relatively simple. Here is what you will need to do:

1. First, make sure that you have Go installed. As we mentioned earlier, you can download and install Go by going to `https://golang.org/dl/`.
2. After installing Go, create a new folder in your computer for Go's workspace. Mine is called `GoProjects`.
3. Inside your Go workspace folder, you will have to create three main folders: `src`, `pkg`, and `bin`. It is very important to create folders with these exact names inside your Go workspace folder. Here is why these three folders are important:
    - The `src` folder will host all of your code files. Whenever you decide to start a new program, you will simply go to the `src` folder and create a new folder with your new program name.
    - The `pkg` folder typically hosts the compiled package files of your code.
    - The `bin` folder typically hosts the binary files that are produced by your Go programs.

4. You will need to set two environmental variables:
   - The first environmental variable is called `GoRoot`, and will include the path to your Go install. `GoRoot` should typically be taken care of by the Go installer. However, if it's missing, or you would like to move your Go installation to a different place, then you need to set `GoRoot`.
   - The second environmental variable is called `GoPath`. `GoPath` includes the path to your Go workspace folder. By default, if not set, `GoPath` is assumed to either to be at `$HOME/go` on Unix systems or `%USERPROFILE%\go` on Windows. There is an entire GitHub page which covers setting up `GoPath` in different operating systems, which can be found at `https://github.com/golang/go/wiki/SettingGOPATH`.

Once your Go environment is set up, you can use the Go tool, which is installed alongside the Go language so that you can compile and run your Go programs.

We'll take a look at some of the basic building blocks of the Go language in the next section.

Packages, variables, data types, and pointers

Packages, variables, data types, and pointers represent the most basic building blocks of the Go language. In this section, we'll cover them one by one from a practical point of view.

Packages

Any Go program consists of one or more packages. Each package is basically a folder, which contains one or more Go files. Every single Go code file you write must belong to a package. Package folders are found inside the `src` folder of your Go workspace.

When you write Go code, you declare your package name at the very top of your Go file. Here is what this looks like in code:

```
package mypackage
```

Here, `mypackage` is the name of the package that my Go file belongs to. It's idiomatic in Go to have your package name in lower case letters. It is usually preferable to name your package folder the same as your package name. So, when you create a new package, simply create a new folder with your package name, and then create your package files inside that folder.

To import an external package and use it in your own package, you need to use the `import` keyword. For example, a popular package in Go's standard library is the `fmt` package, which allows you to write data to the standard output (that is, write to your console screen). Let's assume we want to use the `fmt` package from within our package. Here is what the code would look like:

```
package mypackage
  import "fmt"
```

Some package folders can exist inside folders of other packages. For example, the folder that contains the `rand` package in Go, which is used to generate random numbers, exists inside the folder that contains the `math` package in Go. To import a package like that, you need to use the following syntax:

```
import "math/rand"
```

Now, what if we would like to import multiple packages at once? It's easy—the syntax will end up looking like this:

```
import (
    "fmt"
    "math/rand"
)
```

Go does not allow you to import a package and then not use it to ensure that your code is clean and concise. However, there are some cases (which we'll cover later in this book) where you will want to load a package, but not use it directly. This can be accomplished by appending an underscore before the package name in the import statement. Here is what this would look like:

```
import (
  "database/sql"
  _ "github.com/go-sql-driver/mysql"
)
```

The most famous package name is `main`. Your main package is the first package that runs in your Go program.

To compile a Go program, you will need to navigate to the folder where your `main` package lives in the console, and then type the following command:

```
go install
```

This command will compile your Go program and then place the resulting binary in the `bin` folder of your workspace.

Alternatively, you can run the following command:

```
go build
```

This command will compile and then deploy the resulting binary in the current folder.

If you would like to specify an output path and a filename, you can run the following command:

```
go build -o ./output/myexecutable.exe
```

This will compile your code and then package it in an executable called `myexecutable.exe` at the specified output folder. If your operating system is not Windows, you can ignore the `exe` extension in the preceding example.

Variables and data types

A variable is another basic building block of the Go language. In Go, to declare a variable, you can simply use the `var` keyword. Here is what this looks like:

```
var s string
```

Obviously, `string` is the data type. Let's say we would like to declare more than one variable of type string on the same statement. Here is what this would look like:

```
var s1,s2,s3 string
```

To initialize a variable with an initial value, Go offers a number of options. One option is to initialize the variable while also specifying the variable type. Here is what this looks like:

```
var s1,s2,s3 string = "first-string", "second-string", "third-string"
```

Another option is to initialize the variables without specifying the data type. Here is what this would look like:

```
var s1,s2,s3 = "first-string", "second-string", "third-string"
```

We can then mix data types with the following syntax:

```
var s,i,f = "mystring",12,14.53
```

A popular way to declare and initialize multiple variables at once is as follows:

```
var (
  s = "mystring"
  i = 12
  f = 14.53
  )
```

If you are declaring and initializing your variable inside a function, you don't need to even use the `var` keyword. Instead, you can use `:=`. This is called **type inference**, since you infer the variable type from the provided value. Here is how we would declare and initialize the `s`, `i`, and `f` variables with type inference:

```
s := "mystring"

i := 12

f:=14.53
```

The `var` keyword, however, gives you more control since it allows you to explicitly specify the data type you would like to use for your variable.

Now, let's discuss data types. Go has a standard set of data types that are very similar to data types you'd find in any other statically typed programming language. Here is a summary of Go's standard data types:

Data type(s)	Description
`bool`	A Boolean (either true or false).
`string`	A `string` is a collection of `byte` and can hold any characters. Strings are read only (immutable), so whenever you need to add or remove characters from a string, you are in effect creating a new string.
`int, int8, int16, int32, and int64`	Signed integer types. They represent non-decimal numbers that can be either positive or negative. As you can probably tell from the type names, you can explicitly specify the number of bits that it can allow. If you go with the `int` type, it will pick the number of bits that correspond to your environment. For most modern CPU architectures, it will pick 64 bits, unless you are working with a smaller CPU or older environment. For smaller CPUs or older environments, the choice becomes 32 bits.
`uint, uint8, uint16, uint32, uint64, and uintptr`	Unsigned integer types. They represent non-decimal numbers, which can only be positive. Except for the signage, they are similar to their signed brethren. The `uintptr` type is an unsigned integer type that is large enough to hold a memory address.
`byte`	An alias for `uint8`, it holds 8 bits, which basically represents a byte of memory.
`rune`	An alias for `int32`, it is typically used to represent a Unicode character.

float32 and float64	Simply decimal numbers. For smaller decimal numbers, use the float32 type, as it only allows 32 bits of data. For larger decimal numbers, use the float64 type, as it only allows 64 bits of data.
complex64 and complex128	Complex numbers. Those data types are useful for programs where serious math is needed. The first type, complex64, is a complex number where the real part is a 32-bit float, and the imaginary part is a 32-bit float. The second type, complex128, is a complex number where the real part is a 64-bit float, while the imaginary part is a 64-bit float.

Variables that are declared without an explicit initial values get assigned what is known as **zero values**. Here is a table for zero values:

Type(s)	Zero value
Numeric types	0
Boolean types	false
String type	" "
Pointers	nil

Pointers

The concept of pointers is simple—a **pointer** is a language type that represents the memory locations of your values. Pointers in Go are used everywhere, and that's because they give the programmer a lot of power over the code. For example, having access to your value in memory allows you to change the original value from different parts of your code without the need to copy your value around.

In Go, to create a pointer, you just append * in front of the data type of your value. For example, here is a pointer to an int value:

```
var iptr *int
```

As we mentioned in the previous section, the zero value of a pointer is nil. The behavior of nil is similar to null in languages like Java, that is, if you try to use a nil pointer, an error will get thrown.

Now, let's assume we have a value of type int called x:

```
var x int = 5
```

We also want a pointer to point to the address of x for later use:

```
var xptr = &x
```

The & operand here means that we want the address of x. Whenever you append the & operand before a variable, it basically means that we want to the address of that variable.

What if we have a pointer, and we want to retrieve the value that it points to? This operation is called **de-referencing**, and here is how we can do it:

```
y := *xptr
```

In the preceding code, we de-referenced the pointer xptr to obtain the value that it points to, and then we stored a copy of the value in a new variable called y.

What if we want to change the value that the pointer points to? We can still use de-referencing for that, and here is what this would look like:

```
*xptr = 4
```

Perfect! With this, you should have enough knowledge to use Go pointers in your code.

If you already have experience in pointers from a different programming language like C or C++, you are probably familiar with the concept of pointer arithmetic. This is when you perform arithmetic operations (like addition or subtraction) on pointers to go to different memory addresses. By default, Go does not support pointer arithmetic on vanilla pointers like the ones we described in this section. However, there is a package called unsafe that allows you to do so. The unsafe package is only there to give you the power, should you need it. However, it is highly recommended that you don't use it unless you absolutely have to.

Now, let's explore functions and closures in Go.

Functions and closures

It's time to talk about functions and closures, so sit tight and enjoy the journey. Functions are considered one of the key building blocks in any programming language, as they allow you to define actions in your code.

Let's discuss the basics of functions.

Functions – the basics

Here is how you write a function in Go:

```
func main(){
//do something
}
```

The `main` function is almost always the first function that gets executed in your Go program. The `main` function needs to live inside the `main` package, since `main` is the entry point package for your Go program.

Here is what a function with arguments would look like:

```
func add(a int, b int){
//a+b
}
```

Since the `a` and `b` arguments from the preceding code are of the same type, we can also do this:

```
func add(a,b int){
//a+b
}
```

Now, let's say we want to return a value from our function. Here is what this would look like:

```
func add(a,b int)int{
return a+b
}
```

Go also allows multiple returns, so you can do this:

```
func addSubtract(a,b int)(int,int){
return a+b,a-b
}
```

In Go, there is a concept known as *named returns*, which basically means that you can name your return values in the function header. Here is what this looks like:

```
func addSubtract(a,b int)(add,sub int){
add = a+b
sub = a-b
return
}
```

Functions are also first-class citizens in the Go language, which means that you can assign a function to a variable and use it as a value. Here is an example:

```
var adder = func(a,b int)int{
return a+b
}
var subtractor = func(a,b int) int{
return a-b
}
var addResult = adder(3,2)
var subResult = subtractor(3,2)
```

Because of this, you can also pass functions as arguments to other functions:

```
func execute(op func(int,int)int, a,b int) int{
return op(a,b)
}
```

Here is an example of us making use of the `execute` function we defined previously:

```
var adder = func(a, b int) int {
    return a + b
}
execute(adder,3,2)
```

Go also supports the concept of variadic functions. A **variadic function** is a function that can take an unspecified number of arguments. Here is an example of an `adder` function that takes an unspecified number of `int` arguments and then adds them:

```
func infiniteAdder(inputs ...int) (sum int) {
  for _, v := range inputs {
    sum += v
  }
  return
}
```

The preceding function takes any number of `int` arguments and then sums them all. We'll cover the `for..range` syntax here later in this chapter, under the *Conditional statements and loops* section. We can then call our new function using the following syntax:

```
infiniteAdder(1,2,2,2) // 1 + 2 + 2 + 2
```

We'll look at how functions can be accessed from other packages in the next section.

Functions – accessing functions from other packages

Earlier in this chapter, we covered the concept of packages, and the fact that a Go program is composed of a number of connected packages. So, how do we really connect packages? We connect packages by having the ability to call functions and retrieve types from other packages. But then comes the question, how do we expose a function to other packages?

In Go, there are no `private` or `public` keywords like in most other statically typed programming languages. If you want your function to be `public`, all you need to do is start your function name with an upper case letter. In Go, that is known as making your function **exported**. If, on the other hand, your function starts with a lower case letter, then your function is considered **unexpected**.

To absorb the preceding two paragraphs, let's go through some code. Here is a package called `adder`, which contains a single function called `Add`:

```
package adder

func Add(a,b int)int {
  return a+b
}
```

Now, let's say we want to call `Add` from a different package. Here is what we'd do:

```
package main

//get the adder package
import "adder"

func main() {
  result := adder.Add(4, 3)
  //do something with result
}
```

In the preceding code, we called the exported function `Add` from our main package, at our `main` function. We did two things:

- Used the `import` keyword to load the `adder` package
- In the main function, we called `adder.Add(..)`

As demoed, to call an exported function, you need to use the following syntax:

```
<package name>.<exported function name>
```

If in the `adder` package we had named our function `add` instead of `Add`, the preceding code would not have worked. This is because when the function starts with a lower case letter it would be considered unexpected, which in effect means that it will be invisible to other packages.

Let's see a couple of examples from Go's standard package.

A very popular package from the Go standard packages is the `fmt` package. The `fmt` package can write to the standard output of your environment. It can also format strings and scan data from the standard input, among other things. Here is a simple but very commonly used code snippet:

```go
package main

import (
  "fmt"
)

func main() {
  fmt.Println("Hello Go world!!")
}
```

In the preceding code, we called a function called `Println`, which lives inside the `fmt` package. The `Println` function will take your string message and print it on the standard output. The output of the preceding program is as follows:

Hello Go world!!

Another popular package in the world of Go is `math/rand`, which we can use to generate random numbers. As we mentioned in the *Packages* section, earlier in this chapter, the reason why the package name is not just `rand` is simply because the `rand` package folder exists underneath the folder of the `math` package. So, even though `rand` is more of a sub-package, we just use the package name when we need to call exported functions that belong to it. Here is a simple example:

```go
package main

import (
  "fmt"
  "math/rand"
)

func main() {
  fmt.Println("Let's generate a random int", rand.Intn(10))
}
```

In the preceding code, we imported two packages—the `fmt` package and the `math/rand` package. We then invoked two functions from each of the packages. We first invoked the `Println` function, which belongs to the `fmt` package, to output a string to the standard output. Then, we invoked the `Intn` function, which belongs to the `math/rand` package, to generate a random number between zero and nine.

Now, let's take a look at what constitutes closures.

Closures

A function can also be a closure. A **closure** is a function value that's bound to variables outside its body. This means that a closure can access and change values on those variables. It is hard to understand closures without an example. Here is another flavor of the adder function, which returns a closure:

```
func adder() func(int) int {
    sum := 0
    return func(x int) int {
        sum += x
        return sum
    }
}
```

The closure in the preceding example has access to the `sum` variable, which means that it will remember the current value of the `sum` variable, and will also be able to change the value of the `sum` variable. Again, this is best explained with another example:

```
func adder() func(int) int {
    sum := 0
    return func(x int) int {
        sum += x
        return sum
    }
}

func main() {
    // when we call "adder()", it returns the closure
    sumClosure := adder() // the value of the sum variable is 0
    sumClosure(1) //now the value of the sum variable is 0+1 = 1
    sumClosure(2) //now the value of the sum variable is 1+2=3
    //Use the value received from the closure somehow
}
```

We have covered the basics of Go. In the following section, we'll move on and discuss Go data structures.

Go data structures

In this section, we'll discuss more key concepts of the Go language. It's time to explore the foundational data structures that we need to build non-trivial programs in the Go language.

In the following sections, we'll discuss the various Go data structures, including arrays, slices, maps, Go structs, and methods.

Arrays

An array is a common data structure that exists in any programming language. In Go, an array is a collection of values with the same data type, and a pre-defined size.

Here is how to declare an array in Go:

```
var myarray [3]int
```

The preceding array is of type `int` and of size 3.

We can then initialize the array like this:

```
myarray = [3]int{1,2,3}
```

Or, we can do this:

```
//As per the array declaration, it has only 3 items of type int

myarray[0] = 1 //value at index 0
myarray[1] = 2 //value at index 1
myarray[2] = 3 //value at index 2
```

Alternatively, similarly to other variables, we can declare and initialize the array on the same line, like this:

```
var myarray = [3]int{1,2,3}
```

Or, if we are declaring and initializing the array inside a function, we can use the `:=` notation:

```
myarray := [3]int{1,2,3}
```

Go provides a built-in function called `len()`, which returns the size/length of your array. For example, let's say we run the following code:

```
n := len(myarray)
fmt.Println(n)
```

The output will simply be 3, since the size of `myarray` is 3.

Go also allows you to capture subarrays of your main array. To do that, you need to follow the following syntax:

```
array[<index1>:<index2>+1]
```

For example, let's say I declare a new array that looks like this:

```
myarray := [5]int{1,2,3,4,5}
```

I can obtain a subarray from index two of my array till index three using the following syntax:

```
myarray[2:4]
```

The output of the preceding code will be as follows:

```
[3 4]
```

The two indexes that were passed to the preceding syntax were 2 to indicate that we would like to start from index two, and then 4 to indicate that we would like to stop at index four (*3+1=4*).

Inside the square brackets of the preceding syntax, you can also leave either side empty. Let's say you leave the left-hand side empty, like this:

```
myarray[:4]
```

This indicates that you want a subarray from index zero until index three.

However, let's say you leave the right-hand side empty, like this:

```
myarray[2:]
```

This indicates that the subarray will start from index two until the end of your original array.

Let's say you do something like this:

```
mySubArray := myarray[2:4]
```

mySubArray is not merely a copy of a subpart of myarray. In fact, both arrays will point to the same memory. Let's elaborate by using an example. Here is a simple program:

```
package main

import (
  "fmt"
)

func main() {
  myarray := [5]int{1,2,3,4,5}
  mySubArray := myarray[2:4]
  mySubArray[0] = 2
  fmt.Println(myarray)
}
```

This program output myarray, but it does so after we change a value in mySubArray. As you can see in the preceding code, the original values in myarray were 1, 2, 3, 4, and 5. However, because we changed the value at index 0 of mySubArray, which is index 2 of myarray, the output will end up being as follows:

```
[1 2 2 4 5]
```

Perfect! We now have a solid idea about how to make use of arrays in Go. Let's move on to slices.

Slices

There is a very obvious limitation in Go's array data structure—you must specify the size whenever you declare a new array. In real life, there are numerous scenarios where we will not know the number of elements to expect beforehand. Almost every modern programming language comes with its own data structure to address this requirement. In Go, this special data structure is called a **slice**.

From a practical point of view, you can think of slices as simply dynamic arrays. From a syntax point of view, slices look very similar to arrays, except that you don't need to specify the size. Here is an example:

```
var mySlice []int
```

As you can see, slice declarations are very similar to array declarations, except for the fact that you don't need to specify the number of elements on a slice.

Here is us initializing the preceding slide with some initial values:

```
mySlice = []int{1,2,3,4,5}
```

Let's declare and then initialize this with some initial values in one go:

```
var mySlice = []int{1,2,3,4,5}
```

Since slices can grow in size, we are also allowed to initialize an empty slice:

```
var mySlice = []int{}
```

If you would like to set an initial number of elements in your slice without having to write the initial values by hand, you can utilize a built-in function called `make`:

```
var mySlice = make([]int,5)
```

The preceding code will declare and initialize an `int` slice with an initial length of `5` elements.

To write efficient Go code that can benefit from slices, you need to first understand how slices work internally.

A slice can simply be considered as a pointer to a part of an array. A slice holds three main pieces of information:

- A pointer to the first element of the subarray that the slice points to.
- The length of the subarray that's exposed to the slice.
- The capacity, which is the remaining number of items available in the original array. The capacity is always either equal to the length or greater.

This sounds too theoretical, so let's utilize the power of code and some visualization to provide a practical explanation about how slices really work.

Let's assume we created a new slice:

```
var mySlice = []int{1,2,3,4,5}
```

Internally, the new slice we created points to an array with the 5 initial values that we set:

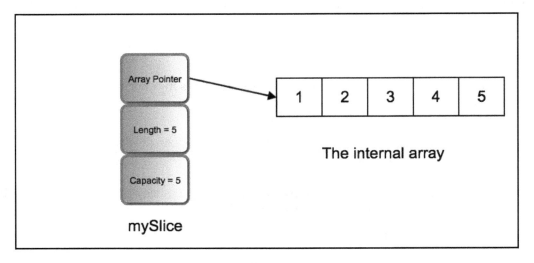

As you can see from the preceding diagram, `mySlice` held three pieces of information:

- The first is a pointer to the array underneath, which holds the data
- The second is the length of the slice, which is 5 in this case
- The third is the full capacity of the slice, which is also 5 in this case

The preceding diagram, however, doesn't really clarify how the capacity of the slice can be different from its length. To uncover the practical differences between length and capacity, we'll need to dig a bit deeper.

Let's say we decided to extract a subslice from the original slice:

```
var subSlice = mySlice[2:4]
```

Reslicing `mySlice` will not produce a new, smaller copy of the array underneath. Instead, the preceding line of code will produce the following slice:

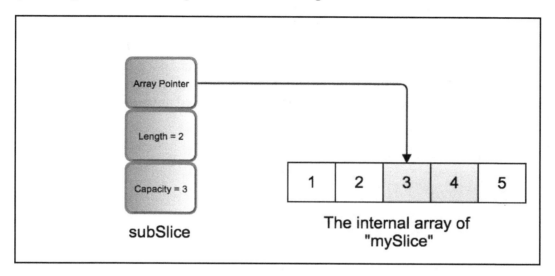

Since `subSlice` includes the elements at index two and index three of `mySlice`, the length of `subSlice` is two (remember that an array index starts at zero, which is why index two is the third element and not the second). The capacity is different, however, and that is because the original array has three elements left, starting from index two, so the capacity is three and not two, even though the length is two.

So, in other words, the length of `subSlice` is two because `subSlice` only cares about two elements. However, the capacity is three because there are three elements left in the original array, starting from index two, which is the index that the `subSlice` array pointer points to.

There is a built-in function called `cap`, which we can use to get the capacity of a slice:

```
cap(subSlice) //this will return 3
```

The built-in function called `len` that we use for arrays works with slices as well, since it will give you the length of the slice:

```
len(subSlice) //this will return 2
```

You might be wondering by now, why should I care about the differences between length and capacity? I can just use the length and ignore the capacity altogether, since the capacity only gives you information about a hidden internal array.

The answer is very simple—**memory utilization**. What if `mySlice` had 100,000 elements instead of just five? This means that the internal array would have had 100,000 elements as well. This huge internal array will exist in our program's memory as long as we use any sub-slices extracted from `mySlice`, even if the sub-slices we use only care about two elements.

To avoid that kind of memory bloat, we need to explicitly copy the fewer elements we care about into a new slice. By doing this, once we stop using the original large slice, Go's garbage collector will realize that the huge array is not needed anymore and will clean it up.

So, how do we achieve that? This can be done through a built-in function called `copy`:

```
//let's assume this is a huge slice
var myBigSlice = []int{1,2,3,4,5,6}
//now here is a new slice that is smaller
var mySubSlice = make([]int,2)
//we copy two elements from myBigSlice to mySubSlice
copy(mySubSlice,myBigSlice[2:4])
```

Perfect! With this, you should have a fairly practical understanding about slice internals and how to avoid memory bloats in slices.

We keep saying that slices are like dynamic arrays, but we haven't seen how to actually grow the slice yet. Go offers a simple built-in function called `append`, which is used to add values to a slice. If you reach the end of your slice capacity, the `append` function will create a new slice with a bigger internal array to hold your expanding data. `append` is a variadic function, so it can take any number of arguments. Here is what this looks like:

```
var mySlice = []int{1,2} //our slice holds 1 and 2
mySlice = append(mySlice,3,4,5) //now our slice holds 1,2,3,4,5
```

One last important thing to mention is the built-in function called `make`. We already covered the `make` function earlier and how it can be used to initialize a slice:

```
//Initialize a slice with length of 3
var mySlice = make([]int,3)
```

The argument 3 in the preceding code represents the slice's length. What we haven't mentioned yet though is the fact that `make` can also be used to specify the capacity of the slice. This can be achieved by using the following code:

```
//initialize a slice with length of 3 and capacity of 5
var mySlice = make([]int,3,5)
```

If we don't provide the capacity to the `make()` function, the length argument value becomes the capacity as well, so in other words, we get the following:

```
//Initialize a slice with length of 3, and capacity of 3
var mySlice = make([]int,3)
```

Now, it's time to talk about maps.

Maps

HashMaps are very popular, and extremely important data structures in any programming language. A **map** is a collection of key value pairs, where you use the key to obtain the value that corresponds to it. Using maps greatly speeds up your software due to the fact that with a map, retrieving a value through a key is a very quick operation.

In Go, you can declare a map like this:

```
var myMap map[int]string
```

The preceding code declares a map where the keys are of type `int`, and the values are of type `string`.

You can initialize a map using the `make` function:

```
myMap = make(map[int]string)
```

You can't use a map before you initialize it, otherwise an error will be thrown. Here is another way to initialize a map:

```
myMap = map[int]string{}
```

What if you want to initialize the map with some values? You can do this:

```
myMap = map[int]string{1: "first", 2: "Second", 3: "third"}
```

To add values to an existing map, you can do this:

```
myMap[4] = "fourth"
```

To obtain a value from a map, you can do the following:

```
//x will hold the value in "myMap" that corresponds to key 4
var x = myMap[4]
```

You can also check if a key exists in a map by using the following syntax, assuming that your code is inside a function block:

```
//If the key 5 is not in "myMap", then "ok" will be false
//Otherwise, "ok" will be true, and "x" will be the value
x,ok := myMap[5]
```

You can delete a value from a map by using the built-in `delete` function:

```
//delete key of value 4
delete(myMap,4)
```

Struct

A struct in Go is a data structure that is composed of fields, where each field has a type. Here is what a Go struct looks like:

```
type myStruct struct{
    intField int
    stringField string
    sliceField []int
}
```

The preceding code creates a `struct` type that is called `myStruct`, which contains three fields:

- `intField` of type `int`
- `stringField` of type `string`
- `sliceField` of type `[]int`

You can then initialize and use that `struct` type in your code:

```
var s = myStruct{
intField: 3,
stringField: "three",
sliceField : []int{1,2,3},
}
```

The preceding method of initialization is also known as **struct literals**. There is a shorter version of it that looks like this:

```
var s = myStruct{3,"three",[]int{1,2,3}}
```

You can also use what is known as *dot notation*, which looks as follows:

```
var s = myStruct{}
s.intField = 3
s.stringField = "three"
s.sliceField= []int{1,2,3}
```

You can obtain a pointer to a `struct` by doing this:

```
var sPtr = &myStruct{
intField:3,
stringField:"three",
sliceField: []int{1,2,3},
}
```

A dot notation can be used with a Go struct pointer, since Go will understand what needs to be done without the need to do any pointer de-referencing:

```
var s = &myStruct{}
s.intField = 3
s.stringField = "three"
s.sliceField= []int{1,2,3}
```

If the Go struct field names start with lower case letters, they will not be visible to external packages. If you want your struct or its fields to be visible to other packages, start the struct and/or field name with upper case letters.

Now, let's talk about Go methods.

Methods

A method is basically a function that you attach to a type. For example, let's assume we have a `struct` type called `Person`:

```
type Person struct{
    name string
    age int
}
```

Go allows us to attach a method to that type like this:

```
func (p Person) GetName()string{
  return p.name
}
```

The part between the `func` keyword and the function name, `GetName()`, is known as the **receiver** of the method.

Let's say we declare a value of type `Person`, like this:

```
var p = Person{
name: "Jason",
age: 29,
}
```

Now, we can invoke the `GetName` method of value p, as follows:

```
p.GetName()
```

Let's create another method called `GetAge()`, which returns the `age` of the attached `person`. Here is the code to do so:

```
func (p Person) GetAge()int{
  return p.age
}
```

Now, we'll see what type embedding is.

Type embedding

But what if you would like a struct to inherit the methods of another struct? The closest feature that the Go language offers to the concept of inheritance is known as *type embedding*. This feature is best explained through an example. Let's go back to the `Person struct` type:

```
type Person struct{
    name string
    age int
}

func (p Person) GetName()string{
  return p.name
}

func (p Person) GetAge()int{
  return p.age
}
```

Now, let's say that we would like to create a new `struct` type called `Student`, which has all the properties and methods of `Person`, plus some more:

```
type Student struct{
    Person
    studentId int
}

func (s Student) GetStudentID()int{
    return s.studentId
}
```

Notice that in the preceding code, we included the type `Person` inside the struct definition of type `Student`, without specifying a field name. This will effectively make the `Student` type inherit all the exported methods and fields of the `Person` `struct` type. In other words, we can access the methods and fields of `Person` directly from an object of type `Student`:

```
s := Student{}
//This code is valid, because the method GetAge() belongs to the embedded
type 'Person':
s.GetAge()
s.GetName()
```

In Go, when a type gets embedded inside another type, the exported methods and fields of the embedded type are said to be *promoted* to the parent or embedding type.

Let's explore how to build interfaces in Go in the next section.

Interfaces

After covering methods, we must cover interfaces, which make use of methods to produce efficient and scalable code in the Go language.

An interface can be very simply described as a Go type that hosts a collection of methods.

Here is a simple example:

```
type MyInterface interface{
    GetName()string
    GetAge()int
}
```

The preceding interface defines two methods—`GetName()` and `GetAge()`.

Earlier, we attached two methods with the same signature to a type called `Person`:

```
type Person struct{
    name string
    age int
}
func (p Person) GetName()string{
  return p.name
}
func (p Person) GetAge()int{
  return p.age
}
```

In Go, an interface can be implemented by other types, like Go structs. When a Go type implements an interface, a value of the interface type can then hold that Go type data. We'll see what that means very shortly.

A very special feature in Go is the fact that for a type to implement or *inherit* an interface, the type only needs to implement the methods of said interface.

In other words, the `Person` struct type from the preceding piece of code implements the `myInterface` interface type. This is due to the fact that the `Person` type implements `GetName()` and `GetAge()`, which are the same methods that were defined by `myInterface`.

So, what does it mean when `Person` implements `MyInterface`?

It means that we can do something like this:

```
var myInterfaceValue MyInterface
var p = Person{}
p.name = "Jack"
p.age = 39
// some code
myInterfaceValue = p
myInterfaceValue.GetName() //returns: Jack
myInterfaceValue.GetAge() //returns: 39
```

We can also do this:

```
func main(){
    p := Person{"Alice",26}
    printNameAndAge(p)
}
```

```
func PrintNameAndAge(i MyInterface){
    fmt.Println(i.GetName(),i.GetAge())
}
```

Interfaces are used quite a bit in APIs and in scalable software. They allow you to build software with flexible functionality. Here is a trivial example of how it helps you build flexible software.

Let's say we want to create a new person type that appends a title to the name:

```
type PersonWithTitle {
    name string
    title string
    age int
}

func (p PersonWithTitle) GetName()string{
    //This code returns <title> <space> <name>
    return p.title + " " + p.name
}

func (p PersonWithTitle) GetAge() int{
    return p.age
}
```

The preceding type also implements MyInterface, which means we can do this:

```
func main(){
    pt := PersonWithTitle{"Alice","Dr.",26}
    printNameAndAge(pt)
}

func PrintNameAndAge(i MyInterface){
    fmt.Println(i.GetName(),i.GetAge())
}
```

The PrintNameAndAge() function signature will not need to change, since it relies on the interface instead of the concrete type. However, the behavior will differ a bit since we changed the concrete struct type from Person to PersonWithTitle. This ability allows you to write flexible APIs and packages that don't need to change whenever you need to add more concrete types to your code.

There are cases where you might want to get back the concrete type value from an interface value. Go includes a feature called **type assertion** that can be used for just that. Here is the most useful form of type assertion:

```
person, ok := myInterfaceValue.(Person)
```

The preceding code assumes that we are inside a function block. If `myInterfaceValue` does not hold a value of type `Person`, the preceding code will return an empty struct for the first return, and false for the second return. Therefore, `ok` will be false, whereas `Person` will be empty.

On the other hand, if `myInterfaceValue` holds a value of type `Person`, then `ok` will become true, and the `Person` variable will hold the data that's retrieved from `myInterfaceValue`.

Now, let's explore how to add logic to our code, by covering conditional statements and loops.

Conditional statements and loops

In Go, there are two keywords for conditional statements—`if`, and `switch`. Let's take a practical look at each one of them.

The if statement

The `if` statement looks like this:

```
if <condition>{
}
```

So, let's assume we want to compare whether a value, `x`, is equal to `10`. Here is what the syntax would look like:

```
if x == 10{
}
```

In Go, you can also execute some initialization in your `if` statement. Here is what this syntax would look like:

```
if x := getX(); x == 5{
}
```

Like other programming languages, an `if` statement is never complete without an `else` clause. Here is what an `if else` looks like in Go:

```
if x==5{
}else{
}
```

How about an `else` clause with a condition?

```
if x == 5{
}else if x >10{
} else {
}
```

The switch statement

Now, let's look at the `switch` statement. Here is what it looks like:

```
switch x {
    case 5:
       fmt.Println("5")
    case 6:
       fmt.Println("6")

default:

  fmt.Println("default case")
}
```

If you haven't noticed already, there is no `break` keyword. In Go, each case breaks automatically, and doesn't need to be told to do so.

Similar to `if` statements, you can do an initialization in your `switch` statement:

```
switch x := getX();x {
    case 5:
       fmt.Println("5")
    case 6:
       fmt.Println("6")

default:

  fmt.Println("default case")
}
```

In Go, a `switch` statement can act like a group of `if else`. This gives you the ability to write long `if else` chains with much nicer code:

```
switch{
case x == 5:
//do something
case x > 10:
// do something else
default:
//default case
}
```

In some scenarios, you want your switch cases not to break automatically, and instead fall through to the next case. For this, you can use the `fallthrough` keyword:

```
switch{
case x > 5:
//do something
fallthrough
case x > 10:
// do something else. If x is greater than 10, then the first case will
execute first, then this case will follow
default:
//default case
}
```

Following conditional statements, let's take a look at loops.

Loops

In Go, there is a single keyword that you can use when you want to write a loop—`for`. There are no other keywords to indicate a loop in Go.

Let's look at the following code. Let's say we want to loop from 1 to 10; here is how this is done:

```
for i:=1;i<=10;i++{
//do something with i
}
```

As in other languages, your `for` statement needs to include the following:

- An initial value (`i:=1`) in your code—this is optional
- A condition to indicate whether to keep iterating or not (`i<=10`)
- The value of the next iteration (`i++`)

What if we have a slice or an array and we want to iterate over it in a loop? Go comes to the rescue with the concept of `for .. range`. Let's assume we have a slice called `myslice` and that we want to iterate over it. Here is what the code would look like:

```
myslice := []string{"one","two","three","four"}
for i,item := range myslice{
//do something with i and item
}
```

In the preceding piece of code, `i` represents the index of the current iteration. For example, if we are at the second item of `myslice`, then the value of `i` will be equal to 1 (because the index starts at 0). The `item` variable, on the other hand, represents the value of the slice item at the current iteration. For example, if we are at the third item of the slice, then we are at item value `three`.

There are cases where we don't care about the index. For this, we can use the following syntax:

```
for _,item := range myslice{
//do something with item
}
```

What about if we only care about the index? For that, we can do this:

```
for i := range myslice{
//do something with item
}
```

Someone might ask, why would I need only the index and not the items of the slice themselves? The answer is simple—when you obtain the item from the `for..range` statement, you only obtain a copy of the item, which means that you won't be able to change the original item that lives in the slice should the need arise. However, when you obtain the index, this gives you the power to change the item inside the slice. There are cases where you would need to change the values inside a slice while you are iterating over it. This is when you use the index. Here is a trivial example:

```
myslice := []string{"one","two","three","four"}
  for i := range myslice {
     myslice[i] = "other"
  }
  fmt.Println(myslice)
  //output is: other other other other
```

But what about the `while` loop? If you come from any programming language other than Go, you must be fully aware of the concept of the `while` loop. As we mentioned earlier, in Go, all loops make use of the `for` keyword, so in other words, `for` is Go's `while` as well. Here is an example:

```
for i>5{
//do something
}
```

As in other programming languages, Go supports the `break` and `continue` keywords. The `break` keyword inside a loop would cause the loop to break, even if it is not done. The `continue` keyword, on the other hand, will force a loop to jump to the next iteration.

Now, we'll talk about `panic`, `recover`, and `defer`

Panics, recovers, and defers

In Go, there is a special built-in function called `panic`. When you invoke `panic` in your code, your program is interrupted, and a panic message is returned. If a `panic` gets triggered and you don't capture it in time, your program will stop execution and will exit, so be very careful when you use a `panic`. Here is a code example:

```
func panicTest(p bool) {
  if p {
    panic("panic requested")
  }
}
```

In the preceding example, we wrote a function that checks a flag, p. If p is true, then we throw a panic. The argument to the `panic` function is the message that wants the panic to return. Here is a more complete program that you can run in Go's playground (http://play.golang.org):

```
package main

import "fmt"

func main() {
  panicTest(true)
  fmt.Println("hello world")
}

func panicTest(p bool) {
  if p {
```

```
    panic("panic requested")
  }
}
```

When I executed that code from the main function in Go's playground (http://play.golang.org), I got the following error:

```
panic: panic requested

goroutine 1 [running]:
main.panicTest(0x128701, 0xee7e0)
    /tmp/sandbox420149193/main.go:12 +0x60
main.main()
    /tmp/sandbox420149193/main.go:6 +0x20
```

The panic caused the program to be terminated, which is why hello world was never printed. Instead, we got the panic message.

So, now that we understand how panics work, an obvious question arises—how do we capture a panic and prevent it from killing our program?

Before we answer that question, we first need to introduce the concept of defer. The defer keyword can be used to indicate that a piece of code must only be executed after the surrounding function returns. As always, this will make much more sense after we look at a code example:

```
func printEnding(message string) {
  fmt.Println(message)
}

func doSomething() {
  //In here we use the keyword "defer"
  //This will call printEnding() right after doSomething()

  defer printEnding("doSomething() just ended")

  //In here, we just print values from 0 to 5
  for i := 0; i <= 5; i++ {
    fmt.Println(i)
  }
}
```

In the preceding code, when we made use of defer, we effectively asked for the printEnding() function to be executed right after doSomething() finishes its execution.

The `defer` statement basically pushes a function call to a list, and the list of saved calls is executed after the surrounding function returns. `Defer` is most commonly used to clean up resources, like closing a file handler, for example.

Here is the full version of the preceding program:

```
package main

import (
  "fmt"
)

func main() {
  doSomething()
}

func printEnding(message string) {
  fmt.Println(message)
}

func doSomething() {
  defer printEnding("doSomething() just ended")
  for i := 0; i <= 5; i++ {
    fmt.Println(i)
  }
}
```

And here is the output of that program:

```
0
1
2
3
4
5
doSomething() just ended
```

Now, what if we put `defer` multiple times in our function?

```
package main

import (
  "fmt"
)

func main() {
  doSomething()
}
```

```
func printEnding(message string) {
  fmt.Println(message)
}

func doSomething() {
  defer printEnding("doSomething() just ended 2")
  defer printEnding("doSomething() just ended")
  for i := 0; i <= 5; i++ {
    fmt.Println(i)
  }
}
```

The `defer` statements typically enter a stack data structure, which means they execute based on the first-in-last-out rule. So, this basically means that the first `defer` statement in the code will execute last, while the next one will execute right before it and so on. To paint a clearer picture, let's look at the program's output:

```
0
1
2
3
4
5
doSomething() just ended
doSomething() just ended 2
```

Perfect! We are now ready to answer our earlier question—how can we capture and handle a `panic` before it terminates our program? We now know about `defer` and how it ensures that a piece of code of our choosing gets executed right after the surrounding function exits. So, defers can definitely be used to insert a piece of code after a `panic` occurs, but are defers enough? The answer is no—there is a built-in function known as `recover()` that we can use to capture a `panic` and return the panic's message.

Again, a code snippet is worth a thousand words:

```
package main

import "fmt"

func main() {
  panicTest(true)
  fmt.Println("hello world")
}

func checkPanic() {
  if r := recover(); r != nil {
    fmt.Println("A Panic was captured, message:", r)
```

```
    }
}

func panicTest(p bool) {
    // in here we use a combination of defer and recover
    defer checkPanic()
    if p {
        panic("panic requested")
    }
}
```

The preceding code will produce the following output:

```
A Panic was captured, message: panic requested
hello world
```

As you can see, we utilized a combination of defer and the recover() function to capture the panic to prevent it from terminating our program. If no panic occurred, the recover() function will return nil. Otherwise, the recover() function will return the error value of the panic. If we use recover() alone, it won't be effective without being combined with defer.

Summary

This chapter took you on a practical learning journey of the building blocks of the Go language. We covered all of the fundamental features of Go that you are likely to see in any Go program. As we progress, you will see the building blocks that we covered in this chapter being utilized again and again.

In the next chapter, we'll cover one of the most beloved features of the Go language by diving into how to handle concurrency in Go.

Questions

1. What is GoPath used for?
2. How do you write a while loop in Go?
3. What are named results?
4. What is the difference between a function and a method?
5. What is type assertion?

6. What is `defer` used for?
7. What is a `panic` in Go?
8. How do we recover from a `panic`?
9. What is the difference between an array and a slice in Go?
10. What is an interface?
11. What is a struct?
12. What is a map?

Further reading

For more information on what was covered in this chapter you can go through the following links:

- **Go website**: `golang.org`
- **Installing Go**: `https://golang.org/doc/install`
- **Go standard packages**: `https://golang.org/pkg/`
- **How to Write Go Code**: `https://golang.org/doc/code.html`
- **Go tour**: `tour.golang.org`
- **Slices internals**: `https://blog.golang.org/go-slices-usage-and-internals`
- **Effective Go**: `https://golang.org/doc/effective_go.html`
- **Composition with Go**: `https://www.ardanlabs.com/blog/2015/09/composition-with-go.html`

3
Go Concurrency

Welcome to the second chapter of our journey to learn about full stack development in Go. In this chapter, we'll continue on our path to understanding the foundations of the Go language, by covering the important topic of **concurrency** in the Go language. Go arguably possesses one of the most effective and easy-to-use concurrency features of the languages in its class. Many developers who switch to Go do so because of Go's concurrency. This chapter assumes some basic knowledge of programming and the concept of threads. In a similar way to the previous chapter, we'll mainly focus on the most important and foundational concepts.

The following topics will be covered in this chapter:

- What is concurrency?
- Goroutines
- Go channels
- `select` statements
- The `sync` package

What is concurrency?

So, what is concurrency? The term is used quite a bit in the software industry, even though not all developers understand its meaning. In this section, we'll attempt to uncover the practical meaning of concurrency from the point of view of the Go language, and why it is useful to you.

In Go, **concurrency** means the ability of your program to cut itself into smaller pieces, then the ability to run the different independent pieces at different times, with the goal of executing all the tasks as quickly as possible based on the amount of resources available.

The preceding definition might appear (for some people) as though we are defining threads. However, the concept of concurrency is more general than the concept of threads. Let's first briefly define threads if you are not very familiar with the concept.

A thread is a feature that the OS gives you that allows you to run pieces of your program in parallel. Let's say that your program is composed of two main parts, **Part 1** and **Part 2**, and you write your code such that **Part 1** runs on **Thread One**, and **Part 2** runs on **Thread Two**. In this case, both parts of your program will run parallel to each other at the same time; the following diagram illustrates how this will look:

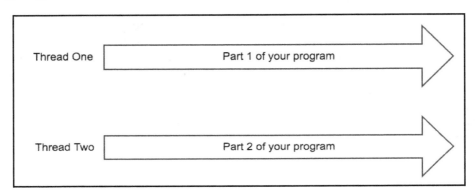

That all sounds good; however, there is a gap in modern software between the number of truly independent threads and the number of concurrent pieces of software that your program needs to execute. In modern pieces of software, you might need thousands of pieces of your program to run independently at the same time, even though your OS might be supplying only four threads!

Concurrency is very important in modern software, due to the need to execute independent pieces of code as fast as possible without disturbing the overall flow of the program. Let's take the simple example of a web server; a web server typically accepts requests from a web client, such as a web browser. Let's say that a request is accepted from Jack, who lives somewhere in Europe, while another request comes at the same time to the web server from Chin, who lives in Asia. You wouldn't want your program to delay Chin's request because of the fact that Jack's request arrived at the same time. Their requests should be processed at the same time and as independently as possible. This is simply why concurrency is an indispensable feature in modern production software.

In Go and other modern programming languages, this gap is addressed by essentially cutting your program into numerous small and independent pieces, and then *multiplexing* those pieces among the available threads. This becomes much clearer with a visual representation.

Let's say we have a piece of software that is composed of 10 different pieces that we would like to run concurrently, even though we only have two real OS threads. Go has the ability to take those 10 different pieces, schedule when will be the best time to run each piece, and then distribute them among the available threads based on some very clever algorithms. Here's a simple view of how this can look:

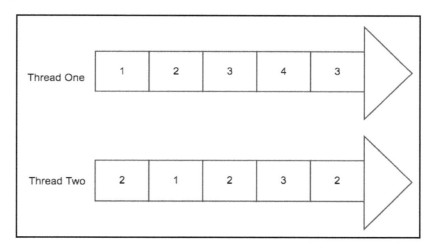

The 10 pieces of your program will feel like they are running at the same time, even though, in reality, they were cleverly distributed to make them finish their tasks as soon as possible based on the available resources. Go takes care of all the complexity of scheduling and distributing the 10 pieces of code on the available threads, while providing you with a very clean API that hides away all the complexities of the algorithms involved. This allows you to focus on writing powerful software to serve your needs, without worrying about the low-level concepts such as managing threads, low-level resource allocation, and scheduling.

Let's take a look at goroutines in the next section.

Goroutines

It's now time to dig deeper into the clean API that Go provides in order to write concurrent software with ease.

A goroutine is simply defined as a *light-weight thread* that you can use in your program; it's not a real thread. In Go, when you define a piece of code as a new goroutine, you basically tell the Go runtime that you would like this piece of code to run concurrently with other goroutines.

Every function in Go lives in some goroutine. For example, the main function that we discussed in the previous chapter, which is usually the entry point function for your program, runs on what is known as the **main goroutine**.

So, how do you create a new goroutine? You just append the `go` keyword before the function that you would like to run concurrently. The syntax is quite simple:

```
go somefunction()
```

Here, `somefunction()` is the piece of code that you would like to run concurrently. Whenever you create a new goroutine, it will get scheduled to run concurrently, and will not block your current goroutine.

Here is a trivial, but more complete piece of code to help us understand the concept of goroutines:

```
package main

import (
 "fmt"
 "time"
)

func runSomeLoop(n int) {
 for i := 0; i < n; i++ {
 fmt.Println("Printing:", i)
 }
}
func main() {
 go runSomeLoop(10)
 //block the main goroutine for 2 seconds
 time.Sleep(2 * time.Second)
 fmt.Println("Hello, playground")
}
```

The preceding code is a simple program that runs a function called runSomeLoop() on a new goroutine. This means that runSomeLoop() will run concurrently to the main() function. In the program, we made use of a function called Sleep(), which exists in the time package. This function will block the main goroutine in order to give runSomeLoop() a chance to run and finish. If we don't block the main goroutine in this example, the main goroutine will likely finish, and then exit the program before runSomeLoop() gets a chance to fully run. There are cases when This is a byproduct of the fact that goroutines are concurrent, which is why invoking a new goroutine does not block your current goroutine.

Here's how the output of the program will look:

```
Printing: 0
Printing: 1
Printing: 2
Printing: 3
Printing: 4
Printing: 5
Printing: 6
Printing: 7
Printing: 8
Printing: 9
Hello, playground
```

This shows us that the runSomeLoop() goroutine managed to run at the same time when the main goroutine was sleeping. When the main goroutine woke up, it printed Hello, playground before it exited.

So, what if we removed the time.Sleep() function that blocked the main goroutine? Take a look at the following code block:

```
package main

import (
  "fmt"
)

func runSomeLoop(n int) {
  for i := 0; i < n; i++ {
    fmt.Println("Printing:", i)
  }
}
func main() {
  go runSomeLoop(10)
  fmt.Println("Hello, playground")
}
```

You will get the following result:

```
Hello, playground
```

You can see that `runSomeLoop()` didn't get the chance to run before the main goroutine exited.

Goroutines are very light from a memory and resources point of view; a production Go program will typically run hundreds and thousands of goroutines. The ability to produce goroutines with such simple API is arguably one of the most powerful features of the Go language, according to many of Go's users.

Let's take a look at Go channels in the next section.

Go channels

An important question can now be addressed; what if we need to share a piece of data between two different goroutines?

In programs that make use of multiple threads, the common approach to share data between different threads is to lock the variables that are shared between the threads. This is typically known as the **sharing memory approach**. The following diagram demonstrates how two threads will share memory, by sharing a variable called **X**:

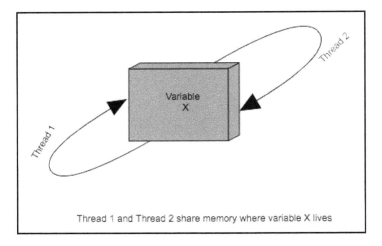

Thread 1 and Thread 2 share memory where variable X lives

In Go, there is a very popular motto:

"Do not communicate by sharing memory; instead, share memory by communicating."

What does that mean? It simply means that Go does not typically prefer sharing memory (there are exceptions, however) between threads through the lock approach. Instead, Go prefers to communicate the data from one goroutine to another. This *communicate* part is achieved through the Go channels. The following diagram demonstrates how this looks visually:

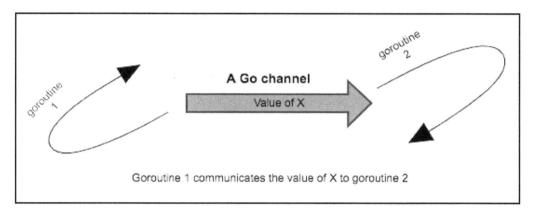

Goroutine 1 communicates the value of X to goroutine 2

Let's take a look at regular and buffered channels in the next sections.

Regular channels

To declare a channel in Go, you simply use the make keyword, as follows:

```
myChannel := make(chan int)
```

In the preceding code, we created and initialized a channel called myChannel that can hold int values. This channel can then be used to send an int value from one goroutine to another.

Here is how to receive a value from a channel:

```
//myIntValue will host the value received from the channel
myIntValue := <-myChannel
```

Here is how to send a value to a channel:

```
myChannel <- 4
```

Whenever you execute a send or a receive operation on a regular Go channel, your goroutine will block until the value is fully sent or received. This simply means that if you send a value via a channel but there is no other goroutine waiting for it on the other end, your goroutine will block. On the other hand, if you are attempting to receive a value via a channel but there is no other goroutine sending it on the other end, your goroutine will block. This behavior ensures that your code is synchronized, your values are fresh and up to date, and avoids the numerous problems that you can typically face in other programming languages when you use locks.

Let's take a look at a complete program showcasing two goroutines communicating, in order to learn more about Go channels:

```go
package main

import (
  "fmt"
  "time"
)

func runLoopSend(n int, ch chan int) {
  for i := 0; i < n; i++ {
    ch <- i
  }
  close(ch)
}

func runLoopReceive(ch chan int) {
  for {
    i, ok := <-ch
    if !ok {
      break
    }
    fmt.Println("Received value:", i)
  }
}

func main() {
  myChannel := make(chan int)
  go runLoopSend(10, myChannel)
  go runLoopReceive(myChannel)
  time.Sleep(2 * time.Second)
}
```

In the preceding code, we created a channel called `myChannel`, which we then pass to two goroutines: `runLoopSend()` and `runLoopReceive()`. The `runLoopSend()` function will keep sending values to this channel, whereas the `runLoopReceive()` function will keep receiving values from this channel.

The preceding code will provide the following output:

```
Received value: 0
Received value: 1
Received value: 2
Received value: 3
Received value: 4
Received value: 5
Received value: 6
Received value: 7
Received value: 8
Received value: 9
```

Let's first focus on `runLoopSend()` because there is a new concept that we are showcasing here. Take a look at the following code line:

```
close(ch)
```

This syntax can be used to close a channel. Once a channel is closed, you cannot send data to it anymore, otherwise, a panic will occur.

Now, let's take a look at `runLoopReceive`, particularly at this following line:

```
i, ok := <-ch
```

The preceding line is a special syntax to inspect whether a channel is closed. If the channel is not closed, the value of `ok` will be true, while `i` will get the value getting sent via the channel. On the other hand, if the channel is closed, `ok` will be false. In the `runLoopReceive` goroutine, we break out of the `for` loop if `ok` is false.

There is actually another, more elegant way to write this `for` loop:

```go
for {
    i, ok := <-ch
    if !ok {
        break
    }
    fmt.Println("Received value:", i)
}
```

We can replace the preceding code with the following code:

```
for i := range ch {
  fmt.Println("Received value:", i)
}
```

The `for..range` syntax is allowed on channels as it allows you to keep receiving data from a channel until the channel gets closed.

The output of the program will simply be as follows:

```
Received value: 0
Received value: 1
Received value: 2
Received value: 3
Received value: 4
Received value: 5
Received value: 6
Received value: 7
Received value: 8
Received value: 9
```

Buffered channels

A buffered channel is a special type of channel that holds a buffer that contains a number of items. Unlike a regular channel, a buffered channel doesn't block unless the following takes place:

- Its buffer is empty and we are trying to receive a value from the channel.
- Its buffer is full and we are trying to send a value to the channel.

To declare a buffered channel, we use the following syntax:

```
myBufferedChannel := make(chan int,10)
```

The preceding syntax creates a buffered channel that can hold 10 `int` values.

To send a value to the buffered channel, we use the same syntax as with regular channels. Each send operation adds one item to the buffer, as follows:

```
myBufferedChannel <- 10
```

To receive a value from a buffered channel, we utilize the same syntax as well. Each receive operation removes one item from the buffer, as follows:

```
x := <-myBufferedChannel
```

Let's take a look at the `select` statement construct in the next section.

The select statement

The `select` statement is an important construct in Go. It allows you to control multiple channels at the same time. With `select`, you can send or receive values to different channels, and then execute code based on the channel that unblocks the first.

This will be best explained by an example; let's take a look at the following piece of code:

```
select {
    case i := <-ch:
      fmt.Println("Received value:", i)
    case <-time.After(1 * time.Second):
      fmt.Println("timed out")
}
```

In the preceding example, we utilized the `select` statement to exercise control over two different channels. The first channel is called `ch`, which we attempted to receive a value from. In comparison, the second channel is produced from the `time.After()` function. The `time.After()` function is very popular in Go, and especially in `select` statements. The function generates a channel that only receives a value after the specified timeout, in effect producing a blocking channel for a predefined period of time. You can use `time.After()` in your code with the `select` statement in cases where you would want to timeout a receive or a send operation on another channel.

Here is another example of sending a `select` statement with a timeout channel, but this time it's a combination of receive and send operations:

```
select {
    case i := <-ch1:
      fmt.Println("Received value on channel ch1:", i)
    case ch2 <- 10:
      fmt.Println("Sent value of 10 to channel ch2")
    case <-time.After(1 * time.Second):
      fmt.Println("timed out")
}
```

The preceding code will synchronize between three channels: `ch1`, `ch2`, and the `time.After()` channel. The `select` statement will wait on those three channels and then, depending on whichever channel finishes first, the appropriate `select` case will be executed.

The `select` statement also supports the `default` case. The `default` case will execute immediately if none of the channels are ready; here is an example:

```
select {
    case i := <-ch1:
        fmt.Println("Received value on channel ch1:", i)
    case ch2 <- 10:
        fmt.Println("Sent value of 10 to channel ch2")
    default:
        fmt.Println("No channel is ready")
}
```

In the preceding code, if both `ch1` and `ch2` are blocked by `time`, the `select` statement is executed, and then the `default` case will trigger.

If multiple channels finish at the same time while being controlled by a `select` statement, the channel case to be executed is picked at random.

Let's take a look at the sync package in the next section.

The sync package

The last topic we will cover in this chapter is the `sync` package. The `sync` package is what you will use when you absolutely need to create a lock-in Go. Even though we mentioned that Go prefers the use of channels to communicate data between goroutines, there are cases where a lock or a **mutual exclusion object** (**mutex**) is unavoidable. An example of a scenario where locks are utilized in Go's standard package is the `http` package, where a lock is used to protect the set of listeners to a particular `http` server object. This set of listeners can be accessed from numerous goroutines so that they get protected by a mutex.

The word *mutex*, in the world of computer programming, refers to an object that allows multiple threads to access the same resource (such as shared memory). Mutex is so named because it allows only one thread to access data at one time.

The workflow of a mutex in a piece of software typically works as follows:

1. A thread acquires the mutex
2. No other threads can acquire the mutex as long as one thread has it
3. The thread that acquired the mutex can access some resources without any disturbance from the other threads
4. When its tasks are done, the thread that acquired the mutex releases the mutex so that other threads can compete for it again

In Go, you make use of goroutines and not full threads. So, when you use mutexes in Go, they will manage the resource access between goroutines.

Let's take a look at the simple mutex, read-write mutex and wait groups in the next sections.

The simple mutex

In Go, a simple lock is a pointer to a mutex `struct` type, which belongs to the `sync` package. We can create a mutex as follows:

```
var myMutex = &sync.Mutex{}
```

Let's assume that we have a map called `myMap` of the `map[int]int` type that we'd like to protect from the concurrent access of multiple goroutines:

```
myMutex.Lock()
myMap[1] = 100
myMutex.Unlock()
```

If we ensure that all goroutines that need to edit `myMap` have access to `myMutex`, we can protect `myMap` against multiple goroutines changing it at the same time.

The read-write mutex

Go also supports a read-write lock. A read-write lock differentiates between read and write operations. So, whenever you only perform concurrent read operations, the goroutines won't block. However, whenever you perform a write operation, all other reads and writes get blocked until the write lock is released. As always, this is best explained with an example, such as the following code:

```
var myRWMutex = &sync.RWMutex{}
```

A read-write lock in Go is represented by a pointer to a Go struct of the `sync.RWMutex` type, which is what we initialized in the preceding code snippet.

To perform a read operation, we make use of the `RLock()` and `RUnlock()` methods of the Go struct:

```
myRWMutex.RLock()
fmt.Println(myMap[1])
myRWMutex.RUnlock()
```

To perform a write operation, we make use of the `Lock()` and `Unlock()` methods:

```
myRWMutex.Lock()
myMap[2] = 200
myRWMutex.Unlock()
```

The `*sync.RWMutex` type can be found all over the place in Go's standard package.

Wait groups

The concept of wait groups is very important for building production level software in Go; it allows you to wait for multiple goroutines to finish before you proceed with the rest of your code.

To fully grasp the benefit of wait groups, let's go back to an earlier code sample:

```
package main

import (
  "fmt"
  "time"
)

func runLoopSend(n int, ch chan int) {
  for i := 0; i < n; i++ {
    ch <- i
  }
  close(ch)
}

func runLoopReceive(ch chan int) {
  for {
    i, ok := <-ch
    if !ok {
      break
    }
```

```
      fmt.Println("Received value:", i)
   }
}

func main() {
  myChannel := make(chan int)
  go runLoopSend(10, myChannel)
  go runLoopReceive(myChannel)
  time.Sleep(2 * time.Second)
}
```

In the preceding code, we had to make the main goroutine sleep for two seconds in order to wait for the other two goroutines to finish. However, what if the other goroutines took more than two seconds? It was never guaranteed that this simple sleep would produce the result that we are seeking. Instead, we could have done the following:

```
package main

import (
  "fmt"
  "sync"
)

// Create a global waitgroup:
var wg = &sync.WaitGroup{}

func main() {
  myChannel := make(chan int)
  //Increment the wait group internal counter by 2
  wg.Add(2)
  go runLoopSend(10, myChannel)
  go runLoopReceive(myChannel)
  //Wait till the wait group counter is 0
  wg.Wait()
}

func runLoopSend(n int, ch chan int) {
  //Ensure that the wait group counter decrements by one after //our
function exits
  defer wg.Done()
  for i := 0; i < n; i++ {
    ch <- i
  }
  close(ch)
}

func runLoopReceive(ch chan int) {
  //Ensure that the wait group counter decrements after our  //function
```

```
exits
  defer wg.Done()
  for {
    i, ok := <-ch
    if !ok {
      break
    }
    fmt.Println("Received value:", i)
  }
}
```

A `WaitGroup struct` type in Go is a type that keeps an internal counter; as long as the internal counter is not 0, the wait group will block your goroutine. In the preceding code, we created a global pointer variable to `WaitGroup`; we called it `wg`. This variable will be visible to all of our functions in this simple program. Before we triggered the two goroutines, we incremented the wait group internal counter by 2 using the `wg.Add(2)` method. After that, we proceeded to create our two goroutines. For each of the goroutines we added the following code:

```
defer wg.Done()
```

This uses a combination of `defer` and the `wg.Done()` method in order to ensure that whenever the goroutine function finishes execution, `wg.Done()` gets called. The `wg.Done()` method will decrement the internal wait group counter by one.

Finally, at the end of our main goroutine, we call `wg.Wait()`, which will block the current goroutine until the internal counter of the wait group is zero. This will, in turn, force the main goroutine to wait until all the goroutines in our program finish executing.

The final output to the preceding code is as follows:

```
Received value: 0
Received value: 1
Received value: 2
Received value: 3
Received value: 4
Received value: 5
Received value: 6
Received value: 7
Received value: 8
Received value: 9
```

Summary

In this chapter, we covered some key concepts in the world of production-level Go programming. We covered concurrency from a practical point of view, then we dove into some of the APIs that Go provides to allow you to write efficient concurrent software with minimal complexity.

In the next chapter, we'll start switch topics from Go to frontend programming by covering the building blocks of the popular React framework.

Questions

1. What is concurrency?
2. What is a thread?
3. How is the concept of concurrency different from parallel threading?
4. What is a goroutine?
5. What does *share memory by communicating* mean?
6. What is a Go channel?
7. What is the difference between a regular Go channel and a buffered Go channel?
8. When should you use a `select` statement?
9. What is the difference between `sync.Mutex` and `sync.RWMutex`?
10. When should you use wait groups?

Further reading

For more information, you can go through the following links:

- **Concurrency in Golang**: `http://www.minaandrawos.com/2015/12/06/concurrency-in-golang/`
- **Concurrency is not parallelism**: `https://blog.golang.org/concurrency-is-not-parallelism`
- **Package** `sync`: `https://golang.org/pkg/sync/`

Section 2: The Frontend

In this section, the reader will take a learning journey into modern frontend technologies that are key for building full stack software. The reader will also learn how to use Go at the frontend via the GopherJS framework. In this part, we'll start building our GoMusic store. This part will cover the first half of the full stack.

This section consists of the following chapters:

- Chapter 4, *Frontend with React.js*
- Chapter 5, *Building a Frontend for GoMusic*

4
Frontend with React.js

In this chapter, we'll take the first step and learn about the upper half of the full stack, which is the frontend. To properly build any software product, you need to have sufficient practical knowledge to build a good-looking user interface. This is vital for building a software product that other people enjoy using.

We'll discuss the powerful React framework, which is one of the most popular frontend frameworks on the market today. React allows you to build dynamic websites that can respond to data changes in real time. This allows you to build websites that are responsive and intelligent. Most of the popular websites on the internet today are built with React. We'll be covering React from a very practical point of view, so we will dive head-on into how to write React apps, instead of tackling theoretical or side topics.

In this chapter, we'll discuss the following topics:

- How to construct React applications
- Installing React
- JSX and React elements
- React components
- Props
- States
- React developer tools

Prerequisites and technical requirements

The React framework simply consists of a collection of JavaScript modules that we can use to build beautiful, responsive UIs. Because of that, you need some JavaScript knowledge to follow this chapter.

A very good resource to get re-introduced to JavaScript can be found at `https://developer.mozilla.org/en-US/docs/Web/JavaScript/A_re-introduction_to_JavaScript`.

In this chapter, we'll be primarily using ES6, which can simply be considered the new version of JavaScript.

There are four core features of ES6 that we'll come across in this chapter:

- **Classes**: A class can be considered as a *special function* in JavaScript, where you can define internal methods. For more information, please visit `https://developer.mozilla.org/en-US/docs/Web/JavaScript/Reference/Classes`.
- **Arrow functions**: An arrow function is JavaScript's version of an anonymous function. For more information, please visit `https://developer.mozilla.org/en-US/docs/Web/JavaScript/Reference/Functions/Arrow_functions`.
- **The `let` keyword**: The `let` keyword is used to declare a block scope local variable. For more information, please visit `https://developer.mozilla.org/en-US/docs/Web/JavaScript/Reference/Statements/let`.
- **The `const` keyword**: The `const` keyword is used to declare local scope variables that are constant and cannot change from their initial value. For more information, please visit `https://developer.mozilla.org/en-US/docs/Web/JavaScript/Reference/Statements/const`.

The GoMusic project

In this chapter, we'll leverage the power of React to build a products page for the GoMusic store. The GoMusic store is the main full stack project that we'll be building throughout this book, and it is basically an online store of musical instruments. The frontend will be built with React, whereas the backend will be built with Go.

Here is the product page we're building today:

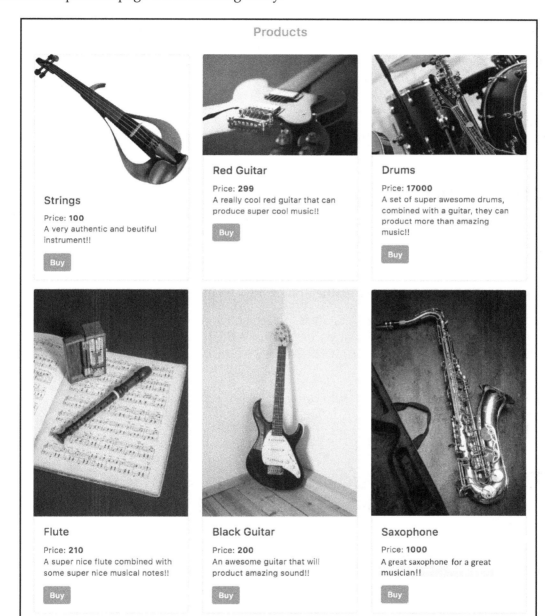

We'll follow a step-by-step approach to building this page. This web page will not be ordinary. We'll make use of the powerful React development tools to update this page in real time whenever we make a change. To further demonstrate the capabilities of React and its tools, the web page will rely on a JSON file, which will contain information about the images, the names, the prices, and the descriptions of the musical instruments we are trying to sell. Whenever we update the JSON file, the web page will automatically update with the new information in the JSON file.

To build the GoMusic website, we require Node.js and **Node Package Manager** (**npm**), which we will see in the following section.

Node.js and the npm

We'll also be using the npm. The npm is a very popular package that hosts almost all well-known Node.js and JavaScript packages. We need the npm to install React as well as the helper tools we will be using to build our React applications.

The npm typically gets distributed with Node.js. So, if you already have a recent version of Node.js installed on your computer, the npm should be there as well.

If you don't have Node.js already installed, please go to `https://nodejs.org/en/` to install Node.js on your computer. Make sure that you have the latest versions of the tools involved. So, if you have Node, but it's an older version, go ahead and update it to a newer version.

You can find more information about npm installation at `https://www.npmjs.com/get-npm`.

Let's take a look at HTML, CSS and Bootstrap in the next section.

HTML, CSS, and Bootstrap

This chapter focuses primarily on React and it assumes familiarity with frontend basics such as HTML and CSS.

Some basic knowledge of HTML and CSS should be enough for you to understand this chapter. HTML is the language that's used to build web pages, whereas CSS is the language that's used to style web pages (add colors and so on).

If you were exposed to HTML and CSS in the past, that should be enough. However, if you prefer to explore HTML more before you proceed, check out `https://developer.mozilla.org/en-US/docs/Learn/HTML/Introduction_to_HTML`. For exploring CSS, this link is a great resource: `https://developer.mozilla.org/en-US/docs/Learn/CSS/Introduction_to_CSS`.

We will utilize the powerful Bootstrap 4 framework to build our frontend views, so familiarity with Bootstrap will help in this chapter as well.

You can find information regarding Bootstrap at `https://getbootstrap.com/docs/4.1/getting-started/introduction/`.

One of the most practical ways to get started with Bootstrap is to use their startup template, which can be found here: `https://getbootstrap.com/docs/4.1/getting-started/introduction/#starter-template`.

Project code

There is a GitHub repository for the code that we'll cover in this project, you can find it at `https://github.com/PacktPublishing/Hands-On-Full-Stack-Development-with-Go/tree/master/Chapter04`.

Let's take a look at the React framework in the next section.

The React framework

React (or React.js) is a JavaScript library for building web user interfaces; it was first released by Facebook in 2013, and has grown exponentially in popularity since then. The library is currently being maintained by Facebook, Instagram, as well as a passionate community. React can build performant and interactive websites.

In the next section we see how to construct React applications.

How to construct React applications

To understand and build applications in React, you must first understand how the library works, and the pieces that work together to compose your React application. In this section, we'll explain the sequence of steps you need to follow to build a React application.

Here is the simplest way to explain how to build a React app:

1. Create *React elements* for your application:
   - An element is one of the most basic building blocks in React. It represents a piece of visual user interface, such as an image, a line with bold font, or a button.
   - You create an element by employing a mixture of JSX, CSS, and JavaScript.

2. Wrap your *elements* with React components:
   - A component is simply a JavaScript class or a function that is composed of React elements.
   - A React application is mostly a number of React components that exchange data.
   - An example of a component would be a single product card from our products page:

3. Use *props* to pass data between your React components:
   - A prop allows one component to send data to another component
   - In our project, props is how we pass the product image, name, prices, and description to the product card component

4. Use *state* to manage and change data inside your React components:
    - Unlike a prop, a React `state` object is internal to your React component
    - Whenever the data in your `state` object changes, the React library re-renders the parts of your application that were affected by the data change
    - In our project, the `state` object is what changes whenever new products are added to our product page

In the next section we will set up our React project.

Setting up the project

It's time to set up our React project. In this section, we'll install the tools that are needed to get our project ready to start writing a React application.

Installing React

Now, we need to install React. Fortunately, this step was made simple by the introduction of a powerful tool called Create React App. This tool bundles a number of features that allow us to create new React apps, construct them in real-time, and then build them so that they're ready for production.

The tool can be retrieved through the npm package manager. To install the tool, you need to run the following command:

```
npm install -g create-react-app
```

This command will install the tool globally, which will allow you to use the tool from anywhere.

Now, in the Terminal, go to the folder where you want your tool to run. To create a new React app in that folder, run the following command:

```
create-react-app first-react-tutorial
```

 Make sure you have the latest version of Node and npm installed in order to avoid errors.

This will create a brand new application called `first-react-tutorial`, under a new folder with the same name.

Once the app is created, we are ready to write some code. But first, let's see how this new app looks; navigate to the app folder, and then run the `npm start` script. Here is how it looks:

```
cd first-react-tutorial
npm start
```

This will run your brand new React app on local port `3000`, it should also open a browser to view the new app, and the URL will be `http://localhost:3000`. Here is how a vanilla React app looks:

Let's prepare the new project in the next section.

Preparing the new project

The React app that gets generated using the Create React App tool comes with a lot of features. For the purpose of this chapter, we only need to write a simple React app; here is how the generated app folder structure looks:

In this chapter, we'll mainly focus on building a simple React app, so we don't need some of the fancy features that come with the generated app. To simplify things, let's delete all the files and folders inside the `src` folder of the generated app. After that, let's just create a single empty JavaScript file called `index.js`. Here is how this will look:

Perfect—now, we are ready to write our simple products page. The first step is to include Boostrap in our HTML so that we can make use of Bootstrap's powerful styling. If you open the `public` folder, you will find an `index.html` file. This file contains some initial HTML that you can use in your React app. We'll modify this HTML file a bit to integrate Bootstrap, and we'll also include a `div` with an ID called `root`. Here's how `index.html` should look after the changes:

```
<!DOCTYPE html>
<html lang="en">
  <head>
    <meta charset="utf-8">
    <meta name="viewport" content="width=device-width, initial-scale=1,
shrink-to-fit=no">
    <!-- Bootstrap CSS -->
    <link rel="stylesheet"
href="https://stackpath.bootstrapcdn.com/bootstrap/4.1.1/css/bootstrap.min.
css" integrity="sha384-
WskhaSGFgHYWDcbwN70/dfYBj47jz9qbsMId/iRN3ewGhXQFZCSftd1LZCfmhktB"
crossorigin="anonymous">

    <meta name="theme-color" content="#000000">
    <!--
      manifest.json provides metadata used when your web app is added to
the
      homescreen on Android. See
https://developers.google.com/web/fundamentals/engage-and-retain/web-app-ma
nifest/
    -->
    <link rel="manifest" href="%PUBLIC_URL%/manifest.json">
```

```
    <link rel="shortcut icon" href="%PUBLIC_URL%/favicon.ico">
    <!--
      Notice the use of %PUBLIC_URL% in the tags above.
      It will be replaced with the URL of the `public` folder during the
build.
      Only files inside the `public` folder can be referenced from the
HTML.

      Unlike "/favicon.ico" or "favicon.ico", "%PUBLIC_URL%/favicon.ico"
will
      work correctly both with client-side routing and a non-root public
URL.
      Learn how to configure a non-root public URL by running `npm run
build`.
    -->
    <title>React App</title>
  </head>
  <body>
    <noscript>
      You need to enable JavaScript to run this app.
    </noscript>
    <div id="root"></div>
    <!--
      This HTML file is a template.
      If you open it directly in the browser, you will see an empty page.

      You can add webfonts, meta tags, or analytics to this file.
      The build step will place the bundled scripts into the <body> tag.

      To begin the development, run `npm start` or `yarn start`.
      To create a production bundle, use `npm run build` or `yarn build`.
    -->
    <script src="https://code.jquery.com/jquery-3.3.1.slim.min.js"
integrity="sha384-
q8i/X+965DzO0rT7abK41JStQIAqVgRVzpbzo5smXKp4YfRvH+8abtTE1Pi6jizo"
crossorigin="anonymous"></script>
    <script
src="https://cdnjs.cloudflare.com/ajax/libs/popper.js/1.14.3/umd/popper.min
.js" integrity="sha384-
ZMP7rVo3mIykV+2+9J3UJ46jBk0WLaUAdn689aCwoqbBJiSnjAK/l8WvCWPIPm49"
crossorigin="anonymous"></script>
    <script
src="https://stackpath.bootstrapcdn.com/bootstrap/4.1.1/js/bootstrap.min.js
" integrity="sha384-
smHYKdLADwkXOn1EmN1qk/HfnUcbVRZyYmZ4qpPea6sjB/pTJ0euyQp0Mk8ck+5T"
crossorigin="anonymous"></script>
  </body>
</html>
```

You can just copy the preceding code and paste it into the `index.html` file inside your `public` folder.

The next step is to put the musical instrument's images in your project. You can download the images from this project's GitHub page: `https://github.com/PacktPublishing/Hands-On-Full-Stack-Development-with-Go/tree/master/Chapter04/public/img`.

Go ahead and create a new folder called `img` inside your `public` folder; copy all the images to that folder.

The next step is to create a JSON file that describes each musical instrument that we would like to show on the product page. As we mentioned previously, our React app will rely on this JSON file to figure out which products to view. The file is called `cards.json`, and here is what we should put there initially:

```json
[{
"id" : 1,
"img" : "img/strings.png",
"imgalt":"string",
"desc":"A very authentic and beautiful instrument!!",
"price" : 100.0,
"productname" : "Strings"
}, {
"id" : 2,
"img" : "img/redguitar.jpeg",
"imgalt":"redg",
"desc":"A really cool red guitar that can produce super cool music!!",
"price" : 299.0,
"productname" : "Red Guitar"
},{
"id" : 3,
"img" : "img/drums.jpg",
"imgalt":"drums",
"desc":"A set of super awesome drums, combined with a guitar, they can
product more than amazing music!!",
"price" : 17000.0,
"productname" : "Drums"
},{
"id" : 4,
"img" : "img/flute.jpeg",
"imgalt":"flute",
"desc":"A super nice flute combined with some super nice musical notes!!",
"price" : 210.0,
"productname" : "Flute"
}]
```

Now, our `public` folder should look like this:

Let's take a look at JSX and React elements in the next section.

JSX and React elements

JSX can be defined as an extension for JavaScript that looks a whole lot like HTML. JSX can be used in React to create React elements. Basically, if you know HTML, you know JSX! In React docs, React elements are simply defined as a description of what you want to see on the screen.

React actually does not require JSX to work—you can replace JSX with some vanilla JavaScript. However, JSX is recommended when developing React applications, and is embraced by the vast majority of the React community. Let's look at some examples.

Remember the **Buy** button from the products page?

This button is a visual element that we can describe with JSX, as follows:

```
<a href="#" className="btn btn-primary">Buy</a>
```

You can see that JSX looks similar to HTML. The only major difference between the two that we'll note in this chapter is the fact that in JSX, we use the `className` keyword instead of `class` when we define the class name that our element belongs to. In the preceding code snippet, I made use of Bootstrap's CSS to style my element.

Another difference between JSX and HTML is that JSX makes use of the camel-case naming convention. For example, the `tabindex` HTML property becomes `tabIndex` in JSX.

The Bootstrap button component can be found at `https://getbootstrap.com/docs/4.1/components/buttons/`. The `href` attribute doesn't point to a real link because we are only building the frontend piece.

Because JSX is a JavaScript extension, you can integrate it in your JavaScript code with ease. For example, you can simply do this:

```
const btnElement = <a href="#" className="btn btn-primary">Buy</a>;
```

You can embed JavaScript code inside JSX by using curly brackets. For example, we can do something like this:

```
const btnName = "Buy";
const btnElement = <a href="#" className="btn btn-primary">{btnName}</a>;
```

Or, you can do something like the following code snippet:

```
const btnName = "Buy";
const btnClass = "btn btn-primary";
const btnElement = <a href="#" className={btnClass}>{btnName}</a>;
```

An element can have children, similar to how we would think of HTML elements. For example, here is an example of a parent `div` element that includes the button element as a child:

```
<div className="card-body">
    <a href="#" className="btn btn-primary">Buy</a>
</div>
```

React elements are cheap to create since they are just plain objects. To render a React element into the **Document Object Model** (**DOM**), we use `ReactDOM.render ()`, as follows:

```
const btnElement = <a href="#" className="btn btn-primary">Buy</a>;
ReactDOM.render(btnElement,document.getElementById('root'));
```

The preceding code will render the button element into a root DOM node.

Now, we have enough information to build one of our product cards using JSX. As a reminder, here is what a product card looks like:

Let's assume that we already have the product information as variables, as follows:

```
const img = "img/strings.png";
const imgalt = "string";
const desc = "A very authentic and beautiful instrument!!";
const price = 100;
const productName = "Strings";
```

With this information at our disposal, here is how we can write a React element in JSX to represent a product card:

```
<div className="col-md-6 col-lg-4 d-flex align-items-stretch">
    <div className="card mb-3">
        <img className="card-img-top" src={img} alt={imgalt} />
        <div className="card-body">
```

```
                    <h4 className="card-title">{productname}</h4>
                    Price: <strong>{price}</strong>
                    <p className="card-text">{desc}</p>
                    <a href="#" className="btn btn-primary">Buy</a>
            </div>
        </div>
    </div>
```

Except for the use of `className` instead of `class`, and the use of curly brackets, `{}`, to host the JavaScript code, the preceding code looks exactly like a piece of HTML code. We simply built a `div` element with several children.

In the preceding code snippet, we used `div` tags, an `img` tag, an `h4` tag, and an `a` tag to build our React element. All of those tags are well-known HTML tags that any frontend developer would probably encounter every day.

For styling, I used the power of Bootstrap to make our product card look beautiful. We used Bootstrap's grid system to ensure that the card will be positioned nicely on the browser's screen.

We also utilized Boostrap's wonderful card component, which can be found here: `https://getbootstrap.com/docs/4.1/components/card/`.

All of the images were obtained from `https://www.pexels.com`, which offers free images to use in your project.

Let's take a look at React components in the next section.

React components

After constructing the elements that represent your visual views, you will need to wrap them with React components to be able to properly use them in your React project.

A React component is typically composed of the following:

- React elements, which we discussed in the *JSX and React elements* section
- Props, which we will discuss in the *Props* section
- State, which we will discuss in the *State* section

Before we jump into props and state, let's cover some basics. A component is typically written as a JavaScript class or a function. Let's write a simple component to get a feeling for what they are really about.

Remember the card element we covered in the *JSX and React elements* section? Here is how it looked:

```
<div className="col-md-6 col-lg-4 d-flex align-items-stretch">
    <div className="card mb-3">
        <img className="card-img-top" src={img} alt={imgalt} />
        <div className="card-body">
            <h4 className="card-title">{productname}</h4>
            Price: <strong>{price}</strong>
            <p className="card-text">{desc}</p>
            <a href="#" className="btn btn-primary">Buy</a>
    </div>
    </div>
</div>
```

In a React production app, we need to write a component that hosts this element. Here is how the React component will look:

```
import React from 'react';
class Card extends React.Component {
    render() {
        const img = "img/strings.png";
        const imgalt = "string";
        const desc = "A very authentic and beautiful instrument!!";
        const price = 100;
        const productName = "Strings";
        return (
            <div className="col-md-6 col-lg-4 d-flex align-items-stretch">
                <div className="card mb-3">
                    <img className="card-img-top" src={img} alt={imgalt}
/>
                    <div className="card-body">
                        <h4 className="card-title">{productname}</h4>
                        Price: <strong>{price}</strong>
                        <p className="card-text">{desc}</p>
                        <a href="#" className="btn btn-primary">Buy</a>
                    </div>
                </div>
            </div>
        );
    }
}
```

In our project's src folder, copy the preceding code to index.js.

Now, let's inspect the preceding code. Here is what you need to know:

- A React component is a JavaScript class that inherits the `React.Component` type
- The most important method in a React component class is `render()`, since this method returns the React element that your component produces
- A component name starts with an uppercase letter, which is why `Card` started with *C* instead of *c*

You might be wondering why a component name has to start with an uppercase letter.

It's because in React, once you create a component, you can use it as a DOM tag in JSX. So to differentiate between a native DOM tag, such as `div`, and a component DOM tag, such as `Card`, we use upper case as the first letter for components.

Because you can use components as DOM tags in JSX, you can render them with `reactDOM.render()`, as follows:

```
reactDOM.render(<Card/>,document.getElementById('root'));
```

The preceding code will render our component under the `root div` of our HTML document.

Let's take a look at the design of the React application in the next section.

React application design

Now that we understand components, it's time to discuss how to design a React application with the power of components. A React application is composed of a number of components that talk to each other. There should be a main container component, which acts as an entry point to other components. The React community recommends against writing components that inherit from other components. Instead, the community recommends composition to be used. So, whenever we talk about parent and child components, we don't mean that child components inherit the parent component's classes, we just mean that the parent component contains one or more of the child components.

Composition means that all of your component classes should inherit from `React.Component`, and then the parent component renders child components to build your web application. This is best explained by an example.

For our product page, the proper design would involve two components: a CardContainer component, which will host the list of product cards we are trying to view, and a Card component, which will represent a single product card.

The CardContainer component is the parent, and the Card components are the children:

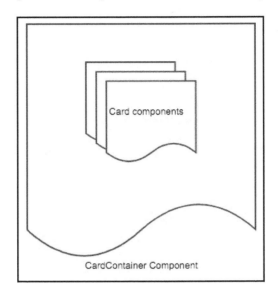

Both objects will inherit from React.Component. The CardContainer component will render a list of Card components to build the product page that supports multiple products. However, before we dive into the code for CardContainer, we need to understand how the CardContainer will pass the musical instrument product data to Card, which is what the next section will address.

Let's look at props and state in the next sections.

Props

So, this all looks good. However, in reality, since we have multiple products and not just one, we need a list of Card components, and not just one. It doesn't make sense to hardcode this component multiple times to correspond to each product. So, instead, we want to write the card component once. The CardContainer component we discussed in the *React application design* section should pass the product information to the Card component. So, we basically have a parent component that needs to pass some information to a child component.

You might wonder: why do we need the `CardContainer` component to pass data to the `Card` component, and not have the `Card` component look for its own data? The answer is simple: it was found that the best design for React applications is to have data state handled at the uppermost parent component where the data makes sense, then pieces of the data get passed down to smaller child components as needed. This design allows the child components to be in sync with one another, and in sync with their parents.

In our application, the uppermost component where all the product's information data should be handled is `CardContainer`, whereas the smaller child components that only need access to individual product information is handled in the `Card` components. In the world of React, this passing of data from parent component to child components is done using the `props` object. Props simply stands for properties.

To access the properties within any React component, we just need to call `this.props`. Let's assume that the product information was already passed to our `Card` component using props. Here is how the `Card` code will now look:

```
import React from 'react';
class Card extends React.Component {
    render() {
        return (
            <div className="col-md-6 col-lg-4 d-flex align-items-stretch">
                <div className="card mb-3">
                    <img className="card-img-top" src={this.props.img}
alt={this.props.imgalt} />
                    <div className="card-body">
                        <h4 className="card-
title">{this.props.productname}</h4>
                            Price: <strong>{this.props.price}</strong>
                            <p className="card-text">{this.props.desc}</p>
                            <a href="#" className="btn btn-primary">Buy</a>
                    </div>
                </div>
            </div>
        );
    }
}
```

In the preceding code, we simply accessed the `props` object through `this.props`, and since we assumed that the product information was already passed to us through props, the `props` object had all the information that we needed.

So, now comes the important question: how was the information passed from the parent component (CardContainer, in our case) to the child components (Card, in our case) using props?

The answer is quite simple; since a component name becomes a DOM tag in JSX, we can simply represent a component in JSX, as follows:

```
<Card img="img/strings.png" alt="strings" productName="Strings"
price='100.0' desc="A very authentic and beautiful instrument!!" />
```

In the preceding code, we utilized JSX to create a React element that represents a single product card component. The element tag name is Card, whereas the props are passed as attributes in JSX. If you look at the Card component code that we covered right before this, you will find that the names of the props correspond to the attribute names we passed within the React element that we created previously. In other words, the props were img, alt, productName, price, and desc. Those were the same names as the attributes in the preceding React element.

So, let's create a very simple CardContainer component that hosts only two cards, and see how this looks. Based on what we know so far, to create a React component, you need to do the following:

- Create a class that inherits from React.Component
- Override the render() method of React.Component

Here is how the code looks:

```
class CardContainer extends React.Component{
  render(){
      return(
          <div>
              <Card key='1' img="img/strings.png" alt="strings"
productName="Strings" price='100.0' desc="A very authentic and beautiful
instrument!!" />
              <Card key='2' img="img/redguitar.jpeg" alt="redg"
productName="Red Guitar" price='299.0' desc="A really cool red guitar that
can produce super cool music!!" />
          </div>
      );
   }
}
```

There are two important things that we need to cover from the preceding code:

- We put the two cards inside a parent `div` element. This is important because the `render()` method needs to return a single React element.
- We added a `key` attribute, even though it was not part of the `Card` component. The key property is a reserved property in React. Keys are important to use when working with lists of elements. Keys must be unique for each item. A key only needs to be unique on an item, compared to its sibling items. In our case, we have a list of cards, so that's why we used the `key` prop. React uses keys to figure out which items would need to get re-rendered, and which items stayed the same. A React component cannot access the `key` property through the `props` object. React monitors whether keys get added, removed, or changed. Then, it makes decisions on which components need to get re-rendered, and which components don't need to be touched.

The `render()` method in the preceding code can actually get refactored further:

```
render() {
  //hardcoded card list
  const cards = [{
    "id" : 1,
    "img" : "img/strings.png",
    "imgalt":"string",
    "desc":"A very authentic and beautiful instrument!!",
    "price" : 100.0,
    "productname" : "Strings"
  }, {
    "id" : 2,
    "img" : "img/redguitar.jpeg",
    "imgalt":"redg",
    "desc":"A really cool red guitar that can produce super cool music!!",
    "price" : 299.0,
    "productname" : "Red Guitar"
  }];
  //get a list of JSX elements representing each card
  const cardItems = cards.map(
    card => <Card key={card.id} img={card.img} alt={card.imgalt}
productName={card.productname} price={card.price} desc={card.desc} />
  );
  return (
    <div>
      {cardItems}
    </div>
  );
}
```

In the preceding code, we still hardcode the product card information for simplicity, but this time we use JavaScript's `map()` method to create a list of React elements. We then include our elements inside a parent `div` element, and return it as the result of our `render()` method.

The preceding code can actually get refactored even further, since it's a bit verbose to assign every single attribute with a value from a card item. Instead, React supports the following syntax:

```
const cardItems = cards.map(
    card => <Card key={card.id} {...card} />
);
```

In the preceding syntax, we just used `...` to pass all the properties of a card item to a `Card` component. This code works because the properties of the card object have the same names as the properties that are expected through the `props` object by the `Card` component. We still explicitly assigned the `key` attribute, because the `Card` object didn't have a `key` property—it had an `id` property instead.

The `CardContainer` component becomes the entry component to our product page, instead of the `Card` component. This means that we should render `CardContainer` instead of `Card` under the `root` div of our HTML document:

```
ReactDOM.render(
    <CardContainer />,
    document.getElementById('root')
);
```

State

The last major topic we need to cover in regards to the React library is the `state` object. We already learned that we use the `props` objects to pass data from one component to another. However, we can't just hardcode our data in a production-level application like we did in the *Props* section. The musical instruments' product information needs to be obtained from somewhere, and not hardcoded in our React code. In a real application, the data should come from a server-side API. However, for the purpose of this chapter, we'll obtain the product information from a JSON file called `cards.json`. In React, our application data needs to live inside the `state` object.

Let's take a look at how to initialize and set our `state` object in the next section.

Initializing the state object

The `state` object should be initialized at the constructor of the React component class that needs this state. For our product page, the data we need to store is simply the product information. Here is us initializing the `state` object:

```
class CardContainer extends React.Component {
  constructor(props) {
    //pass props to the parent component
    super(props);
    //initialize the state object for this component
    this.state = {
     cards: []
    };
  }

  /*
  Rest of the card container code
  */
}
```

A constructor for a component object expects `props` as an argument, so the first thing we need to do is pass `props` to the parent `React.Component` object.

The second step is to initialize the `state` object of our component. `state` objects are internal to our components, so the `state` object we initialize here is not shared with other components. Our `state` object will contain a list called `cards`, and is where we will store our musical instrument product card list.

Setting our state

The next obvious step is to set our `state` object with a list of product cards. To set data in a React `state` object, we must use a method called `setState()`, which belongs to our component object. Here is an example of us setting our `state` object with the information of two product cards:

```
this.setState({
    cards: [{
            "id" : 1,
            "img" : "img/strings.png",
            "imgalt":"string",
            "desc":"A very authentic and beautiful instrument!!",
            "price" : 100.0,
```

```
            "productname" : "Strings"
        }, {
            "id" : 2,
            "img" : "img/redguitar.jpeg",
            "imgalt":"redg",
            "desc":"A really cool red guitar that can produce super cool
music!!",
            "price" : 299.0,
            "productname" : "Red Guitar"
        }]
});
```

The `render()` method of our `CardContainer` component will need to change to look like this:

```
render(){
    const cards = this.state.cards;
        let items = cards.map(
            card => <Card key={card.id} {...card} />
        );
        return (
            <div className='container pt-4'>
                <h3 className='text-center text-primary'>Products</h3>
                <div className="pt-4 row">
                    {items}
                </div>
            </div>
        );
}
```

In the preceding code, we did two main things:

- Obtained the product card information from our `state` object
- Added some extra styling using the Bootstrap framework to make our product page look better

Obviously, we are still hardcoding our product data inside our component code, which is not right. As we mentioned earlier, our list of product card data needs to be in a file called `cards.json`, which we created in the *Preparing the new project* section. We need to add some code to grab data from this file, and then change the state accordingly. We will use the `fetch()` method, which is common in modern browsers, to obtain the contents of the `cards.json` file, and then we'll populate the state with the obtained data:

```
fetch('cards.json')
  .then(res => res.json())
  .then((result) => {
```

```
    this.setState({
    cards: result
  });
});
```

The preceding code is more than enough to fill up our `state` object. In a real production app, we would fetch an API address instead of a local file. But where should we put that code?

In React components, there are some life cycle methods that are supported. A life cycle method is a method that gets called whenever component life cycle events occur. An example of a component life cycle event is when the component gets mounted into the tree—the method that gets called whenever this event happens is called `componentDidMount()`. When you override this method, any code you write there will get executed whenever your component mounts. It is advised to write initialization code that involves loading data from remote locations in `componentDidMount()`. In our case, we are not really loading data from a remote location, since the `card.json` file is local to our app, however in a real production application, the data will live remotely. So, let's just write our initialization code inside `componentDidMount()` with the understanding that `fetch()` will need to change in the future to grab the data from a remote API:

```
componentDidMount() {
    fetch('cards.json')
    .then(res => res.json())
    .then((result) => {
        this.setState({
        cards: result
        });
    });
}
```

Perfect—this was the last piece of code we needed to finish up our `CardContainer` component. Here is how the entire class looks:

```
class CardContainer extends React.Component {
  constructor(props) {
  super(props);
  this.state = {
  cards: []
  };
  }

  componentDidMount() {
  fetch('cards.json')
  .then(res => res.json())
  .then((result) => {
```

```
this.setState({
cards: result
});
});
}

render() {
const cards = this.state.cards;
let items = cards.map(
card => <Card key={card.id} {...card} />
);
return (
<div className='container pt-4'>
<h3 className='text-center text-primary'>Products</h3>
<div className="pt-4 row">
{items}
</div>
</div>
);
}
}
```

We have covered enough ground to learn how to build a working application in React.

Developer tools

The React community is indeed a very passionate one. Facebook has released a bunch of tools that can be used to debug and troubleshoot React apps; you can find the repository for the dev tools at https://github.com/facebook/react-devtools. The dev tools are available as a Chrome extension, a Firefox extension, or as a standalone app.

For the purpose of this chapter, we'll have a brief look at the Chrome extension, which you can find at https://chrome.google.com/webstore/detail/react-developer-tools/fmkadmapgofadopljbjfkapdkoienihi.

Once you install the Chrome React Developer Tools extension, you can run it from Chrome's developer tools:

Once you open Chrome's developer tools, you will find a **React** tab in your developer tools pane:

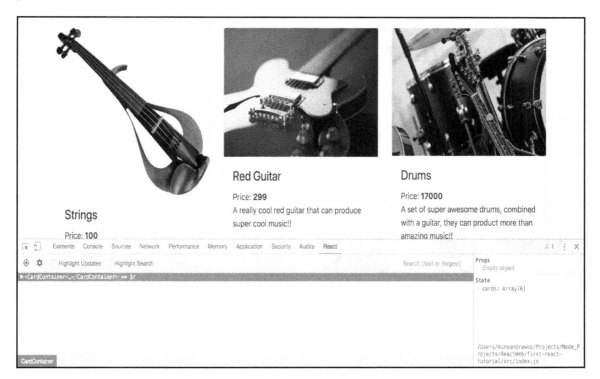

You will find your React components in this window. The entry to the React component to our product page was `CardContainer`, as shown in the preceding screenshot.

For each component that's exposed through the dev tools, you can dive deeper into the children components and their properties:

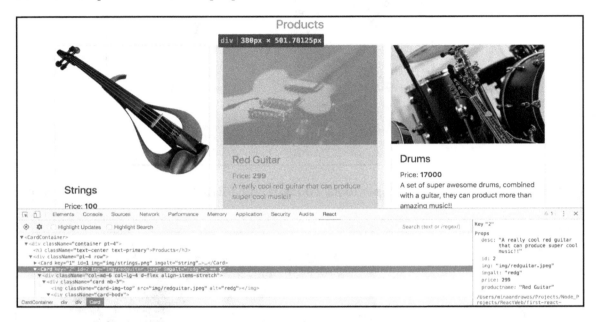

This will allow you to further inspect your React app and troubleshoot it properly, without much complexity. I advise that you take a moment to try out the dev tools for yourself and explore what they can do.

Summary

In this chapter, we learned how to design and build a working React application. We covered all the key pieces that make React work, such as React elements, components, props, and states. We also learned about JSX and how similar it is to HTML. Once you learn React, you will find it a very enjoyable framework to build web products with. There is a reason why it is so popular with developers worldwide.

In the next chapter, we'll utilize the knowledge we gained here to build the frontend of our GoMusic website.

Questions

1. What is React?
2. What is JSX?
3. What is a React element?
4. What are props?
5. What is a React state?
6. What is a React component?
7. What are the two things you should do inside a component constructor?
8. What is the most important method in a React component class?
9. What does a life cycle method mean?
10. What is a `key` property, and why is it important?

Further reading

For more information regarding what was covered in this chapter, you can check out the following links:

- **React website**: https://reactjs.org/
- **React docs**: https://reactjs.org/docs/hello-world.html
- **React tutorial**: https://reactjs.org/tutorial/tutorial.html

5
Building a Frontend for GoMusic

It's now time to build the first major piece of the project of this book. As mentioned in `Chapter 4`, *Frontend with React.js*, we'll be building an online store for musical instruments, which we will name GoMusic. In this chapter, we'll build most of the frontend of the online store by utilizing the impressive power of the React framework. Our GoMusic store will support the fundamental features of any online store:

- Users should be able to buy any product they like.
- Users should have access to a promotional page, which provides current sales and promotions.
- Users should be able to create their own accounts, and sign into them for a more personalized experience.

The following are the three main components of our frontend that we will be learning about in this chapter:

- Main pages, which all users of our web application should see
- Modal dialog windows, which help with buying products, accounts creation, and signing in
- User pages, which show a personalized page for the logged-in user

In this chapter, we will cover the following topics:

- Writing non-trivial React applications
- Integrating credit card services with our frontend with Stripe
- Writing modal windows in our code
- Designing routes in our code

Prerequisites and technical requirements

In Chapter 4, *Frontend with React.js*, we covered the foundations of how to build a React.js application, so read it before attempting to follow along with this chapter.

The requirements are the same for this chapter. Here is a quick recap of the required knowledge and tools:

- npm.
- The React framework.
- The Create React App tool, which you can simply install using the following command:

```
npm install -g create-react-app
```

- The Bootstrap framework.
- Knowledge of ES6, HTML, and CSS. In this chapter, we will use HTML forms in more than one component.

The code and files for this chapter can be found in GitHub: https://github.com/ PacktPublishing/Hands-On-Full-Stack-Development-with-Go/tree/master/Chapter05.

Building GoMusic

Now it's time to build our online store. Our first step is to use the Create React App tool to create a new React application. Open your Terminal, navigate to the folder where you would like the GoMusic application to live, then run the following command:

```
create-react-app gomusic
```

This command will create a new folder, called gomusic, which will contain a skeleton React application waiting to be constructed.

Now navigate to your `gomusic` folder using the following command:

```
cd gomusic
```

Inside, you'll find three folders: `node_modules`, `public`, and `src`. Before we start writing our application, we'll need to remove some files from the `src` folder.

Delete the following files from the `src` folder:

- `app.css`
- `index.css`
- `logo.svg`

Next, we'll need to go the `public` folder. To make things simpler, replace the contents of your `public` folder with those found at our project's GitHub page: `https://github.com/PacktPublishing/Hands-On-Full-Stack-Development-with-Go/tree/master/Chapter05/public`.

The contents of the GitHub page contain images that we'll be using in our project, the JSON files that will describe our data, as well as the modified HTML file, which will include support for jQuery and the Bootstrap frameworks.

In the next section, we'll take a look at the main pages in our application.

Main pages

The main pages of our GoMusic application are the pages that all users should see, whether they are logged into their GoMusic accounts or not. There are three main pages:

- The products page, which is our **Home** page
- The **Promotions** page
- The **About** page

The first page is the products page. Here is how it looks:

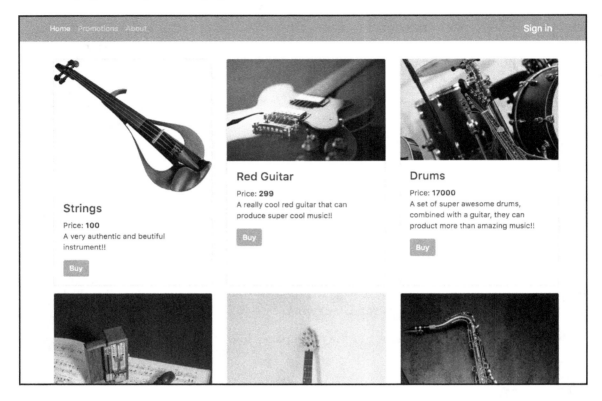

As shown in the preceding screenshot, we will support a navigational menu that will allow us to navigate between the three main pages. The **Home** option will host the products page, which all users should see.

The second page is our **Promotions** page, which should look very similar to the **Home** page, except that it will show less products with lower prices. The prices in this page should show up in red to emphasize the sale:

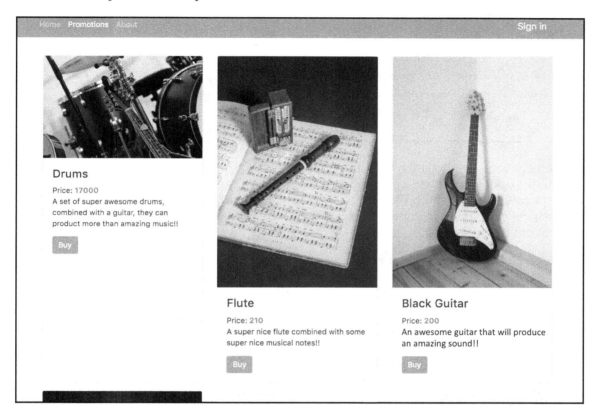

The third page is our **About** page, which should just show some information about the GoMusic store:

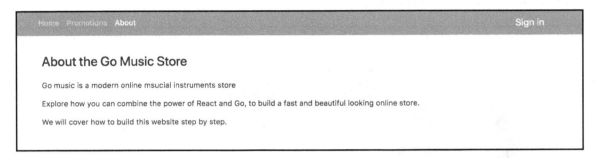

You probably also noticed the **Sign in** option at the rightmost edge of our navigational menu; this option will open up a modal dialog window, which will allow our users to create accounts and sign in. We'll be covering the modal dialog windows in the *Modal dialog windows and handling credit cards* section. For each of our main pages, we'll create a React component to represent it.

Create the following files in the src folder:

- Navigations.js: This file will host the code for the navigational menu component.
- ProductCards.js: This file will host the code for the **Home** and **Promotions** page components.
- About.js: This file will host the code for the **About** page component.

Now, let's start with the navigational menu component.

The navigational menu

The first component that we need to build to connect all our main pages together would be the navigational menu:

In the React framework, in order to build a functioning navigational menu with ease, we need to make use of the power of a package called react-router-dom. To install this package, open your Terminal, then run the following command:

```
npm install --save react-router-dom
```

Once the package is installed, we can make use of it in our code. Now, let's open up the Navigation.js file and start writing some code.

The first thing we need to do is to import the packages that we need to build our menu. We'll utilize two packages:

- The react package
- The react-router-dom package

We will need to export a class called NavLink from react-router-dom. The NavLink class is a React component that we can use in our code in order to create links that can navigate to other React components:

```
import React from 'react';
import {NavLink} from 'react-router-dom';
```

Next, we need to create a new React component called Navigation. Here's how it looks:

```
export default class Navigation extends React.Component{
}
```

Inside our new component, we'll need to override the render() method, as mentioned in Chapter 4, *Frontend with React.js*, in order to write the view of the component:

```
export default class Navigation extends React.Component{
    render(){
        //The code to describe how our menu would look like
    }
}
```

Inside our `render()` method, we'll make use of the Bootstrap framework in combination with the `NavLink` component that we imported, in order to build our navigational menu. Here is how the code inside the `render()` method should look:

```
export default class Navigation extends React.Component{
    render(){
        //The code to describe how our menu would look like
        return (
            <div>
                <nav className="navbar navbar-expand-lg navbar-dark bg-
success fixed-top">
                    <div className="container">
                        <button type="button" className="navbar-brand
order-1 btn btn-success"  onClick={() => {
this.props.showModalWindow();}}>Sign in</button>
                        <div className="navbar-collapse"
id="navbarNavAltMarkup">
                            <div className="navbar-nav">
                                <NavLink className="nav-item nav-link"
to="/">Home</NavLink>
                                <NavLink className="nav-item nav-link"
to="/promos">Promotions</NavLink>
                                <NavLink className="nav-item nav-link"
to="/about">About</NavLink>
                            </div>
                        </div>
                    </div>
                </nav>
            </div>
        );
    }
}
```

The code makes use of the Bootstrap framework to style and build the navigation bar. Also, when the **Sign in** button gets clicked, we invoke a function called `showModalWindow()`, which is expected to get passed to us as a React prop. The job of this function is to show the **Sign in** modal window:

```
<button type="button" className="navbar-brand order-1 btn btn-success"
onClick={() => { this.props.showModalWindow();}}>Sign in</button>
```

Perfect: with the preceding code out of the way, we now have a functional component that can be utilized to show the navigational menu. We will explore this function in the *The user page navigational menu* section.

Let's take a look at the Products and Promotions page in the next section.

The Products and Promotions pages

Now let's move to writing the product's page component. The code is similar to the products page that we wrote in `Chapter 4`, *Frontend with React.js*. Let's open the `ProductsCards.js` file, then write the following code:

```
import React from 'react';

class Card extends React.Component {
    render() {
        const priceColor = (this.props.promo)? "text-danger" : "text-dark";
        const sellPrice =
(this.props.promo)?this.props.promotion:this.props.price;
        return (
            <div className="col-md-6 col-lg-4 d-flex align-items-stretch">
                <div className="card mb-3">
                    <img className="card-img-top" src={this.props.img}
alt={this.props.imgalt} />
                    <div className="card-body">
                        <h4 className="card-
title">{this.props.productname}</h4>
                        Price: <strong
className={priceColor}>{sellprice}</strong>
                        <p className="card-text">{this.props.desc}</p>
                        <a className="btn btn-success text-white"
onClick={()=>{this.props.showBuyModal(this.props.ID,sellPrice)}}>Buy</a>
                    </div>
                </div>
            </div>
        );
    }
}
```

The preceding code represents a single product card component. It makes use of Bootstrap to style our card.

The code is almost the same as the product cards we built in Chapter 4, *Frontend with React.js*, except for few differences:

- We changed the **Buy** button color to green by making use of Bootstrap's `.btn-success` class.
- We added an option to change the **Price** color through a variable called `priceColor`; the variable looks at a prop called `promo`. If `promo` is true, we'll use a red color; if the `promo` prop is false, we'll use the black color.
- The **Buy** button here opens up a modal window by calling the `showBuyModal()` function. We will discuss the modal windows in more detail in the *Modal dialog windows and handling credit cards* section.

The code will produce two flavors of a product card based on the value of the `promo` prop. If the `promo` prop is false, the product card will look like this:

If the `promo` prop is true, the product card will look like this:

The next thing we need to write in the `ProductsCards.js` file is the `CardContainer` component. This component will be responsible for showing the product cards together in one page. Here is our card container in action:

Strings

Price: **100**
A very authentic and beautiful instrument!!

Red Guitar

Price: **299**
A really cool red guitar that can produce super cool music!!

Drums

Price: **17000**
A set of super awesome drums, combined with a guitar, they can product more than amazing music!!

Flute

Price: **210**
A super nice flute combined with some super nice musical notes!!

Black Guitar

Price: **200**
An awesome guitar that will produce an amazing sound!!

Saxophone

Price: **1000**
A great saxophone for a great musician!!

Let's create the component:

```
export default class CardContainer extends React.Component{
    //our code
}
```

The component should look very similar to the one we wrote in `Chapter 4`, *Frontend with React.js*. The next step is to write the constructor of our component. This component will rely on a `state` object where the card's information is stored. Here is how the constructor should look:

```
export default class CardContainer extends React.Component{
    constructor(props) {
        super(props);
        this.state = {
            cards: []
        };
    }
}
```

As per `Chapter 4`, *Frontend with React.js*, we put the card's information in a file called `cards.json`, which should now exist in our `public` folder. The file contains a JSON array of objects, where each object contains data about one card, such as ID, image, description, prices, and product name. Here is sample data from the file:

```
[{
    "id" : 1,
    "img" : "img/strings.png",
    "imgalt":"string",
    "desc":"A very authentic and beautiful instrument!!",
    "price" : 100.0,
    "productname" : "Strings"
}, {
    "id" : 2,
    "img" : "img/redguitar.jpeg",
    "imgalt":"redg",
    "desc":"A really cool red guitar that can produce super cool music!!",
    "price" : 299.0,
    "productname" : "Red Guitar"
},{
    "id" : 3,
    "img" : "img/drums.jpg",
    "imgalt":"drums",
    "desc":"A set of super awesome drums, combined with a guitar, they can
product more than amazing music!!",
```

```
"price" : 17000.0,
    "productname" : "Drums"
}]
```

In the `public` folder of GoMusic, we also added a file called `promos.json`, which hosts data about sales and promotions. The data in `promos.json` is in the same data format as `cards.json`.

Now, with the `CardContainer` constructor out of the way, we need to override the `componentDidMount()` method, in order to write the code to obtain the card data from either `cards.json`, or `promos.json`. When showing the main products page, we'll obtain our product card's data from `cards.json`. Whereas, when showing the promos and sales page, we'll obtain our product card's data from `promos.json`. Since the source of the card data is not unique, we'll use a prop for this purpose. Let's call the prop `location`. Here is how the code will look:

```
componentDidMount() {
  fetch(this.props.location)
  .then(res => res.json())
  .then((result) => {
  this.setState({
  cards: result
  });
  });
}
```

In the preceding code, we utilized the popular `fetch()` method to retrieve data from the address stored in `this.props.location`. If we are viewing the main products page, the value of location will be `cards.json`. If we are viewing the **Promotions** page, the value of location will be `promos.json`. Once we retrieve the card data, we'll store it in the `state` object of our `CardContainer` component.

Finally, let's write the `render()` method of our `CardContainer` method. We will get the product cards from our component's `state` object, then feed the product cards' data as props to our `Card` components. Here is how the code will look:

```
render(){
      const cards = this.state.cards;
      let items = cards.map(
          card => <Card key={card.id} {...card} promo={this.props.promo}
showBuyModal={this.props.showBuyModal} />
      );
      return (
          <div>
              <div className="mt-5 row">
```

```
                {items}
            </div>
        </div>
    );
}
```

We also pass the `showBuyModal` prop to the card component; this prop represents the function that we will implement in the *Creating a parent StripeProvider component* section to open the buy modal window. The `showBuyModal` function will be expected to take the product ID represented as the card, as well as the selling price of the product, as input.

The preceding code is very similar to the `CardContainer` code we wrote in Chapter 4, *Frontend with React.js*. The only addition is that we now also pass a `promo` prop to the `Card` component. The `promo` prop lets us know whether the product card in question is a promotion.

Let's take a look at the **About** page in the next section.

The About page

Now let's add an **About** page. Here's how it will look:

About the Go Music Store

Go music is a modern online msucial instruments store

Explore how you can combine the power of React and Go, to build a fast and beautiful looking online store.

We will cover how to build this website step by step.

Let's navigate to the `src` folder in our project. Create a new file called `About.js`. We'll start by importing the `react` package:

```
import React from 'react';
```

Next, we need to write a React component. Typically, we'd create a new class that would inherit from `React.Component`. However, we'll explore a different coding style that would be better suited to the **About** page.

For simpler components, where a full class is not needed, we simply use what is known as *functional components*. Here is how the `About` component would look when written as a functional component:

```
export default function About(props){
    return (
        <div className="row mt-5">
            <div className="col-12 order-lg-1">
                <h3 className="mb-4">About the Go Music Store</h3>
                <p>Go music is a modern online musical instruments
store</p>
                <p>Explore how you can combine the power of React and Go,
to build a fast and beautiful looking online store.</p>
                <p>We will cover how to build this website step by
step.</p>
            </div>
        </div>);
}
```

A functional component is just a function that takes a props object as an argument. The function returns a JSX object that represents the view that we would like the component to show. The preceding code is equivalent to writing a class that inherits from `React.Component`, then overriding the `render()` method to return our view.

In more recent versions of React, a functional component can support a `state` object, through a feature known as React *Hooks*. A React Hook gives you the ability to initialize and utilize a state in a functional component. Here is a simple example of a `state` counter from the React documentation:

```
import React, { useState } from 'react';

function Example() {
  // Declare a new state variable, which we'll call "count"
  const [count, setCount] = useState(0);

  return (
    <div>
      <p>You clicked {count} times</p>
      <button onClick={() => setCount(count + 1)}>
        Click me
      </button>
    </div>
  );
}
```

We do not use React Hooks in our code here. However, if you are curious about the feature, you can explore it by visiting `https://reactjs.org/docs/hooks-intro.html`.

Before we move to the next section, it's worth mentioning that the `Card` component could have been written as a functional component as well, since it was relatively simple, and didn't need a constructor or any special logic beyond the `render()` method.

Now, let's talk about how to build dialog windows in our React app.

Modal dialog windows and handling credit cards

Now it's time to cover the modal windows in our website. A modal window is a small temporary window that is overlaid on your main website. There are two main modal windows that we need to build:

- The **Buy Item** modal window
- The **Sign in** modal window

The Buy Item modal window outline

Let's start with the **Buy Item** modal window. This modal window should show up when a user clicks on the **Buy** button of a product card; in other words, when you click on the **Buy** button:

Once the **Buy** button is clicked, the following modal window should appear:

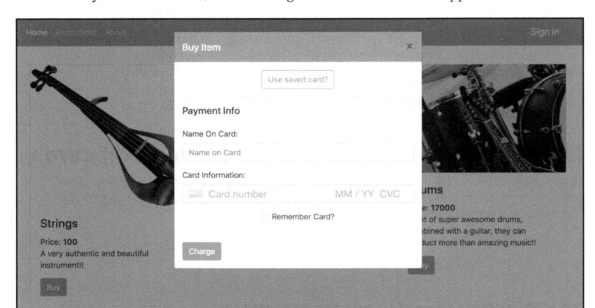

As you can see, the modal is basically a smaller window that showed up over our main website. It allows the user to input some important data before going back to the main website. Modal windows are very powerful tools in any modern website, so let's start writing one. The modal window we are building today needs to be capable of taking credit card information.

Before we start writing code, we'll need to install an important package called reactstrap. This package exposes features offered by the bootstrap framework through React components; it has a very handy Modal component that we can use to build reactive modal windows. Let's run the following command from our favorite Terminal. The command can be executed from the project's main folder:

```
npm install --save reactstrap
```

The first step is to go to the src folder, then create a new file called modalwindows.js. This file is where we will write all of our modal windows. Next, let's import the React library:

```
import React from 'react';
```

We then import the modal-related components from the reactstrap package:

```
import { Modal, ModalHeader, ModalBody } from 'reactstrap';
```

Since we are starting with the **Buy Item** modal window, let's write a React component called BuyModalWindow:

```
export class BuyModalWindow extends React.Component{
}
```

We use the export keyword here, because this class will need to be exported to other files. Again, we will make use of the power of the Bootstrap frontend framework to build our modal window. When we wrote our Card component, we designed our Buy button to open a modal window with the #buy ID. So, here is our #buy modal window:

```
export class BuyModalWindow extends React.Component{
    render() {
        return (
          <Modal id="buy" tabIndex="-1" role="dialog"
isOpen={props.showModal} toggle={props.toggle}>
              <div role="document">
                  <ModalHeader toggle={props.toggle} className="bg-success
text-white">
                      Buy Item
                  </ModalHeader>
                  <ModalBody>
                      {/*Credit card form*/}
                  </ModalBody>
              </div>
          </Modal>
          );
    }
}
```

In the preceding code, we built a React component that encapsulates a nice modal window with a green header, a Close button, and an empty body. The Credit card form code is not included yet; we'll get to that in the *Credit card handling with React and Stripe* section. The code makes use of the Modal component, which is provided by the reactstrap package. The reactstrap package also provides a ModalHeader component for us to specify how the modal header will look, as well as a ModalBody component to define the body of our modal window.

The Modal component hosts two very important React props that we need to address:

- **The** isOpen **prop**: A Boolean that needs to be set to true when we need the modal to show up, otherwise the value is false
- **The** toggle **prop**: A callback function that is used to toggle the value of isOpen when needed

Let's do a quick tweak to our code first. Since the BuyModalWindow component doesn't include any other methods besides the render() method, we can write it as a functional component:

```
export function BuyModalWindow(props){
  return (
        <Modal id="buy" tabIndex="-1" role="dialog"
isOpen={props.showModal} toggle={props.toggle}>
            <div role="document">
                <ModalHeader toggle={props.toggle} className="bg-success
text-white">
                    Buy Item
                </ModalHeader>
                <ModalBody>
                    {/*Credit card form*/}
                </ModalBody>
            </div>
        </Modal>
    );
}
```

Perfect, now let's fill the empty body of our modal window. We need to write a Credit card form to be the body of our modal window.

In the next section we'll take a look at credit card handling for our application.

Credit card handling with React and Stripe

The idea of building a form that just takes credit card information might sound simple at first. However, the process involves more than just building a bunch of text boxes. In production environments, we need to be able to validate the information being entered to the credit card, and we need to figure out a secure way to handle credit card data. Since credit card information is extremely sensitive, we cannot treat it simply like any other piece of data.

Luckily, there are several services out there that you can use to handle credit cards in your frontend code. In this chapter, we'll make use of Stripe (`https://stripe.com/`), which is one of the most popular services for handling payments with credit cards. Like almost any other web service in a production environment, you would need to visit its website, create an account, and get an API key to use in your product code. With Stripe, the registration also involves providing your business bank account so that they can deposit money into your account.

However, they also provide some test API keys that we can utilize for development and initial testing, which is what we'll be utilizing today.

Stripe helps with every step involved in charging credit cards in your application. Stripe validates credit cards, charges them with the approved amounts you provide, and then puts that money in your business bank account.

In order to fully integrate Stripe or almost any other payment service with your code, you need to write code at the frontend and the backend. In this chapter, we'll be covering most of the code needed at the frontend. We'll be visiting this topic again at a later chapter when working on the backend, in order to write the full integration. Let's get started.

Due to the huge popularity of the React frontend framework, Stripe provides special React libraries and APIs that we can use to design visual elements that can take credit card data. These visual elements are known as React Stripe elements (`https://github.com/stripe/react-stripe-elements`).

React Stripe elements provide the following functionalities:

- They provide some UI elements that can take credit card data, such as credit card numbers, expiry dates, CVC numbers, and ZIP codes.
- They can do advanced validation on the data entered. For example, for credit card fields, they can tell whether a Master Card or Visa is being entered.
- After Stripe elements accept the data provided to them, they give you a token ID that represents the credit card in question and you can then enter this token ID in the backend to use the card in your application.

Perfect. So, now that we have enough background about Stripe, let's start writing some code.

There are a number of steps that you must cover in your code in order to properly integrate credit card handling with your frontend code:

1. Create a React component to host your `Credit card form` code. Let's call it the `child` React component; you'll see very shortly why it's a `child` component.

2. Inside that component, make use of the Stripe elements, which are just some React components provided by Stripe in order to build the credit card input fields. These fields are simply the text boxes that take credit card information, such as the credit card number and expiry date.

3. Inside this `child` component, write the code to submit the validated credit card token to the backend.

4. Create another React component. This component will act as a parent to the React component that hosted the Stripe elements. The parent React component will need to do the following:

   - Host a stripe component that processes Stripe's API key, also known as `StripeProvider`.
   - Inside the `StripeProvider` component, you need to host the `child` React component.
   - Before you can host the `child` React component, you need to inject it with special Stripe code that wraps it with Stripe props and functions. The method to inject a component with Stripe code is called `injectStripe`.

Let's implement the preceding steps one by one.

Creating a child React component to host Stripe elements

First, we need to install the Stripe react packages. In the Terminal, we need to navigate to our `gomusic` project folder, then run the following command:

```
npm install --save react-stripe-elements
```

Next, let's visit the `index.html` file located at `frontend/public/index.html`. Then, right before the HTML closing tag, which is the line right before `</head>`, type `<script src="https://js.stripe.com/v3/"></script>`. This will ensure the Stripe code will be loaded when the end user loads our GoMusic application in their browser.

Now let's write some code. Inside our `src` folder, let's create new file called `CreditCards.js`. We start by importing the packages that we need for our incoming code to work:

```
import React from 'react';
import { injectStripe, StripeProvider, Elements, CardElement } from 'react-
stripe-elements';
```

Time to write our `child` React component, which will host our credit card form:

```
class CreditCardForm extends React.Component{
    constructor(props){
        super(props);
    }
}
```

In order for our code to be as realistic as possible, we need to adhere to the three states associated with processing a credit card:

- **Initial status**: No cards have been processed yet.
- **Success status**: Card has been processed and succeeded.
- **Failed status**: Card has been processed but failed.

Here is the code to represent these three states:

```
const INITIALSTATE = "INITIAL", SUCCESSSTATE = "COMPLETE", FAILEDSTATE =
"FAILED";
class CreditCardForm extends React.Component{
    constructor(props){
        super(props);
    }
}
```

Next, let's write three methods to represent the three states:

```
const INITIALSTATE = "INITIAL", SUCCESSSTATE = "COMPLETE", FAILEDSTATE =
"FAILED";
class CreditCardForm extends React.Component{
    constructor(props){
        super(props);
    }
    renderCreditCardInformation() {}
    renderSuccess() {}
    renderFailure(){}
}
```

These three methods will be called based on our current status. We need to save our current state in our React `state` object so that we can retrieve it at any time inside our component:

```
const INITIALSTATE = "INITIAL", SUCCESSSTATE = "COMPLETE", FAILEDSTATE =
"FAILED";
class CreditCardForm extends React.Component{
    constructor(props){
        super(props);
        this.state = {
            status: INITIALSTATE
        };
    }
    renderCreditCardInformation() {}
    renderSuccess() {}
    renderFailure(){}
}
```

The status will change based on the success or failure of the credit card transaction. It's time to write the `render()` method of our React component. Our `render()` method will simply look at our current status by inspecting `this.state.status`, then based on the status, it will render the appropriate view:

```
const INITIALSTATE = "INITIAL", SUCCESSSTATE = "COMPLETE", FAILEDSTATE =
"FAILED";
class CreditCardForm extends React.Component{
    constructor(props){
        super(props);
        this.state = {
            status: INITIALSTATE
        };
    }
    renderCreditCardInformation() {}
    renderSuccess() {}
    renderFailure(){}
    render() {
        let body = null;
        switch (this.state.status) {
            case SUCCESSSTATE:
                body = this.renderSuccess();
                break;
            case FAILEDSTATE:
                body = this.renderFailure();
                break;
            default:
                body = this.renderCreditCardInformation();
        }
```

```
        return (
            <div>
                {body}
            </div>
        );
    }
}
```

What's left is to write the code for the three render methods. Let's start with the most complex, which is `renderCreditCardInformation()`. This is where we'll use the Stripe element components. Here is the view that this method needs to produce:

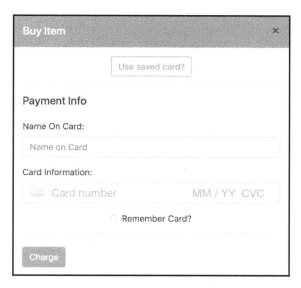

We'll start by writing the JSX elements that represent the **Use Saved Card?** button at the beginning as well as the **Remember Card?** checkbox close to the end. We'll write those elements separately because later we'll need to hide them from users who are not logged in:

```
renderCreditCardInformation() {
        const usersavedcard = <div>
            <div className="form-row text-center">
                <button type="button" className="btn btn-outline-success
text-center mx-auto">Use saved card?</button>
            </div>
            <hr />
        </div>

        const remembercardcheck = <div className="form-row form-check text-
center">
```

```
                <input className="form-check-input" type="checkbox" value=""
    id="remembercardcheck" />
                <label className="form-check-label"
    htmlFor="remembercardcheck">
                    Remember Card?
                </label>
            </div>;
            //return the view
        }
```

In the preceding code, we again used the Bootstrap framework to design the button and the checkbox.

Making use of Stripe elements to handle credit card information

Now it's time to design the user interface for the credit card payment information. Here is the piece that we need to build:

Payment Info

Name On Card:

    Name on Card

Card Information:

    Card number   MM / YY CVC

The most interesting part is the **Card Information** field:

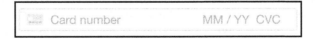

This is where we'll make use of the Stripe elements components, in order to integrate Stripe's UI and validation with our user interface. If you recall, there is a package called `CardElement` that we imported at the beginning of our `CreditCards.js` file. `CardElement` is nothing but a React component that is provided by Stripe in order to build credit card field UIs in your React applications. This is our Stripe element that we'll be using in our code. We can simply utilize it through JSX like any other component:

```
<CardElement \>
```

Stripe elements components support a prop called `style`, which allows you to define how the style of the element should look. The `style` prop takes a JavaScript object that defines how the style should look for the Stripe element. The following code shows a `style` object that looks right at home with the Bootstrap framework visually:

```
const style = {
    base: {
        'fontSize': '20px',
        'color': '#495057',
        'fontFamily': 'apple-system,BlinkMacSystemFont,"Segoe
UI",Roboto,"Helvetica Neue",Arial,sans-serif'
    }
};
```

For our card's Stripe element to take the preceding `style` object, we just need to do this:

```
<CardElement style={style}/>
```

Perfect. Now let's build the rest of our `renderCreditCardInformation()` method. With the Stripe card element out of the way, we need to build the HTML form that will host the Stripe card element along with the **Name On Card** field in our credit card pay modal window. Here is the JSX code for the UI:

```
<div>
                    <h5 className="mb-4">Payment Info</h5>
                    <form>
                        <div className="form-row">
                            <div className="col-lg-12 form-group">
                                <label htmlFor="cc-name">Name On Card:</label>
                                <input id="cc-name" name='cc-name'
className="form-control" placeholder='Name on Card'
onChange={this.handleInputChange} type='text' />
                            </div>
                        </div>
                        <div className="form-row">
                            <div className="col-lg-12 form-group">
                                <label htmlFor="card">Card Information:</label>
                                <CardElement id="card" className="form-control"
style={style} />
                            </div>
                        </div>
                    </form>
</div>
```

The preceding code only shows an HTML form that hosts the **Name On Card** as well as the card element visual component. We also made use of a method called `handleInputChange()`, which triggers when we input the **Name On Card** field. This method changes the `state` object of our component based on the new **Name On Card** value of our HTML form. This is the recommended React way to handle forms—create state to correspond to your HTML form values:

```
handleInputChange(event) {
    this.setState({
        value: event.target.value
    });
}
```

It's time to write the full code for the credit card information window, including the **Remember Card?** and **Use Saved Card?** options. Here's how the full `renderCreditCardInformation()` method should look:

```
renderCreditCardInformation(){
    const style = {
        base: {
            'fontSize': '20px',
            'color': '#495057',
            'fontFamily': 'apple-system,BlinkMacSystemFont,"Segoe
UI",Roboto,"Helvetica Neue",Arial,sans-serif'
        }
    };
    const usersavedcard = <div>
        <div className="form-row text-center">
            <button type="button" className="btn btn-outline-success
text-center mx-auto">Use saved card?</button>
        </div>
        <hr />
    </div>

    const remembercardcheck = <div className="form-row form-check text-
center">
        <input className="form-check-input" type="checkbox" value=""
id="remembercardcheck" />
        <label className="form-check-label"
htmlFor="remembercardcheck">
            Remember Card?
        </label>
    </div>;
    return (
        <div>
            {usersavedcard}
            <h5 className="mb-4">Payment Info</h5>
```

```
<form onSubmit={this.handleSubmit}>
    <div className="form-row">
        <div className="col-lg-12 form-group">
            <label htmlFor="cc-name">Name On Card:</label>
            <input id="cc-name" name='cc-name'
className="form-control" placeholder='Name on Card'
onChange={this.handleInputChange} type='text' />
        </div>
    </div>
    <div className="form-row">
        <div className="col-lg-12 form-group">
            <label htmlFor="card">Card Information:</label>
            <CardElement id="card" className="form-control"
style={style} />
        </div>
    </div>
    {remembercardcheck}
    <hr className="mb-4" />
    <button type="submit" className="btn btn-success btn-
large" >{this.props.operation}</button>
</form>
        </div>
    );
}
```

The preceding code makes use of our `remembercardcheck` and `usersavedcard` elements. We also assume that there is a method called `handleSubmit`, which will get triggered when our HTML form gets submitted. The `handleSubmit` method will be discussed in the *Submitting a credit card token to the backend* section.

Perfect. Now let's write up the remaining methods in our `CreditCardForm` component: `renderSuccess()` and `renderFailure()`. We'll start with `renderSuccess()`:

The code is simple:

```
renderSuccess(){
        return (
            <div>
                <h5 className="mb-4 text-success">Request
Successfull....</h5>
                <button type="submit" className="btn btn-success btn-large"
onClick={() => { this.props.toggle() }}>Ok</button>
            </div>
        );
}
```

The preceding code is linked to the **Buy** modal window through the `toggle` method, which will get passed to our component here as a prop. As mentioned, the `toggle` method can be used to open or close a modal window. Since the modal window will be open when this code gets executed, the modal window will close once the **Ok** button is pressed. The full syntax for the `toggle` method will be defined later in our code, specifically when we cover the main code in the `App.js` file.

Here's how the `renderFailure()` method looks:

The code for the preceding UI looks like this:

```
renderFailure(){
        return (
            <div>
                <h5 className="mb-4 text-danger"> Credit card information
invalid, try again or exit</h5>
                {this.renderCreditCardInformation()}
            </div>
        );
}
```

Submitting a credit card token to the backend

Now let's go back to the `handleSubmit()` method, which should trigger whenever the credit card HTML form submits. When you make use of a Stripe element component, it not only validates the credit card information, but it also returns a `token` object that represents the credit card entered. This `token` object is what you'll use in the backend to charge this card.

The `handleSubmit()` method code needs to take care of a number of things:

1. Retrieve the token that corresponds to the credit card entered
2. Send the token to our backend server
3. Render a success or a failure state based on the outcome

Here's how the code will look:

```
async handleSubmit(event){
        event.preventDefault();
        console.log("Handle submit called, with name: " +
this.state.value);
        //retrieve the token via Stripe's API
  let { token } = await this.props.stripe.createToken({ name:
this.state.value });
        if (token == null) {
            console.log("invalid token");
            this.setState({ status: FAILEDSTATE });
            return;
        }

        let response = await fetch("/charge", {
            method: "POST",
            headers: { "Content-Type": "text/plain" },
            body: JSON.stringify({
                token: token.id,
```

```
            operation: this.props.operation,
        })
    });
    console.log(response.ok);
    if (response.ok) {
        console.log("Purchase Complete!");
        this.setState({ status: SUCCESSSTATE });
    }
}
```

If you look closely at the preceding code, you will notice that we made use of a method called `this.props.stripe.createToken()`, which we assumed is embedded in our props, in order to retrieve the credit card token:

```
let { token } = await this.props.stripe.createToken({ name:
this.state.value });
```

The method is called `createToken()`. We passed the **Name On Card** value as an argument (which was stored in our `state` object). The `createToken()` method can only be available if we inject our React component with Stripe code. We will see how to do that in the next section.

We also made use of JavaScript's `fetch()` method, in order to send an HTTP POST request to relative URL. The POST request will include our Stripe token ID as well as the type of operation of the request. We pass an operation type here because I would like to use this request in the future to either take money from a card or save a card for later use. We'll be talking more about the other end of the POST request when it's time to cover the backend code.

Creating a parent StripeProvider component

The next step is to create a parent component to host our `CreditCardForm` component. Here is what we need to do:

1. Inject our `CreditCardForm` component with the Stripe API code. This is done using the `injectStripe()` method.
2. Provide our Stripe API key to our component. This is done using the `StripeProvider` React component, which is provided by Stripe.
3. Host the `CreditCardForm` component inside our parent component. This is done using the `Elements` component.

This will make much more sense when we see the code:

```
export default function CreditCardInformation(props){
    if (!props.show) {
        return <div/>;
    }
    //inject our CreditCardForm component with stripe code in order to be
able to make use of the createToken() method
    const CCFormWithStripe = injectStripe(CreditCardForm);
    return (
        <div>
            {/*stripe provider*/}
            <StripeProvider apiKey="pk_test_LwL4RUtinpP3PXzYirX2jNfR">
                <Elements>
                    {/*embed our credit card form*/}
                    <CCFormWithStripe operation={props.operation} />
                </Elements>
            </StripeProvider>
        </div>
    );
}
```

The preceding code should exist in our CreditCards.js file, which also contained our CreditCardForm component code. We also passed the operation as a prop, which we then later used when we submitted the credit card request to our backend. Also notice export default at the beginning of our CreditCardInformation component definition. This is because we will be importing and using this component in other files.

Now that we've followed all the steps to write a credit card form that can integrate with Stripe, it's time to go back to our buy modal window to embed the credit card form in it. Our buy modal window existed in the modalwindows.js file. As a reminder, here is the code that we covered earlier for the buy modal window:

```
export function BuyModalWindow(props) {
    return (
        <Modal id="buy" tabIndex="-1" role="dialog"
isOpen={props.showModal} toggle={props.toggle}>
            <div role="document">
                <ModalHeader toggle={props.toggle} className="bg-
success text-white">
                    Buy Item
                </ModalHeader>
                <ModalBody>
                    {/*Credit card form*/}
                </ModalBody>
            </div>
        </Modal>
```

```
    );
}
```

First we need to import the `CreditCardInformation` component to our `modalwindows.js`. So, we need to add this line to the file:

```
import CreditCardInformation from './CreditCards';
```

All that we need to do now is to embed our `CreditCardInformation` component in the modal body:

```
export function BuyModalWindow(props) {
    return (
        <Modal id="buy" tabIndex="-1" role="dialog"
isOpen={props.showModal} toggle={props.toggle}>
            <div role="document">
                    <ModalHeader toggle={props.toggle} className="bg-
success text-white">
                        Buy Item
                    </ModalHeader>
                    <ModalBody>
                        <CreditCardInformation show={true} operation="Charge"
toggle={props.toggle} />
                    </ModalBody>
                </div>
        </Modal>
    );
}
```

And with that, we are done with the **Buy** modal window. Now let's move to the **Sign in** window.

The Sign in and Register modal windows

Before we jump into the code, let's first explore how the **Sign in** and **Register** modal windows should look. Click on the **Sign in** button in our navigation bar:

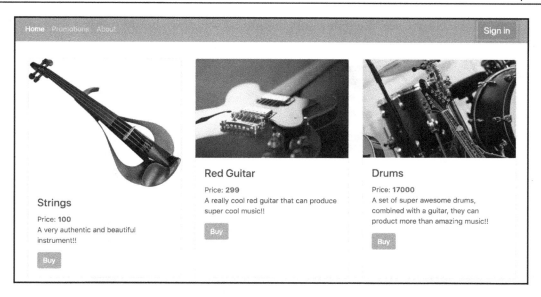

The following modal window should appear:

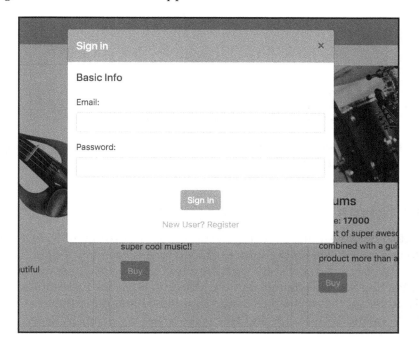

If we click on the **New User? Register** link, the modal window should expand to show the registration form for new users:

In order to build those modal windows correctly, we need to cover how to properly handle forms with multiple inputs in the React framework.

Handling forms in the React framework

Since the React framework relies on being in control of your frontend state, forms represent a challenge to this vision. This is because, in HTML forms, each input field handles its own state based on the user input. Let's say we have a text box and the user makes some changes to it; the text box will change its state based on what the user enters. In React however, it is preferred that any state change should be handled in the state object using the setState() method. There are multiple ways to handle forms in React.

We'll make use of various ways of handling HTML forms. React encourages what is known as the *controlled components* approach, which simply means that you design your component in a way such that your `state` object becomes the single source of truth.

But how? The answer is simple:

1. You monitor your HTML form input fields inside your component.
2. Whenever a form input field changes, you change your `state` object to hold the new value of the form input field.
3. Your `state` object now will hold the latest values of your form input.

The Sign in page

Let's start with the **Sign in** page. As a reminder, here's how it looks:

This is basically a form with two text input fields, a button, a link, and some labels. The first step is to create a React component to host the **Sign in** form. In the `modalwindows.js` file, let's create a new component called `SignInForm`:

```
class SignInForm extends React.Component{
    constructor(){
        super(props);
    }
}
```

Next, we need to create a `state` object in our component:

```
class SignInForm extends React.Component{
    constructor(){
        super(props);
        this.state = {
            errormessage = ''
        };
    }
}
```

Our `state` object currently hosts a single field called `errormessage`. Whenever the sign-in process fails, we'll fill up the `errormessage` field with the error message that occurred.

After that, we need to bind two methods: one to handle form submission and one to handle form input change:

```
class SignInForm extends React.Component{
    constructor(){
        super(props);
        //this method will get called whenever a user input data into our
form
        this.handleChange = this.handleChange.bind(this);
        //this method will get called whenever the HTML form gets submitted
        this.handleSubmit = this.handleSubmit.bind(this);
        this.state = {
            errormessage = ''
        };
    }
}
```

Now it's time to write our `render()` method. The `render()` method will need to perform the following tasks:

- Show the **Sign in** form, collect the user input, then submit the form
- Show an error message if the sign in failed, then enable the user to sign in again

Here is how the code will look:

```
render(){
        //error message
        let message = null;
        //if the state contains an error message, show an error
        if (this.state.errormessage.length !== 0) {
            message = <h5 className="mb-4 text-
danger">{this.state.errormessage}</h5>;
        }
```

```
        return (
            <div>
                {message}
                <form onSubmit={this.handleSubmit}>
                    <h5 className="mb-4">Basic Info</h5>
                    <div className="form-group">
                        <label htmlFor="email">Email:</label>
                        <input name="email" type="email" className="form-
control" id="email" onChange={this.handleChange}/>
                    </div>
                    <div className="form-group">
                        <label htmlFor="pass">Password:</label>
                        <input name="password" type="password"
className="form-control" id="pass" onChange={this.handleChange} />
                    </div>
                    <div className="form-row text-center">
                        <div className="col-12 mt-2">
                            <button type="submit" className="btn btn-
success btn-large">Sign In</button>
                        </div>
                        <div className="col-12 mt-2">
                            <button type="submit" className="btn btn-link
text-info" onClick={() => this.props.handleNewUser()}> New User?
Register</button>
                        </div>
                    </div>
                </form>
            </div>
        );
    }
}
```

There are some important points that we need to cover from the preceding code:

- For each input element, there is an attribute called `name`. This attribute is used to identify each input element. This is important because when we set our `state` object to reflect the value on each input, we need to identify the input name.
- Also for each input element, there is an attribute called `onChange`. This attribute is how we call our `handleChange()` method whenever a user inputs data on our HTML form.
- At the end of our form, if the user decides to click on the **New user? Register** link, we call a method called `handleNewUser()`, which is passed to us by the component props. We'll cover this method in the next section.

Let's talk about the `handleChange()` method, which will populate our `state` object with the data that the user inputs into the HTML **Sign in** form. For that, we'll use a modern JavaScript feature called *computed property name*. Here is how the code looks:

```
handleChange(event){
    const name = event.target.name;
    const value = event.target.value;
    this.setState({
        [name]: value
    });
}
```

In the preceding code, we made use of the `name` property of the event target, which corresponds to the name attributes that we assigned in the HTML form. After the user inputs the username and the password, our `state` object will end up looking like this:

```
state = {
    'email': 'joe@email.com',
    'password': 'pass'
}
```

The last piece in our `SignInForm` would be the `handleSubmit()` method. We'll cover this method in more detail when it's time to cover the backend in Chapter 6, *RESTful Web APIs in Go with the Gin Framework*. So, for now, here's a filler for the `handleSubmit()` method:

```
handleSubmit(event){
    event.preventDefault();
    console.log(JSON.stringify(this.state));
}
```

The Registration form

The next form we need to cover is the **Registration** form. As a reminder, here is how it looks:

This form will be in the same file as the **Sign in** form, which was `modalwindows.js`. The code for the **Registration** form will be very similar to the code we just covered for the **Sign in** form. The difference is that the form for **Registration** has some more fields than the **Sign In** form, otherwise the code is very similar. Here is the code for the **Registration** form:

```
class Registeration extends React.Component{
    constructor(props) {
        super(props);
        this.handleSubmit = this.handleSubmit.bind(this);
        this.state = {
            errormessage: ''
        };
        this.handleChange = this.handleChange.bind(this);
        this.handleSubmit = this.handleSubmit.bind(this);
    }

    handleChange(event) {
        event.preventDefault();
        const name = event.target.name;
        const value = event.target.value;
        this.setState({
            [name]: value
        });
```

```
    }

    handleSubmit(event) {
        event.preventDefault();
        console.log(this.state);
    }

    render() {
        let message = null;
        if (this.state.errormessage.length !== 0) {
            message = <h5 className="mb-4 text-
danger">{this.state.errormessage}</h5>;

        }
        return (
            <div>
                {message}
                <form onSubmit={this.handleSubmit}>
                    <h5 className="mb-4">Registeration</h5>
                    <div className="form-group">
                        <label htmlFor="username">User Name:</label>
                        <input id="username" name='username'
className="form-control" placeholder='John Doe' type='text'
onChange={this.handleChange} />
                    </div>

                    <div className="form-group">
                        <label htmlFor="email">Email:</label>
                        <input type="email" name='email' className="form-
control" id="email" onChange={this.handleChange} />
                    </div>
                    <div className="form-group">
                        <label htmlFor="pass">Password:</label>
                        <input type="password" name='pass1'
className="form-control" id="pass1" onChange={this.handleChange} />
                    </div>
                    <div className="form-group">
                        <label htmlFor="pass">Confirm password:</label>
                        <input type="password" name='pass2'
className="form-control" id="pass2" onChange={this.handleChange} />
                    </div>
                    <div className="form-row text-center">
                        <div className="col-12 mt-2">
                            <button type="submit" className="btn btn-
success btn-large">Register</button>
                        </div>
                    </div>
                </form>
```

```
                </div>
            );
        }
    }
```

Perfect! With this out of the way, we have finished the **Sign in** form as well as the **Registration** form. We just need to write the containing modal window code that will host either the **Sign in** form or the **Registration** form. The modal window will need to achieve the following tasks:

- Show the **Sign in** form
- If the user clicks on the **New User? Register** option, the **Registration** form should appear

Let's create a new React component in the `modalwindows.js` file and call it `SignInModalWindow`:

```
export class SignInModalWindow extends React.Component{

}
```

To design this component properly, we need to think about the fact that this component has two modes—specifically, whether it should show the **Sign in** page for existing users, or show the new **Registration** page for new users. In the world of React, we need to make use of our `state` object, in order to keep track of whether we are showing the **Sign in** page or the **Registration** page. The initial state would be to show the **Sign in** page, then if the user clicks on the **New User? Register** link, we change our state to the **Registration** page:

```
export class SignInModalWindow extends React.Component{
  constructor(props) {
      super(props);
      this.state = {
      showRegistrationForm: false
      };
      this.handleNewUser = this.handleNewUser.bind(this);
  }
```

In the preceding code, besides initializing our `state` object, we also bounded a method called `handleNewUser()`. This method is what we'll call when a user clicks on the **New User? Register** link to load the **Registration** form instead of the **Sign in** page. This method should change the value of our `state` object to reflect the fact that we need to now load the **Registration** form:

```
handleNewUser() {
      this.setState({
```

```
            showRegistrationForm: true
    });
}
```

This sounds good. However, the **New User? Register** link existed in the `SignInForm` React component, so how do we call the `handleNewUser()` method here from our `SignInForm` component?

The answer is simple: we pass the method as a prop to `SignInForm`, and then `SignInForm` calls the method whenever the **New User? Register** link is clicked. If you go back a few pages, you will find that we did indeed link the **New User? Register** link in the `SignInForm` React component to a function prop called `handleNewUser()`, which gets called whenever the link is clicked. At the time, we said that we'll cover this prop in a little bit, and here we are.

Now the remaining piece of the `SignInModalWindow` component is the required `render()` method, which will sum up what we need to do. Here is what the `render()` method needs to do:

- Check the `state` object. If it shows that we need to show the **Registration** form, load the **Registration** form component, `RegistrationForm`, otherwise keep `SignInForm`.
- For the `SignInForm`, pass the `handleNewUser()` method as a prop. This is a common design pattern in the React world.
- Load the modal window code. As usual, we'll make use of the powerful Bootstrap framework to style our form.
- Include either `SignInForm` or `RegistrationForm` in the modal window, based on what our `state` object dictates:

```
render(){
        let modalBody = <SignInForm handleNewUser={this.handleNewUser} />
        if (this.state.showRegistrationForm === true) {
            modalBody = <RegisterationForm />
        }

    return (
            <Modal id="register" tabIndex="-1" role="dialog"
isOpen={this.props.showModal} toggle={this.props.toggle}>
                <div role="document">
                    <ModalHeader toggle={this.props.toggle} className="bg-
success text-white">
                        Sign in
                        {/*<button className="close">
                            <span aria-hidden="true">&times;</span>
```

```
            </button>*/}
        </ModalHeader>
        <ModalBody>
            {modalBody}
        </ModalBody>
    </div>
</Modal>
);
    }
}
```

In the next section, we'll take a look at the user pages in our application.

User pages

It's now time to discuss the user page—what should the user see once they sign into our application? Here is what they should see:

- Their name in the navigation menu, with an option to **Sign out**
- A list of their existing orders

Let's explore how this looks.

The navigation menu should change to look like this:

It now allows to navigate to a page called **My Orders**, which will show the user's previous orders. The other difference is that instead of a **Sign In** button, we now see a **Welcome <username>** drop-down button. When you click on it, the following option should appear:

This is the **Sign Out** button, which the user will need to click on to sign out of their session.

Next, let's have a look at the **My Orders** page:

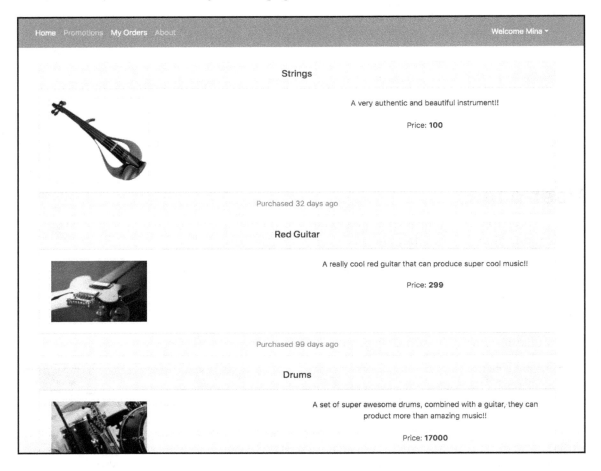

It's a relatively simple page that shows a list of the user's existing orders.

Now, let's write some code for the orders page.

The orders page

Let's start with writing the React component that represent the **My Orders** page. There are two components involved with the **My Orders** page:

- A single order card component
- A parent container component that hosts all the order card components

Let's begin with the single order card component. Here is how it looks:

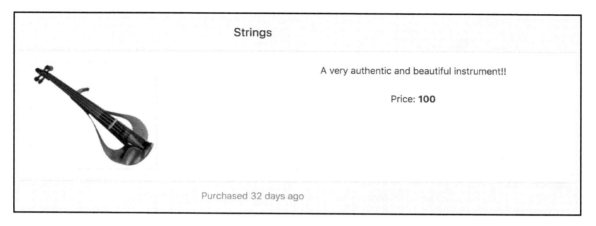

Create a new file called `orders.js` inside the `src` folder. In there, we'll write our new components. At the top of the file, we need to import React:

```
import React from 'react';
```

For the single order card component, let's call it simply `Order`. This component will be simple. Since it will be contained within a parent container component, we can assume that all the order information is passed as props. Also, since we don't need to create any special methods, let's make it a functional component:

```
function Order(props){
    return (
        <div className="col-12">
            <div className="card text-center">
                <div className="card-
header"><h5>{props.productname}</h5></div>
                <div className="card-body">
                    <div className="row">
                        <div className="mx-auto col-6">
                            <img src={props.img} alt={props.imgalt}
className="img-thumbnail float-left" />
                        </div>
                        <div className="col-6">
                            <p className="card-text">{props.desc}</p>
                            <div className="mt-4">
                                Price: <strong>{props.price}</strong>
                            </div>
                        </div>
                    </div>
                </div>
```

```
                    </div>
                    <div className="card-footer text-muted">
                        Purchased {props.days} days ago
                    </div>
                </div>
                <div className="mt-3" />
            </div>
        );
    }
```

As always, the Bootstrap framework makes styling our component a breeze.

Now let's move to the orders container parent component. This one will be a bit more complex because we need to store our orders in the state object of the component:

```
export default class OrderContainer extends React.Component{
    constructor(props) {
        super(props);
        this.state = {
            orders: []
        };
    }
}
```

The orders list needs to come from the backend part of our application. Because of that, the state object should change based on the interaction with the backend of our application. Let's not worry about that part for now because we'll have to cover it when designing the backend of our application in Chapter 6, *RESTful Web APIs in Go with the Gin Framework*. For now, let's jump into the render() method:

```
render(){
        return (
            <div className="row mt-5">
                {this.state.orders.map(order => <Order key={order.id}
{...order} />)}
            </div>
        );
    }
```

The preceding code is simple. We go through the orders in our state object, then load an Order component for each order object that we have. Remember here that when we are dealing with lists, we should use the key prop for the React framework to properly handle changes in the list, as mentioned in Chapter 4, *Frontend with React.js*.

If you look at the GitHub code for this chapter, you'll notice that I actually fetch the orders data from a static file, in order to update the `orders` list in the `state` object. This is temporary, since I need some data to show how the visuals will look.

The user page navigational menu

Let's go back to the `navigation.js` file that was in our `src` folder. We already wrote a `Navigation` React component there in the *The navigational menu* section, which included the default navigation menu if the user is not logged in. We now need to add the pieces that should show up when a user is logged in. The first step is to write a new method, called `buildLoggedInMenu()`, which will show the **Welcome <user>** drop-down button, as well as the sign out option.

Inside the `Navigation` React component, let's add the new method:

```
buildLoggedInMenu(){
        return (
            <div className="navbar-brand order-1 text-white my-auto">
                <div className="btn-group">
                    <button type="button" className="btn btn-success
dropdown-toggle" data-toggle="dropdown" aria-haspopup="true" aria-
expanded="false">
                        Welcome {this.props.user.name}
                    </button>
                    <div className="dropdown-menu">
                        <a className="btn dropdown-item" role="button">Sign
Out</a>
                    </div>
                </div>
            </div>
        );
}
```

The method makes use of JSX with Bootstrap in order to build our drop-down button and sign out option. We assume that the username is passed to us as a prop.

Now, we'll need to modify the `render()` method in order to change the navigation menu when a user is logged in. We'll assume a prop is passed to us that specifies whether the user is logged in. The modified `render()` method also needs a new navigational link to point to the **My Orders** page:

```
render(){
        return (
            <div>
                <nav className="navbar navbar-expand-lg navbar-dark bg-
```

```
success fixed-top">
                     <div className="container">
                         {
                             this.props.user.loggedin ?
                                 this.buildLoggedInMenu()
                                 : <button type="button" className="navbar-
brand order-1 btn btn-success" onClick={() => {
this.props.showModalWindow();}}>Sign in</button>
                         }
                         <div className="navbar-collapse"
id="navbarNavAltMarkup">
                             <div className="navbar-nav">
                                 <NavLink className="nav-item nav-link"
to="/">Home</NavLink>
                                 <NavLink className="nav-item nav-link"
to="/promos">Promotions</NavLink>
                                 {this.props.user.loggedin ? <NavLink
className="nav-item nav-link" to="/myorders">My Orders</NavLink> : null}
                                 <NavLink className="nav-item nav-link"
to="/about">About</NavLink>
                             </div>
                         </div>
                     </div>
                 </nav>
             </div>
         );
     }
}
```

In the preceding code, we assumed a prop had been passed to us that tells us whether the user is logged in (this.props.user.loggedin). If the user is logged in, we do two things:

1. Call the buildLoggedInMenu() method to load the user drop-down button at the end of the navigation menu.
2. Add a link to a path called /myorders. This link will connect to the OrderContainer component. We'll cover how to connect this link to a React component in the next section.

Putting it all together – routes

We now need to write the React component that connects all the preceding components together. You are probably thinking that we already wrote the navigation menu—shouldn't that link everything together? The simple answer is: not yet. In the navigation menu component, we made use of links to point to other pages. However, we did not connect those links to actual react components; the /about link needs to connect to the About React component, the /myorders link needs to connect to the OrderContainer React component, and so on.

We used a React component called NavLink in order to create our links. NavLink was obtained from the react-router-dom package, which we installed in the *The navigational menu* section. The NavLink component is the first step to connect links to React components, while the second step is another type called BrowserRouter. Let's see that in action.

Create a new file called App.js; it should exist in our src folder. This file will host a component that will act as the entry point for all our other components. Because of that, we need to import all the major components that we have created so far in here:

```
import React from 'react';
import CardContainer from './ProductCards';
import Nav from './Navigation';
import { SignInModalWindow, BuyModalWindow } from './modalwindows';
import About from './About';
import Orders from './orders';
```

Next, we need to import a few components from the react-router-dom package:

```
import { BrowserRouter as Router, Route } from "react-router-dom";
```

Now let's write our new component:

```
class App extends React.Component{
}
```

Since this component will have access to all the other components, we need to store global information here. One of the most important pieces of information for our application is whether the user is signed in, because this effects how our application pages look. Because of that, the state object of this component needs to reflect whether a user is logged in:

```
class App extends React.Component{
  constructor(props) {
    super(props);
    this.state = {
```

```
        user: {
          loggedin: false,
          name: ""
        }
      };
    }
  }
```

Let's not worry about how this state is populated for now, because this will need to be covered when we write the backend part of our application. For the time being, let's focus on how to connect each `NavLink` to a React component.

There are three steps involved:

1. Add a component of the `BrowserRouter` type. In our case, we just named it `Router` for simplicity.
2. Inside `BrowserRouter`, put all the instances `NavLink`. In our case, all of our `NavLink` instances are in the `Navigation` component; we imported the `Navigation` component here as `Nav` for simplicity.
3. Inside `BrowserRouter`, use the `Route` component that we imported from the `react-router-dom` package to link a URL path to the React component. Each URL path will correspond to a `NavLink` path.

The preceding steps can be hosted in our `render()` method. Here is how this code looks:

```
render(){
    return (
      <div>
        <Router>
          <div>
            <Nav user={this.state.user} />
            <div className='container pt-4 mt-4'>
              <Route exact path="/" render={() => <CardContainer
location='cards.json' />} />
              <Route path="/promos" render={() => <CardContainer
location='promos.json' promo={true}/>} />
              {this.state.user.loggedin ? <Route path="/myorders"
render={() =><Orders location='user.json'/>}/> : null}
              <Route path="/about" component={About} />
            </div>
            <SignInModalWindow />
            <BuyModalWindow />
          </div>
        </Router>
      </div>
    );
```

```
    }
  }
```

The preceding code implements the three steps that we covered earlier. It also includes `SignInModalWindow` and `BuyModalWindow`. Either modal window will only show up if the user activates them.

We used two different ways to connect a `NavLink` instance to a React component:

- If a component needs a prop as an input, we use `render`:

  ```
  <Route path="/promos" render={() => <CardContainer
  location='promos.json' promo={true}/>} />
  ```

- If a component does not need a prop as an input, we can use the `Route` component:

  ```
  <Route path="/about" component={About} />
  ```

In order for the routing concepts to sync, let's look at what happened with the `About` React component:

- In our navigational menu component (`Navigation` at `Navigation.js`), we used the `NavLink` type that we obtained from `react-router-dom` to create a path called `/about`:`<NavLink className="nav-item nav-link" to="/about">About</NavLink>`.
- In our `App` component, we linked the `/about` path to the `About` React component:

  ```
  <Router>

  <div>
  <Nav user={this.state.user} />
  <div className='container pt-4 mt-4'>
  {/*other routes*/}
  <Route path="/about" component={About} />
  </div>
  {/*rest of the App component*/}
  </div>
  </Router>
  ```

Now, we need to define the `toggle` methods and show methods for the buy and the sign-in modal windows. The `show` methods are basically the methods to call in order to show the buy or sign-in modal windows. The most straightforward way to do this is to use a `state` object of our component to specify whether the modal windows should be on or off. Our application is designed so that only one modal window should be open at a time, which is why we'll control their open/closed state from our `App` component.

Let's start by exploring the `show` methods for the buy and sign-in modal windows:

```
showSignInModalWindow(){
  const state = this.state;
  const newState = Object.assign({},state,{showSignInModal:true});
  this.setState(newState);
}

showBuyModalWindow(id,price){
  const state = this.state;
  const newState =
Object.assign({},state,{showBuyModal:true,productid:id,price:price});
  this.setState(newState);
}
```

The code, in both cases, will clone our `state` object, while adding and setting a Boolean field that indicates that the target modal window should be on. In case of the sign-in modal window, the Boolean field will be called `showSignInModal`, whereas, in the case of the buy modal window, the Boolean field will be called `showBuyModal`.

Now, let's look at the `toggle` methods for the sign in and the buy modal windows. As mentioned, the `toggle` method is used to toggle the state of the modal window. In our case, we just need to reverse the value of the `state` Boolean fields that represent whether our modal windows are open:

```
toggleSignInModalWindow() {
  const state = this.state;
  const newState =
Object.assign({},state,{showSignInModal:!state.showSignInModal});
  this.setState(newState);
}

toggleBuyModalWindow(){
  const state = this.state;
  const newState =
Object.assign({},state,{showBuyModal:!state.showBuyModal});
  this.setState(newState);
}
```

The constructor for our `App` component needs to bind the new methods that we added for them to be used in our code:

```
constructor(props) {
  super(props);
  this.state = {
    user: {
      loggedin: false,
      name: ""
    }
  };
  this.showSignInModalWindow = this.showSignInModalWindow.bind(this);
  this.toggleSignInModalWindow = this.toggleSignInModalWindow.bind(this);
  this.showBuyModalWindow = this.showBuyModalWindow.bind(this);
  this.toggleBuyModalWindow = this.toggleBuyModalWindow.bind(this);
}
```

Next, we need to pass the new methods to the components that need them as prop objects. We also need to pass the `state.showSignInModal` and `state.showBuyModal` flags, because that's how our modal window components will know whether a modal window should be visible:

```
render() {
  return (
    <div>
      <Router>
        <div>
          <Nav user={this.state.user}
showModalWindow={this.showSignInModalWindow}/>
          <div className='container pt-4 mt-4'>
            <Route exact path="/" render={() => <CardContainer
location='cards.json' showBuyModal={this.showBuyModalWindow} />} />
            <Route path="/promos" render={() => <CardContainer
location='promos.json' promo={true}
showBuyModal={this.showBuyModalWindow}/>} />
            {this.state.user.loggedin ? <Route path="/myorders"
render={()=><Orders location='user.json'/>}/> : null}
            <Route path="/about" component={About} />
          </div>
          <SignInModalWindow showModal={this.state.showSignInModal}
toggle={this.toggleSignInModalWindow}/>
          <BuyModalWindow showModal={this.state.showBuyModal}
toggle={this.toggleBuyModalWindow} productid={this.state.productid}
price={this.state.price}/>
        </div>
      </Router>
    </div>
```

```
        );
    }
}
```

There are two remaining code pieces to be covered in this chapter.

The first piece is to make the App component exportable because this component will become the entry point for all our other components. At the end of the App.js file, let's add this line:

```
export default App;
```

The second piece of code we need to write is to link the App React component to the root element of our template HTML code. Create a file called index.js, where we add this code:

```
import React from 'react';
import ReactDOM from 'react-dom';
import App from './App';
import registerServiceWorker from './registerServiceWorker';

ReactDOM.render(<App />, document.getElementById('root'));
registerServiceWorker();
```

This code makes use of the tools that are loaded with the Create React App tool.

Perfect! With this last piece of code out of the way, our chapter is done.

Summary

This chapter took a practical deep dive into how to build a proper frontend application using the React framework. We covered several topics as we built our application, such as routing, handling credit cards and forms, and typical React framework design approaches. You should have enough knowledge at this point to build non-trivial applications in the React framework.

In the next chapter, we'll switch topics and revisit Go. We'll start to cover how to build the backend for our GoMusic application, by introducing the Go open source framework, Gin.

Questions

1. What is `react-router-dom`?
2. What is `NavLink`?
3. What is Stripe?
4. How do we handle credit cards in React?
5. What is a controlled component?
6. What is `BrowserRouter`?
7. What are Stripe elements?
8. What is the `injectStripe()` method?
9. How do we handle routing in React?

Further reading

For more information on the topics covered in this chapter, check out the following links:

- **React router package**: https://reacttraining.com/react-router/
- **Stripe**: https://stripe.com/
- **Stripe React elements**: https://stripe.com/docs/recipes/elements-react
- **Handling forms in React**: https://reactjs.org/docs/forms.html

Section 3: Web APIs and Middleware in Go

In this section, we'll take a deep dive into building web APIs and middleware in the Go language by making use of the popular Gin framework. This section will cover basic and advanced concepts of backend technologies by covering the Gin framework. It will also cover important practical topics, such as testing and profiling production apps. This section will cover the second half of the full stack.

This section consists of the following chapters:

- Chapter 6, *Restful Web APIs in Go with the Gin Framework*
- Chapter 7, *Advanced Go Web Applications with the Gin Framework*
- Chapter 8, *Testing and Benchmarking Your Web API*
- Chapter 9, *Introduction to Isomorphic Go with GopherJS*
- Chapter 10, *Where to Go from Here?*

6
RESTful Web APIs in Go with the Gin Framework

In the previous chapters, we explored how to build an engaging frontend for our application, by utilizing the popular React framework.

It's now time to cover how to build efficient backend code in the Go programming language to work with our frontend. In this chapter, we'll make use of the super-fast Gin framework to build some of the APIs needed for the project of this book (that is, the GoMusic store).

In this chapter, we'll cover the following topics:

- RESTful APIs
- The Gin framework
- Models and bindings
- HTTP handlers

Technical requirements

The code for this chapter can be found at https://github.com/PacktPublishing/Hands-On-Full-Stack-Development-with-Go/tree/master/Chapter06.

RESTful APIs

Any backend software system needs a set of APIs to communicate with the frontend. Full stack software is simply composed of a frontend component from one side that exchanges messages with a backend component from the other side. One of the most popular types of APIs used in full stack software are RESTful APIs.

Let's cover an overview of RESTful APIs in the next section.

Overview

RESTful APIs can simply be defined as a set of rules used to build web services where you retrieve or manipulate resources. A **resource** is typically a kind of document—it could be an HTML document (such as a web page), a JSON document (for pure information sharing), or some other type of document. **JSON** stands for **JavaScript Object Notation**; this is because it basically refers to how you would write the object in JavaScript. It's very popular and is widely used.

For the majority of RESTful APIs, HTTP is utilized as the communication layer for the API:

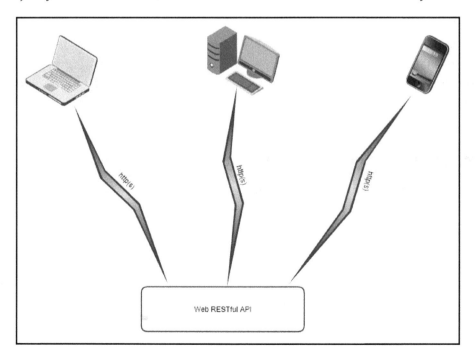

The topic can be very lengthy; however, there are a few simple facts and concepts that you need to know in order to properly write RESTful APIs. In the next few sections, we will provide an overview of the key building blocks behind RESTful APIs.

We'll take a look at the client-server architecture, URLs and the HTTP methods in the next sections.

The client-server architecture

RESTful APIs rely on the client-server architecture. This simply means that for RESTful APIs, you need two main components—a client and a server. A client sends an HTTP request to a server, and the server replies with an HTTP response to the client. A single server typically handles numerous clients at the same time:

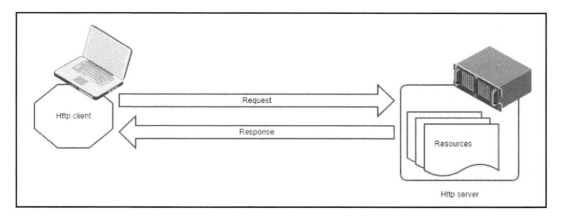

The preceding diagram can be explained with the help of following points:

- The client is the component that initiates the API request. A client either asks for a resource from a server, or sends a resource to a server.
- The server is the component that receives requests and then processes them. A server either sends a resource to a client when requested to do so, or adds/modifies a resource when a client requests this to happen.

URLs

A URL can simply be defined as the address for a particular RESTful API resource.

When a client sends a request to a server, the client sends the request to a URL address that is being watched by the server. Any RESTful API interaction involves a client sending a message to a URL address.

In order to form an understanding about what a URL consists of, let's take `http://www.example.com/user?id=1` as an example.

The preceding URL consists of three main components that we need to be aware of, as follows:

1. **The server location**: This is basically the combination of the protocol and the server domain name, `http://www.example.com/`.
2. **The relative URL path**: This is the relative URL address from the server address, `/user`.
3. **The query**: This is a query used to identify what resources we seek, such as `?id=1`.

The first two components exist in the vast majority of RESTful API interactions, whereas the third component is used for more specialized API calls.

HTTP methods

As mentioned earlier, clients send requests to servers. The requests can be used to retrieve resources from servers, or manipulate resources hosted by servers. However, how can we tell what a particular request wants? This is where HTTP methods are used. An HTTP method is basically how an HTTP request from a client reveals its intention to a server.

There are numerous method types that can be supported by HTTP requests; however, since this book is all about practicality, we'll discuss three of the most commonly used request methods in the world of RESTful APIs:

- **The GET request method**: A GET HTTP request method is used when a client's intention is to retrieve a resource from the server. Whenever you open a web browser such as Google Chrome, and then type in www.google.com, your web browser acts as an HTTP client that sends a GET HTTP request to the www.google.com URL. Google servers then receive your client's request and respond with Google's main page, which is simply an HTML document that is then translated by your web browser to look pretty.

- **The POST request method**: A POST HTTP request method is used when the client's intention is to send data to the server. When a client sends a POST request, it must also include the data that the server is supposed to receive in the message body of the request. The URL address of the request identifies the resource that we are either adding or changing with the new data being sent. There is another HTTP method called PUT, which can be used to add or replace resource. However, we'll be using POST in our code.

- **The DELETE request method**: A DELETE HTTP request method is used when the client's intention is to delete a resource from the server. The URL of the request will identify the resource that we want to delete.

Now that we covered REST APIs, it's time to explore the Gin framework, which is how we'll build a REST API in our Go code.

The Gin framework

Gin is a very popular Go open source framework that is mainly used to build ultra-high performance RESTful APIs. The project can be found at https://github.com/gin-gonic/gin. Gin is not only fast, but it also enjoys a simple and fun-to-use API that makes building production-level RESTful APIs a breeze.

In this section, we will learn how to build a web RESTful API through the Gin framework, by starting the implementation of the backend code that is needed to support our GoMusic store.

Let's take a look at models and the database layer in the next section.

Models and the database layer

Our backend obviously needs a database to store all the data that our RESTful API is supposed to expose. Let's call the database interaction code our *database layer*. In the world of backend software systems, careful and thoughtful design needs to be applied when writing the database layer. This is because the database layer is vital for almost all of the major functionalities in backend systems.

Let's get into the details of models in the next section.

Models

The first step to building a well-designed database layer is to build models for the data. **Data models** can simply be described as data structures that represent the information that we retrieve from the database and use in our APIs. This is best explained by an example.

In our GoMusic application, since it's simply an online store that sells products, we can identify the distinct models that our application needs to support, as follows:

- A product
- A customer
- A customer order

Let's start writing some code; in your project root folder, you need to create a new folder called `backend`. Underneath this, create a folder called `src`, then underneath the `src` folder, create a folder called `models`. Now, inside the `models` folder, create a new file called `models.go`. This is where we'll write our models. The first thing we need to do is to define a package, as follows:

```
package models
```

Next, let's write our `Product` data structure, as follows:

```
type Product struct{
  Image string `json:"img"`
  ImagAlt string `json:"imgalt"`
  Price float64 `json:"price"`
  Promotion float64 `json:"promotion"`
  ProductName string `json:"productname"`
  Description string `json:"desc"`
}
```

You might be wondering about the strange `json:"..."` syntax inside our Go struct; this syntax is known as **struct tags**. In our case, the struct tags are used to indicate how the field in question will look in a JSON document. JSON is a very popular data serialization format that is typically used to share data in RESTful APIs. The preceding Go struct will look like the following code snippet in a JSON format:

```
{
        "img": "/path/to/img.jpeg",
        "imgalt": "image alt",
        "price": 100,
        "promotion":80,
        "productname": "guitar",
        "desc": "A black guitar with with amazing sounds!!"
}
```

From the preceding JSON data block, you can tell how easy it is to represent data in JSON.

If we don't use JSON structure fields in our Go struct, Go will make some default assumptions when converting our Go struct field names to JSON field names. For example, all uppercase first letters in the Go struct fields will convert to lowercase first letters in the JSON document. It is typically preferred to use JSON struct tags in order to be in full control of what the JSON document will look like.

Perfect; now, let's write our Customer data structure, as follows:

```
type Customer struct {
  FirstName string `json:"firstname"`
  LastName string `json:"lastname"`
  Email string `json:"email"`
  LoggedIn bool `json:"loggedin"`
}
```

Next, let's write our Order data structure, as follows:

```
type Order struct{
  Product
  Customer
  CustomerID int `json:"customer_id"`
  ProductID int `json:"product_id"`
  Price float64 `json:"sell_price"`
  PurchaseDate time.Time `json:"purchase_date"`
}
```

The preceding data structure makes use of a Go feature known as *embedding*. Embedding in our example here simply means that we include all the fields of a different Go struct in the current Go struct. We embedded the `Product` and `Customer` Go structs in the `Order` Go struct. This means that all the product and customer Go struct fields, such as `img` and `firstname`, are now part of the `Order` struct.

Let's take a look at the database layer interface in the next section.

The database layer interface

Another major part of well-designed database layers is the database layer interface. In order to fully appreciate the need for a database interface layer, let's imagine a quick scenario. Let's say you build your backend to use database *X*, and all your code relies on direct calls to database *X*. Now, what happens if database *X* turns out to be very expensive and you find a much cheaper and more maintainable database that you can use in your code? Let's call the new database, database *Y*. You now have to revisit every single piece of your code that did queries to database *X* and change it, which may affect much more code than just your database layer.

So, what do we do? We simply create an interface that defines all the behaviors that we expect from the database layer. All our code outside the database layer should only use methods provided by this interface and nothing else. Now, if we want to move from database *X* to database *Y*, we can simply write a new database layer that can communicate with database *Y* and still support our existing database layer interface. By doing this, we ensure that the vast majority of our existing code outside of the database layer will stay the same and behave as expected.

Our next step is to write the database layer interface for our GoMusic application. To do so, we have to first identify the behaviors we seek from our database layer, as follows:

- Get a list of all products
- Get a list of all promotions
- Get a customer by the customer's first and last name
- Get a customer by the customer's `id`
- Get a product by the product's `id`
- Add a user to the database
- Mark a user in the database as signed in
- Mark a user in the database as signed out
- Get a list of customer orders by the customer's `id`

Inside the `backend/src` folder, let's create a new folder called `dblayer`. Inside this folder, we'll create a new file called `dblayer.go`. This is where we'll write our database layer interface. We start our code by declaring the package name and importing the models package, as follows:

```
package dblayer

import (
   "github.com/PacktPublishing/Hands-On-Full-Stack-Development-with-
Go/Chapter06/backend/src/models"
)
```

Next, we write our interface, which encapsulates all the behavior points we covered in this section, as follows:

```
type DBLayer interface{
   GetAllProducts() ([]models.Product, error)
   GetPromos() ([]models.Product, error)
   GetCustomerByName(string, string) (models.Customer, error)
   GetCustomerByID(int) (models.Customer, error)
   GetProduct(uint) (models.Product, error)
   AddUser(models.Customer) (models.Customer, error)
   SignInUser(username, password string) (models.Customer, error)
   SignOutUserById(int) error
   GetCustomerOrdersByID(int) ([]models.Order, error)
}
```

In the next chapter, we'll dive back into the database layer to continue its implementation. But for now, let's focus on our REST API layer and its implementation using the Gin framework.

Implementing RESTful APIs using the Gin framework

As mentioned earlier, the backend code for a full stack application such as GoMusic needs to interact with the frontend component through RESTful APIs. This simply means that a major component of our backend code is the RESTful API layer. This layer is what we'll discuss from this point on until the end of the chapter.

Before we start writing code, we need to first agree on our requirements. The first step of any well-designed RESTful API backend is to first figure out the different interactions between the frontend component and the backend component.

Here is what our RESTful API needs to do:

1. Our backend needs to provide a list of available products to the frontend.
2. Our backend needs to provide a list of available promotions to the frontend.
3. Our frontend needs to send user information to our backend in order to sign in existing users, or add new users.
4. Our frontend needs to send user sign out requests to the backend.
5. Our backend needs to provide a list of existing orders belonging to a specific user.
6. Our frontend needs to send credit card token information to the backend in order to process a charge.

By looking at the preceding points, we can guess which HTTP methods to use for each one:

- For the first, second, and fifth points, we use a GET HTTP request, since the server only needs to provide resources (in our case, these are JSON documents) as responses to client requests.
- For the third, fourth, and sixth points, we use the POST HTTP request, since the server will be expected to add or manipulate resources based on a client request.

Let's take a look at how we can define routes in the next section.

Defining routes

The next step to implement a RESTful API is to define the different URLs that correspond to the different API actions we need to happen. This is also known as defining routes, since the URLs are the routes to our API resources.

We'll go through the RESTful API interactions one by one and define their routes. But first, let's start by creating a new file for our RESTful API.

In the `backend/src` folder, create a new folder called `rest`. Inside the `rest` folder, create a file called `rest.go`. This is where we start using the Gin framework. In your favorite Terminal, type the following command in order to deploy and install the Gin framework to your development environment:

```
go get -u github.com/gin-gonic/gin
```

In the `rest.go` file, start by declaring the package name and importing the Gin framework, as follows:

```
package rest

import (
  "github.com/gin-gonic/gin"
)
```

Then, declare the function that will act as the entry point for our RESTful API. This is where we define the HTTP routes for our RESTful API:

```
func RunAPI(address string) error{
}
```

The preceding method takes one argument that will host the address of our RESTful API server.

In order to make use of Gin, we first need to obtain a **Gin engine**. A Gin engine is the object type that gives us access to assign HTTP methods to URLs to action:

```
func RunAPI(address string) error{
    r := gin.Default()
}
```

Next, we need to start mapping HTTP methods to URLs to action. For that, we need to make use of the Gin engine object that we just created. The following code block is a simple example of where we use the Gin engine to accept a GET request coming to the relative URL, /relativepath/to/url:

```
func RunAPI(address string) error{
    r := gin.Default()
    r.GET("/relativepath/to/url", func(c *gin.Context) {
      //take action
    })
}
```

The anonymous function in the preceding code, `func(c *gin.Context){}`, is where we define the action that we want to be performed when we receive an incoming client request that satisfies our conditions (the /relativepath/to/url relative path, and the GET HTTP method).

The `*gin.Context` type is provided to us by the Gin framework. It supplies us with all the tools that we need to not only explore the incoming request, but also to take action and provide the appropriate response. We will discuss the `*gin.Context` type in more detail in the next section, but for now, let's focus on building the routes. Let's revisit the list of API interactions and write some code to represent each interaction:

1. Our backend needs to provide a list of available products to the frontend using a `GET` request:

```
//get products
  r.GET("/products",func(c *gin.Context) {
     //return a list of all products to the client
     }
  )
```

2. Our backend needs to provide a list of available promotions to the frontend using a `GET` request:

```
//get promos
  r.GET("/promos",func(c *gin.Context) {
     //return a list of all promotions to the client
     }
  )
```

3. Our frontend needs to send user information to our backend in order to sign in existing users or to add new users using a `POST` request:

```
//post user sign in
  r.POST("/users/signin", func(c *gin.Context) {
     //sign in a user
     }
  )
//add user
r.POST("/users",func(c *gin.Context){
     //add a user
     }
)
```

4. Our frontend needs to send user sign out requests to the backend using a `POST` request:

```
//post user sign out
/*
  In the path below, our relative url needs to include the user id
  Since the id will differ based on the user, the Gin framework
allows us to include a wildcard. In Gin, the wildcard will take the
form ':id' to indicate that we are expecting a parameter here with
```

```
the name 'id'
*/
    r.POST("/user/:id/signout",func(c *gin.Context) {
        //sign out a user with the provided id
    }
)
```

5. Our backend needs to provide a list of existing orders belonging to a specific user using a GET request:

```
//get user orders
    r.GET("/user/:id/orders", func(c *gin.Context) {
        //get all orders belonging to the provided user id
    }
)
```

6. Our frontend needs to send credit card token information to the backend in order to process a charge:

```
//post purchase charge
    r.POST("/users/charge", func(c *gin.Context) {
        //charge credit card for user
    }
)
```

Let's see how to build an HTTP handler in the next section.

Creating handlers

The next logical step in building our RESTful API is to define the actions that we need to perform when we receive client requests. This is also known as **building handlers**. So, let's start.

In the `backend/src/rest` folder, create a new file called `handler.go`. In this file, we'll write the code that is needed to handle the actions that correspond to the different API requests that our server is expected to receive.

As always, the first thing we need to do is to declare the package and import the external packages that we need to use, as follows:

```
package rest

import (
    "fmt"
    "log"
```

```
    "net/http"
    "strconv"

    "github.com/PacktPublishing/Hands-On-Full-Stack-Development-with-
Go/Chapter06/backend/src/dblayer"
    "github.com/PacktPublishing/Hands-On-Full-Stack-Development-with-
Go/Chapter06/backend/src/models"
    "github.com/gin-gonic/gin"
)
```

In order to write clean code that allows extensibility, let's write an interface that represents all the methods that a handler needs to support, as follows:

```
type HandlerInterface interface {
  GetProducts(c *gin.Context)
  GetPromos(c *gin.Context)
  AddUser(c *gin.Context)
  SignIn(c *gin.Context)
  SignOut(c *gin.Context)
  GetOrders(c *gin.Context)
  Charge(c *gin.Context)
}
```

Next, let's create a `struct` type and call it `Handler`; this will host all our `Handler` methods. `Handler` will need access to the database layer interface, since all our `Handler` methods will need to either retrieve or change data:

```
type Handler struct{
    db dblayer.DBLayer
}
```

To follow good design principles, we should create a constructor for `Handler`. We'll just create a simple constructor for now, as follows:

```
func NewHandler() (*Handler, error) {
  //This creates a new pointer to the Handler object
  return new(Handler), nil
}
```

The preceding constructor will need to evolve in the future in order to initialize the database layer. However, let's focus on the `Handler` method for now.

In the next few sections, let's focus on what our API needs to do point by point, and then create the corresponding handlers. Each one of the few section will represent an API functionality we need to implement.

Getting a full list of available products

First, let's create a method called GetProducts that takes the *gin.Context type as an argument:

```
func (h *Handler) GetProducts(c *gin.Context) {
}
```

Next, we need to ensure that our database interface is initialized and not nil, then we use the database layer interface in order to obtain the list of products:

```
func (h *Handler) GetProducts(c *gin.Context) {
  if h.db == nil {
    return
  }
  products, err := h.db.GetAllProducts()
}
```

Now, what happens if the call returns an error? We need to return a JSON document to the client with the error. The response to the client also needs to include an HTTP status code that indicates that the request failed. An HTTP status code is a way to report that an error happened in HTTP communication. This is where we start using the *gin.Context type, which includes a method called JSON() that we can use to return JSON documents:

```
func (h *Handler) GetProducts(c *gin.Context) {
  if h.db == nil {
    return
  }
  products, err := h.db.GetAllProducts()
  if err != nil {
    /*
        First argument is the http status code, whereas the second argument
is the body of the request
    */
    c.JSON(http.StatusInternalServerError, gin.H{"error": err.Error()})
    return
  }
}
```

Finally, if there is no error, then we return the list of products we retrieved from the database. Since we defined JSON struct tags in our data models, our data models will get converted to the JSON document formats that we defined:

```
func (h *Handler) GetProducts(c *gin.Context) {
  if h.db == nil {
    return
  }
```

```
    products, err := h.db.GetAllProducts()
    if err != nil {
        c.JSON(http.StatusInternalServerError, gin.H{"error": err.Error()})
        return
    }
    c.JSON(http.StatusOK, products)
}
```

Getting a list of promotions

This handler will be very similar to the GetProducts handler, except that it will use a
different database call to retrieve the list of promotions instead of the list of products:

```
func (h *Handler) GetPromos(c *gin.Context) {
    if h.db == nil {
        return
    }
    promos, err := h.db.GetPromos()
    if err != nil {
        c.JSON(http.StatusInternalServerError, gin.H{"error": err.Error()})
        return
    }
    c.JSON(http.StatusOK, promos)
}
```

Sign in new users or add new users

The method that we'll create in this section, handles a POST request; here, we expect to
receive a JSON document from the client that we need to decode before we can process the
request. Let's assume that our client sends a JSON document that represents the customer.
The code to decode the JSON object will look like the following code block:

```
func (h *Handler) SignIn(c *gin.Context) {
    if h.db == nil {
        return
    }
    var customer models.Customer
    err := c.ShouldBindJSON(&customer)
}
```

The `c.ShouldBindJSON(...)` method is provided to us by the `*gin.Context` type. Its main purpose is to extract JSON documents from our HTTP request body, and then parse it to the provided argument. In our case, the provided argument was a variable of type `*models.Customer`, which is our customer/user data model.

The rest of our `SignIn` method is simple—if no errors occur from decoding the JSON document to the data model, we call the `SignInUser` database layer method to sign in or add the customer to the database:

```
func (h *Handler) SignIn(c *gin.Context) {
  if h.db == nil {
    return
  }
  var customer models.Customer
  err := c.ShouldBindJSON(&customer)
  if err != nil {
    c.JSON(http.StatusBadRequest, gin.H{"error": err.Error()})
    return
  }
  customer,err = h.db.SignInUser(customer)
  if err != nil {
    c.JSON(http.StatusInternalServerError, gin.H{"error": err.Error()})
    return
  }
  c.JSON(http.StatusOK, customer)
}
```

To add a user, the logic will be very similar, except that we add a user instead of signing someone in:

```
func (h *Handler) AddUser(c *gin.Context) {
  if h.db == nil {
    return
  }
  var customer models.Customer
  err := c.ShouldBindJSON(&customer)
  if err != nil {
    c.JSON(http.StatusBadRequest, gin.H{"error": err.Error()})
    return
  }
  customer,err = h.db.AddUser(customer)
  if err != nil {
    c.JSON(http.StatusInternalServerError, gin.H{"error": err.Error()})
    return
  }
  c.JSON(http.StatusOK, customer)
}
```

Sign out requests

For this handler, we expect a URL with a parameter, such as /user/:id/signout. Here is what the handler needs to do:

1. Extract the parameter that is the ID of the user we are signing out. This can be done by calling a method named Param(), which belongs to the *gin.Context type; the following code block demonstrates how this will look:

```go
func (h *Handler) SignOut(c *gin.Context) {
  if h.db == nil {
    return
  }
  p := c.Param("id")
  // p is of type string, we need to convert it to an integer type
  id,err := strconv.Atoi(p)
  if err != nil {
    c.JSON(http.StatusBadRequest, gin.H{"error": err.Error()})
    return
  }
}
```

2. Next, we need to call the SignOutUserById database layer method in order to mark the user as having signed out in the database:

```go
func (h *Handler) SignOut(c *gin.Context) {
  if h.db == nil {
    return
  }
  p := c.Param("id")
  id, err := strconv.Atoi(p)
  if err != nil {
    c.JSON(http.StatusBadRequest, gin.H{"error": err.Error()})
    return
  }

  err = h.db.SignOutUserById(id)
  if err != nil {
    c.JSON(http.StatusInternalServerError, gin.H{"error":
err.Error()})
    return
  }
}
```

Getting orders for a specific user

We expect a URL with a parameter here as well, such as `/user/:id/orders`. The
`:id` parameter represents the ID of the user whose orders we are trying to retrieve. The
code will look like this:

```
func (h *Handler) GetOrders(c *gin.Context) {
  if h.db == nil {
    return
  }
  // get id parameter
  p := c.Param("id")
  // convert the string 'p' to integer 'id'
  id, err := strconv.Atoi(p)
  if err != nil {
    c.JSON(http.StatusBadRequest, gin.H{"error": err.Error()})
    return
  }
  // call the database layer method to get orders from id
  orders, err := h.db.GetCustomerOrdersByID(id)
  if err != nil {
    c.JSON(http.StatusInternalServerError, gin.H{"error": err.Error()})
    return
  }
  c.JSON(http.StatusOK, orders)
}
```

Charging a credit card

This handler involves more functionality than just reading requests and calling the
database. This is because we'll need to interact with Stripe's API to charge a customer's
credit card. We will be covering this method more details in the next chapter. For now, let's
create an empty handler to use in our code, as follows:

```
func (h *Handler) Charge(c *gin.Context) {
  if h.db == nil {
    return
  }
}
```

Putting it all together

After creating our handlers, let's go back to `./backend/src/rest/rest.go`. Instead of mapping our routes to empty handlers, let's map our routes to the handlers that we created in the previous section:

```go
func RunAPI(address string) error {
    //Get gin's default engine
    r := gin.Default()
    //Define a handler
    h, _ := NewHandler()
    //get products
    r.GET("/products", h.GetProducts)
    //get promos
    r.GET("/promos", h.GetPromos)
    //post user sign in
    r.POST("/users/signin", h.SignIn)
    //add a user
    r.POST("/users",h.AddUser)
    //post user sign out
    r.POST("/user/:id/signout", h.SignOut)
    //get user orders
    r.GET("/user/:id/orders", h.GetOrders)
    //post purchase charge
    r.POST("/users/charge", h.Charge)
    //run the server
    return r.Run(address)
}
```

Observe the last line in our function: `r.Run(address)`. We must call this method after we finish defining our API routes and handlers, so that our RESTful API server starts listening to incoming requests from HTTP clients.

Since a number of our routes start with `/user/` and `/users`, the preceding code can be refactored further using a method called `Group()`:

```go
func RunAPI(address string,h HandlerInterface) error {
    //Get gin's default engine
    r := gin.Default()
    //get products
    r.GET("/products", h.GetProducts)
    //get promos
    r.GET("/promos", h.GetPromos)
    /*
        //post user sign in
        r.POST("/user/signin", h.SignIn)
        //post user sign out
```

```
    r.POST("/user/:id/signout", h.SignOut)
    //get user orders
    r.GET("/user/:id/orders", h.GetOrders)
    //post purchase charge
    r.POST("/user/charge", h.Charge)
*/

userGroup := r.Group("/user")
{
  userGroup.POST("/:id/signout", h.SignOut)
  userGroup.GET("/:id/orders", h.GetOrders)
}

usersGroup := r.Group("/users")
{
  usersGroup.POST("/charge", h.Charge)
  usersGroup.POST("/signin", h.SignIn)
  usersGroup.POST("", h.AddUser)
}

return r.Run(address)
}
```

The preceding technique is sometimes known as *grouping routes.* This is when we group HTTP routes, that share part of their relative URLs, into a common code block.

To make our code cleaner, let's rename the preceding function to RunAPIWithHandler(), because the handler can be passed to it as an argument:

```
func RunAPIWithHandler(address string,h HandlerInterface) error{
    //our code
}
```

Then, let's create a function with the old name RunAPI() that represents the default state of RunAPIWithHandler(). This is when we use the default implementation for our HandlerInterface:

```
func RunAPI(address string) error {
  h, err := NewHandler()
  if err != nil {
    return err
  }
  return RunAPIWithHandler(address, h)
}
```

Now, in our `main.go` file, which should live in the `backend/src` folder of our project, we can simply call `RunAPI()`, as follows:

```
func main() {
    log.Println("Main log....")
    log.Fatal(rest.RunAPI("127.0.0.1:8000"))
}
```

But what about connecting our React frontend with the newly created backend? That's simple; in our React application `root` folder, there is a file called `package.json`. In the `package.json` file, we will need to add the following field:

```
"proxy": "http://127.0.0.1:8000/"
```

This field will forward any frontend requests to the address specified as the proxy. If our web server listens on `127.0.0.1:8000`, which is represented by the `address` argument in our `RunAPI()` function, then our web server will receive the incoming requests from our frontend.

Summary

In this chapter, we started with an overview about RESTful APIs. From there we dove into practical topics such as data modeling, defining routes, grouping routes, and creating handlers. We covered the knowledge necessary to write functional web APIs in Go.

We also got our first exposure to the powerful Gin framework, which is very popular for writing production-level RESTful APIs.

In the next chapter, we'll dive deeper into backend web APIs. More advanced topics will be covered like ORMs and security. We will also revisit our application's frontend, and discuss how it connects to the backend that we built.

Questions

1. What is Gin?
2. What is HTTP?
3. What is a RESTful API?
4. What is a URL?
5. What is a handler?
6. What is JSON?
7. What is the `Param()` method used for?
8. What is the `c.JSON()` method used for?
9. What is the `Group()` method used for?

Further reading

For more information, you can go through the following links:

- **Gin:** `https://github.com/gin-gonic/gin`
- **Representational state transfer:** `https://stackoverflow.com/a/29648972`

Advanced Web Go Applications with Gin and React

7

In this chapter, we'll continue building our GoMusic web application. This chapter will cover some advanced concepts, as it will add to what we built in the previous chapter before it dives deeper into how to build advanced backend software. We will cover some important and practical topics such as database layers for connecting our application to a production database, **object-relational mapping** (**ORM**) for simplifying our database layer code, middleware for adding functionality on top of our Web API handlers, authentication to secure our web application, and credit card charging. We will also revisit the frontend of our GoMusic application in order to cover how our frontend would connect to our backend.

Specifically, we'll cover the following topics in this chapter:

- Database layers and ORMs
- Middleware
- Security, authentication, and authorization
- Credit card charging
- Proxying React applications
- Authorizing and authenticating from React applications

This chapter will revisit the frontend layer of our application, in order to evolve our existing React application to utilize the new backend features.

Technical requirements

For this chapter, we recommend that you have the following software installed:

- The Go language
- A code editor or an IDE such as VS Code
- npm and Node.js
- React

Knowledge of the following topics is required:

- Go (Chapter 2, *Building Blocks of the Go Language,* and Chapter 3, *Go Concurrency*)
- JavaScript
- React (Chapter 4, *Frontend with React.js,* and Chapter 5, *Building a Frontend for GoMusic*)
- Some familiarity with relational databases and MySQL

The code for this chapter can be found in this book's GitHub repository at https://github.com/PacktPublishing/Hands-On-Full-Stack-Development-with-Go/tree/master/Chapter07.

The database layer

In the previous chapter, we started writing our database layer. As a reminder, our database layer was hosted in the backend\src\dblayer folder. Our first step was to write the database layer interface, which defined all of the functionality that we expect from the database layer. This is what the database layer interface looked like:

```
type DBLayer interface {
  GetAllProducts() ([]models.Product, error)
  GetPromos() ([]models.Product, error)
  GetCustomerByName(string, string) (models.Customer, error)
  GetCustomerByID(int) (models.Customer, error)
  GetProduct(int) (models.Product, error)
  AddUser(models.Customer) (models.Customer, error)
  SignInUser(username, password string) (models.Customer, error)
  SignOutUserById(int) error
  GetCustomerOrdersByID(int) ([]models.Order, error)
}
```

Now, we need to implement these methods to get some solid functionality in our database layer.

Before we start implementing this functionality, we first need to get a database ready.

Relational databases

A database is one of the key pieces of the backend of any application. This is where the backend layer can persist and retrieve data.

A relational database can simply be described as a database that stores data in a number of tables and then establishes relationships between those tables.

When configuring a database, there are three things we need to define:

- **A database name**: In our case, it will be called GoMusic.
- **Table names**: In our case, for simplicity, we'll go with three tables:
    - **A** customer **table**: This table is where we'll store our app user's information
    - **An** orders **table**: This table should map the customers to the products they bought
    - **A** products **table**: This table will host a list of the available products for GoMusic
- **Indexes and relationships between the tables**: In our case, the orders table will point to both the customer and products tables. Both tables will need an id index. Indexes are used to make queries more efficient and faster.

MySQL is a well-known relational database, and we will be using it in this book. MySQL is a very popular open source database engine and is being used in numerous projects, both large and small.

Here is how our architecture looks like with a database serving data for our application's backend:

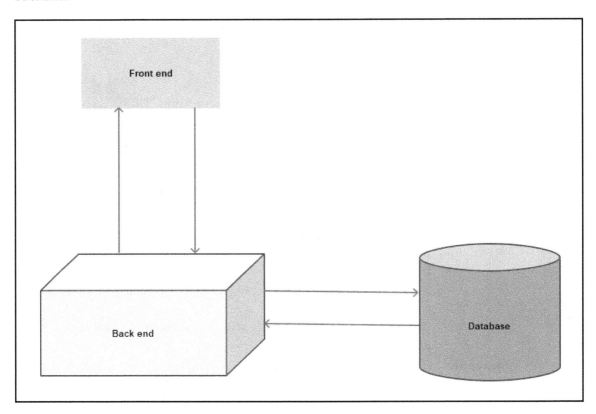

Let's set up MySQL for our application in the next section.

Setting up

Before we start creating databases and tables, we first need to install MySQL. There are Enterprise Editions as well as Community Editions of MySQL. The Community Edition of MySQL is what we would use in a project like ours. This is because the Community Editions are free and can be used for learning and exploration projects. To install the MySQL Community Edition Server, you need to download it from the following link: https://dev.mysql.com/downloads/.

Once we have installed MySQL, we need to install client tools to make use of the database. MySQL usually comes with a tool called **MySQL Workbench**, which is shown in the following screenshot:

The MySQL Workbench tool page

You can use the tools in **MySQL Workbench** to create MySQL databases, tables, indexes, and relationships. Let's go through the tables, one by one.

The customer table

As we mentioned earlier, this is the table where we will store our app user's information. Here is how the `customer` table will look like:

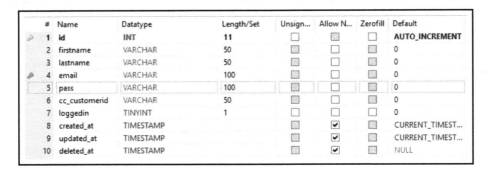

#	Name	Datatype	Length/Set	Unsign...	Allow N...	Zerofill	Default
1	id	INT	11	☐	☑	☐	AUTO_INCREMENT
2	firstname	VARCHAR	50	☑	☐	☑	0
3	lastname	VARCHAR	50	☑	☐	☑	0
4	email	VARCHAR	100	☑	☐	☑	0
5	pass	VARCHAR	100	☑	☐	☑	0
6	cc_customerid	VARCHAR	50	☑	☐	☑	0
7	loggedin	TINYINT	1	☐	☐	☐	0
8	created_at	TIMESTAMP		☑	☑	☑	CURRENT_TIMEST...
9	updated_at	TIMESTAMP		☑	☑	☑	CURRENT_TIMEST...
10	deleted_at	TIMESTAMP		☑	☑	☑	NULL

The table consists of the following ten columns:

1. `id`: This is the unique ID for each customer.
2. `firstname`: This is the first name of the customer.
3. `lastname`: This is the last name of the customer.
4. `email`: This is the customer's email.
5. `pass`: This is the password for the customer. This field must be stored in a hashed form.
6. `cc_customerid`: This is an ID that represents the credit card of the customer. We'll cover this field later in this chapter.
7. `loggedin`: This flag specifies whether the user is logged in or not.
8. `created_at`: This field specifies the date when the customer was added.
9. `updated_at`: This field specifies the last time the row/customer was updated.
10. `deleted_at`: This field specifies the last time the row was deleted.

This table will support two indexes. As mentioned earlier, indexes are used to make queries more efficient and faster. This is done by identifying the columns, which we expect will be used as search keys in our queries. Indexes can also be used to identify fields that are unique and must not be duplicated.

Name	Type / Length
∨ 🔑 PRIMARY KEY	PRIMARY
◈ id	
∨ 🔑 email	UNIQUE
◈ email	

The primary key is the customer `id` field; it's a unique identification number per customer. The unique key is the `email` field. We can't have two or more customers with the same email address.

The orders table

Now, let's look at the `orders` table, which will host a list of the available products for GoMusic:

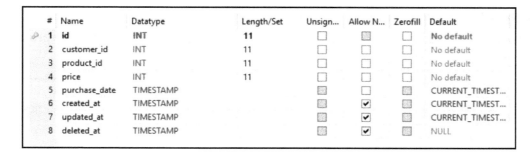

#	Name	Datatype	Length/Set	Unsign...	Allow N...	Zerofill	Default
1	id	INT	11	☐	▨	☐	No default
2	customer_id	INT	11	☐	☐	☐	No default
3	product_id	INT	11	☐	☐	☐	No default
4	price	INT	11	☐	☐	☐	No default
5	purchase_date	TIMESTAMP		▨	☐	▨	CURRENT_TIMEST...
6	created_at	TIMESTAMP		▨	✔	▨	CURRENT_TIMEST...
7	updated_at	TIMESTAMP		▨	✔	▨	CURRENT_TIMEST...
8	deleted_at	TIMESTAMP		▨	✔	▨	NULL

This table consists of the following eight columns:

1. `id`: The unique ID of the order
2. `customer_id`: The ID of the customer making the order
3. `product_id`: The ID of the product the customer bought
4. `price`: The price of the purchase
5. `purchase_date`: The date of the purchase
6. `created_at`: The date/time the row was created
7. `updated_at`: The updated date/time when the row was last updated
8. `deleted_at`: The date/time when the row was deleted, if any

This table will support one index, as shown in the following screenshot:

The index is simply the unique ID index. Each order will have its own unique ID.

The products table

Finally, let's look at the products table. This table will map the customers to the products they bought:

	#	Name	Datatype	Length/Set	Unsign...	Allow N...	Zerofill	Default
🔑	1	id	INT	11	☐	☑	☐	AUTO_INCREMENT
	2	image	VARCHAR	100	☐	☑	☐	NULL
	3	imgalt	VARCHAR	50	☐	☑	☐	NULL
	4	description	TEXT		☐	☑	☐	No default
	5	productname	VARCHAR	50	☐	☑	☐	NULL
	6	price	FLOAT		☐	☑	☐	NULL
	7	promotion	FLOAT		☐	☑	☐	NULL
	8	created_at	TIMESTAMP		☐	☑	☐	CURRENT_TIMEST...
	9	updated_at	TIMESTAMP		☐	☑	☐	CURRENT_TIMEST...
	10	deleted_at	TIMESTAMP		☐	☑	☐	NULL

The table consists of the following 10 columns:

1. id: The unique ID of the product
2. image: The relative location of the product image
3. imgalt: The alternative name for the image
4. description: The product description
5. productname: The name of the product
6. price: The original price of the product
7. promotion: The promotional price of the product
8. created_at: The time when the row was created
9. updated_at: The time when the row was last updated
10. deleted_at: The time when the row was deleted, if any

This table supports just one index, that is, our unique product `id` field:

With this, we should have a good enough database to empower our application. Our database is relatively simple, but it is sufficient to showcase the concepts that we need to cover in this chapter.

Now that we have covered what our database will look like, it's time to cover how to design the code that interacts with our database.

ORM

To design the code that interacts with our database, we will utilize an approach known as *ORM* . ORMs allow you to interact with databases using object-oriented paradigms. ORMs generate code that represent database tables as code objects, and represents queries as methods in your favorite programming language.

In the case of the Go language, we will need to create Go structs to represent each of our tables. We already started writing our models in the previous chapter, that is, `product`, `customer`, and `order`.

Before we continue to write the code, let's first discuss the **Go object-relational mapping** (**GORM**), which is the Go open source package, that offers support for ORMs.

GORM

One of the most popular Go ORM packages is the GORM package, which can be found at `http://gorm.io/`. GORM offers some mature functionality that makes writing backend database layers a breeze. Let's continue writing our database layer by utilizing ORM, step by step:

First, we need to retrieve the GORM package:

```
go get -u github.com/jinzhu/gorm
```

Then, we need to evolve our models so that they can be used properly by GORM.

An ORM needs model objects to accurately reflect the database table columns that are expected to be read and/or manipulated by the ORM library. The ORM can also make use of some meta information, for example, the last time a row was updated, deleted, or created, to ensure proper synchronization between the database and your application at runtime.

In the case of GORM, there is a data type called `gorm.Model`, which is simply a Go struct that hosts fields representing the row `id` field, the `created_at` time, the `updated_at` time, and the `deleted_at` time. It is recommended to embed `gorm.Model` in Go structs that represent your data. In the case of the `customers` table, the Go struct would look like this:

```
type Customer struct {
  gorm.Model
  Name string `json:"name"`
  FirstName string `gorm:"column:firstname" json:"firstname"`
  LastName string `gorm:"column:lastname" json:"lastname"`
  Email string `gorm:"column:email" json:"email"`
  Pass string `json:"password"`
  LoggedIn bool `gorm:"column:loggedin" json:"loggedin"`
  Orders []Order `json:"orders"`
}
```

The preceding code also shows plenty of `struct tags`. The `gorm` struct tags in the preceding example are used to identify the column names that correspond to the field names. So, for instance, the struct field, `FirstName`, is represented by a column called `firstname`. This is identified by the line `gorm:"column:firstname"`.

We also make use of the `json struct` tag in the preceding code to identify what the field will look like in the JSON format. In theory, we don't always need to assign `struct` tags for every single field; however, I find it more practical to do so to avoid confusion.

But how can GORM recognize the fact that the `Customer` Go struct corresponds to the `customers` table in our database? Usually, GORM changes the first letter of our Go struct name to lowercase, and then it adds an 's' at the end, which will convert `Customer` into `customers`. However, GORM also empowers us to explicitly declare the table name that corresponds to the Go struct. This can be done through a method whose signature is `TableName() string`. So, in other words, we can explicitly specify our table name using the following method:

```
func (Customer) TableName() string {
  return "customers"
}
```

Great! Now, inside our `backend\src\models\models.go` file, which sits inside our project folder, let's evolve the data models for the `products` and `orders` tables, similarly to what we did previously:

```
type Product struct {
  gorm.Model
  Image string `json:"img"`
  ImagAlt string `json:"imgalt" gorm:"column:imgalt"`
  Price float64 `json:"price"`
  Promotion float64 `json:"promotion"` //sql.NullFloat64
  PoructName string `gorm:"column:productname" json:"productname"`
  Description string
}

func (Product) TableName() string {
  return "products"
}

type Order struct {
  gorm.Model
  Product
  Customer
  CustomerID int `gorm:"column:customer_id"`
  ProductID int `gorm:"column:product_id"`
  Price float64 `gorm:"column:price" json:"sell_price"`
  PurchaseDate time.Time `gorm:"column:purchase_date" json:"purchase_date"`
}

func (Order) TableName() string {
  return "orders"
}
```

Let's implement of database layer in the next section.

Implementing the database layer

Now, we have to implement the functionality of our database layer.

In the previous chapter, we designed a database layer interface that defined all of the database operations we are expected to need. This is what it looked like:

```
type DBLayer interface {
  GetAllProducts() ([]models.Product, error)
  GetPromos() ([]models.Product, error)
  GetCustomerByName(string, string) (models.Customer, error)
  GetCustomerByID(int) (models.Customer, error)
```

```
GetProduct(int) (models.Product, error)
AddUser(models.Customer) (models.Customer, error)
SignInUser(username, password string) (models.Customer, error)
SignOutUserById(int) error
GetCustomerOrdersByID(int) ([]models.Order, error)
}
```

In our project folder, let's create a new file called `orm.go` in the same folder as `dblayer`. The file will exist in the `{our_project_folder}/backend/src/dblayer` folder.

The GORM package relies on plugins to connect to the different databases that GORM supports. Plugins are Go packages that need to be imported silently in the package where GORM is being used.

To import a plugin package silently in Go, along with the GORM package, we can use the following syntax:

```
import (
    _ "github.com/go-sql-driver/mysql"
    "github.com/jinzhu/gorm"
)
```

Our plugin is the `github.com/go-sql-driver/mysql` package. If you don't already have it installed in your machine, you will need to retrieve it using the `go get` command from your favorite Terminal:

go get github.com/go-sql-driver/mysql

Next, we'll need to create a Go `struct` type, which will implement our `DBLayer` interface.

Our Go struct will host a data type called `*gorm.DB`. The `*gorm.DB` type is our entry point for using GORM's functionality. Here is what the code will look like:

```
type DBORM struct {
    *gorm.DB
}
```

We need to create a constructor for our new type. The constructor will initialize our embedded `*gorm.DB` type.

To obtain an initialized `*gorm.DB` type, we need to use a function called `gorm.Open()`. This function takes two arguments—our database type name, which in our case is `mysql`, and our connection string. A connection string basically contains information regarding how to connect to the specific database that we are trying to access. To make our constructor flexible, we won't hardcode the database name or the connection string. Instead, we'll allow this information to be passed to the constructor. Here is the code:

```
func NewORM(dbname, con string) (*DBORM, error) {
  db, err := gorm.Open(dbname, con)
  return &DBORM{
    DB: db,
  }, err
}
```

It's finally time to start implementing the methods of the `DBLayer` interface.

We'll start by making use of GORM helpful methods, which will spare us from having to write explicit queries. The first method to implement is `GetAllProducts()`. This method simply returns a list of all products, which is the equivalent of a `select *` SQL statement. This can be achieved using GORM's `db.Find()` method, which belongs to the `*gorm.DB` type. Here is the code:

```
func (db *DBORM) GetAllProducts() (products []models.Product, err error) {
  return products, db.Find(&products).Error
}
```

You can see how using an ORM like GORM can produce extremely efficient code. The single line of code in the preceding method executed a `select * from products` query at the `products` table and then returned all of the results. The `Find()` method was able to detect that we seek the products table because we supplied it with an argument of type `[]models.Product`.

Next, we write the `GetPromos()` method, which returns a list of products where the promotion field is not null.

This is simply a select statement with a `where` clause. GORM allows you to achieve this by using a method called `Where()`, combined with the `Find()` method we covered earlier. Here is the code:

```
func (db *DBORM) GetPromos() (products []models.Product, err error) {
  return products, db.Where("promotion IS NOT NULL").Find(&products).Error
}
```

Again, this is simple and efficient. The preceding method simply executed the equivalent of the following query:

```
select * from products where promotion IS NOT NULL
```

The `Where()` method can also take a Go struct value, which represents the condition in our query. We'll see that in our next `DBLayer` method, which is `GetCustomerByName`. This method takes the first and last names of a customer and then returns the customer's information. Here is the code:

```
func (db *DBORM) GetCustomerByName(firstname string, lastname string)
(customer models.Customer, err error) {
   return customer, db.Where(&models.Customer{FirstName: firstname,
LastName: lastname}).Find(&customer).Error
}
```

This method is very similar to the `GetPromos()` method, except that the `Where()` method is fed a Go struct value with the first and last names instead of a string `where` clause. The equivalent of the following query was executed:

```
select * from customers where firstname='..' and lastname='..'
```

Next, we will implement `GetCustomerByID()`, which will retrieve a customer by using their ID in the database.

This time, instead of using a combination of `Where` and `Find`, we will use a method called `First`, which can get the first result that corresponds to a certain condition:

```
func (db *DBORM) GetCustomerByID(id int) (customer models.Customer, err
error) {
   return customer, db.First(&customer, id).Error
}
```

Next, we will implement a method to get a product by ID, which is very similar to `GetCustomerByID()`, except this time the result is a product and not a customer:

```
func (db *DBORM) GetProduct(id int) (product models.Product, error error) {
   return product, db.First(&product, id).Error
}
```

So far, we have been writing methods that execute queries and retrieve results. But now, it's time to start writing methods that add or update rows.

Our next method is `AddUser()`, which basically adds a new user to the database.

This method will also hash the user's password (which we will cover later in the *Security* section), and will set the user as logged in. GORM provides a very handy method called `Create()` so that we can add rows to our database:

```
func (db *DBORM) AddUser(customer models.Customer) (models.Customer, error)
{
  //we will cover the hashpassword function later
  hashPassword(&customer.Pass)
  customer.LoggedIn = true
  return customer, db.Create(&customer).Error
}
```

Next, we need to implement the `SignInUser` method, which basically updates the `loggedin` field in a row representing a specific customer in our customers table.

The `SignInUser` method will identify the user that just logged in based on their email. We will then verify the user's password. If the password is correct, then we update the database. Here is what the code will look like:

```
func (db *DBORM) SignInUser(email, pass string) (customer models.Customer,
err error) {
  //Verify the password, we'll cover this function later
  if !checkPassword(pass) {
    return customer, errors.New("Invalid password")
  }
  //Obtain a *gorm.DB object representing our customer's row
  result := db.Table("Customers").Where(&models.Customer{Email: email})
  //update the loggedin field
  err = result.Update("loggedin", 1).Error
  if err != nil {
    return customer, err
  }
  //return the new customer row
  return customer, result.Find(&customer).Error
}
```

The preceding code covers many of the methods we covered before, except in two places:

- `result := db.Table("Customers").Where(&models.Customer{Email: email})`: This is how we can obtain an object representing the row that we are interested in
- `result.Update("loggedin", 1)`: This is how we update our row

The `SignOutUserById()` method is used to sign out users using their IDs. This will follow the same techniques that we have covered so far:

```
func (db *DBORM) SignOutUserById(id int) error {
  //Create a customer Go struct with the provided if
  customer := models.Customer{
    Model: gorm.Model{
      ID: uint(id),
    },
  }
  //Update the customer row to reflect the fact that the customer is not
logged in
    return db.Table("Customers").Where(&customer).Update("loggedin", 0).Error
}
```

Finally, we implement the `GetCustomerOrdersByID()` method to get customer orders by `customer_id`:

```
func (db *DBORM) GetCustomerOrdersByID(id int) (orders []models.Order, err
error) {
    return orders, db.Table("orders").Select("*")
                .Joins("join customers on customers.id = customer_id")
                .Joins("join products on products.id = product_id")
                .Where("customer_id=?", id).Scan(&orders).Error

}
```

The preceding code is a bit different than the previous methods. This is because we need to execute a couple of joins to produce the results we seek. We need to join three tables: the `orders` table, the `customers` table, and the `products` table. From the `customers` table, we only want customers with IDs that correspond to the provided customer's ID. For the `products` table, we only want products where the product ID corresponds to the product ID of the current order. Luckily, the GORM package provides a method called `Joins`, which can be used to join tables. The preceding code will translate into the following query (assuming that we have a `customer_id` of value `'1'`):

```
SELECT * FROM `orders` join customers on customers.id = customer_id join
products on products.id = product_id WHERE (customer_id='1')
```

And with that, our database layer is almost done. Let's take a look at what is middleware in the next section.

Middleware

Middleware is an important and fun topic in the world of modern web applications. The word *middleware* can mean many things in the software development industry. However, for the purpose of this book, we only care about one definition for it. **Middleware** can simply be defined as code that can run between the time you receive an HTTP request and the time your handler code gets executed on that request. This is best explained through an example.

In the RESTful API that we built for our GoMusic application, let's pick on one of our API endpoints—the /products relative URL. Here was the code that was used to assign this relative URL to an action or a function handler:

```
r.GET("/products", h.GetProducts)
```

Here was the code of the GetProducts handler:

```
func (h *Handler) GetProducts(c *gin.Context) {
  if h.db == nil {
    return
  }
  products, err := h.db.GetAllProducts()
  if err != nil {
    c.JSON(http.StatusInternalServerError, gin.H{"error": err.Error()})
    return
  }
  c.JSON(http.StatusOK, products)
}
```

So far, so good. Here is the workflow for this API resource:

1. An HTTP GET request is received at the /products relative URL address.
2. The GetProducts() method gets executed.

Our web API middleware is simply some code that we can inject between *steps 1* and *2* or even beyond. Technically, the middleware is simply an HTTP handler function that wraps our own handler function. In other words, it's a function that will encapsulate the GetProducts() method, which will allow you to insert functionality before and after your method.

The Gin web framework comes preloaded with two pieces of middleware by default. The framework also allows you to define your own custom middleware when needed.

The two default middlewares that get injected into the Gin web server are **logger middleware** and **recovery middleware**. The logger middleware simply logs the API activity throughout the life of your application. If you run a Go web application that's powered by Gin in a Terminal of your choice, you will see something like this:

```
[GIN] 2018/12/29 - 13:33:19 |?[97;42m 200 ?[0m| 2.7849836s | 127.0.0.1
|?[97;44m GET ?[0m /products
[GIN] 2018/12/29 - 13:33:19 |?[97;42m 200 ?[0m| 65.82ms | 127.0.0.1
|?[97;44m GET ?[0m /img/redguitar.jpeg
[GIN] 2018/12/29 - 13:33:19 |?[97;42m 200 ?[0m| 65.82ms | 127.0.0.1
|?[97;44m GET ?[0m /img/drums.jpg
[GIN] 2018/12/29 - 13:33:19 |?[97;42m 200 ?[0m| 67.4312ms | 127.0.0.1
|?[97;44m GET ?[0m /img/strings.png
[GIN] 2018/12/29 - 13:33:19 |?[97;42m 200 ?[0m| 9.4939ms | 127.0.0.1
|?[97;44m GET ?[0m /img/flute.jpeg
[GIN] 2018/12/29 - 13:33:19 |?[97;42m 200 ?[0m| 9.9734ms | 127.0.0.1
|?[97;44m GET ?[0m /img/saxophone.jpeg
[GIN] 2018/12/29 - 13:33:19 |?[97;42m 200 ?[0m| 18.3846ms | 127.0.0.1
|?[97;44m GET ?[0m /img/blackguitar.jpeg
```

This is basically Gin's logging middleware in action.

On the other hand, Gin's recovery middleware ensures that your application is recovered from panics and writes the HTTP error code 500 in the response when necessary.

There are numerous open source middleware options available for Gin. One list of supported middleware can be found at https://github.com/gin-gonic/contrib.

Let's see how to write a custom middleware in the next section.

Custom middleware

As we mentioned earlier, Gin allows you to author your own middleware so that you can embed some functionality in your web app. Writing custom middleware in Gin is relatively simple, as we can see in the following steps.

The first step is to write the actual code for the middleware.

As we mentioned earlier, a web API middleware is simply an HTTP handler function that encapsulates other HTTP handler functions. Here is what the code would look like for this:

```
func MyCustomMiddleware() gin.HandlerFunc {
  return func(c *gin.Context) {
    //The code that is to be executed before our request gets handled,
  starts here
```

```
    // Set example variable
    c.Set("v", "123")
    //We can then retrieve the variable later via c.Get("v")

  // Now we our request gets handled
  c.Next()

  // This code gets executed after the handler gets handled

  // Access the status we are sending
  status := c.Writer.Status()
  // Do something with the status
  }
}
```

Let's write a very simple middleware that would print
*********************************** before and after the request:

```
func MyCustomLogger() gin.HandlerFunc {
    return func(c *gin.Context) {
        fmt.Println("***********************************")
        c.Next()
        fmt.Println("***********************************")
    }
}
```

The next step is to add this middleware to our Gin engine. This can be done in two ways:

- If we want to keep Gin's default middleware, but then add `MyCustomLogger()`, we can do the following:

```
func RunAPIWithHandler(address string, h HandlerInterface) error {
  //Get gin's default engine
  r := gin.Default()
  r.Use(MyCustomLogger())
  /*
    The rest of our code
    */
}
```

- If, on the other hand, we want to ignore Gin's default middleware and only enable our custom middleware, we can use the following code path:

```
r := gin.New()
r.Use(MyCustomLogger())
```

If we'd like to enable more than one middleware, we just add them as an argument to the `Use()` method, as follows:

```
r := gin.New()
r.Use(MyCustomLogger1(),MyCustomLogger2(),MyCustomLogger3())
```

In the next section, we'll discuss how to secure our web application.

Security

Security is a very important topic when it comes to deploying web applications to production. This topic is massive and can take chapters to cover, if not books. Since the purpose of this book is to cover practical hands-on topics and be to the point, we will cover the most vital nuggets of knowledge that are needed to build a secure web application.

Secure web applications primarily rely on encrypting the data between the web client (browser) and the web server. In other words, they rely on encrypting the data between the frontend and the backend.

As we mentioned earlier, HTTP is the protocol that's utilized between web clients and web servers. HTTP can be secured through a protocol that is known as **TLS** (**Transport Layer Security**). The combination of HTTP and TLS is commonly known as **HTTPS**.

 There is another protocol known as SSL, which was also utilized to secure HTTP. However, TLS is newer and more secure.

Before we discuss the code, let's first cover some important background knowledge about HTTPS and how it works.

Certificates and private keys

HTTPS works as follows:

1. Trust is established between the web client and the web server. This happens through a handshake and through certificates and private keys. We will cover this in more detail later.
2. The web client and the web server agree on an encryption key.
3. The web client and the web server will encrypt their communication using the encryption key they agreed on.

Establishing trust between the client and the server

The certificates and private keys we mentioned in *step 1* of the *Certificates and private keys* section are an entirely different matter. To understand them, you first have to understand the concept of public key encryption or asymmetric cryptography.

A **public key** is used to encrypt data, and it can be shared safely with other parties. However, the public key can't decrypt data. A different key is required to decrypt the data. This key is known as the **private key**, and it must not be shared. The public key can be used by any person to encrypt data. However, only the person with the private key that corresponds to the public key can decrypt the data back to its original human-readable form. The public and private keys are generated using complex computational algorithms. Utilizing a combination of public and private keys is known as asymmetrical cryptography.

In *step 1* of the *Certificates and private keys* section, asymmetrical cryptography is utilized between a web client and web server to agree on a shared encryption key (also known as a shared secret or session key), which is then used in symmetrical cryptography (*steps 2 and 3*). A handshake occurs between the web client and web server, where the client indicates its intent to start a secure communication session with the server. Typically, this entails agreeing on some mathematical details on how the encryption occurs. The server then replies with a *digital certificate*.

 A **digital certificate** (or a public key certificate) is an electronic document that proves the ownership of a public key.

A digital certificate is a digital document that gets issued by a trusted third-party entity. The document contains a public encryption key, the server name that the key belongs to, and the name of the trusted third-party entity, who verifies that the information is correct and that the public key belongs to the expected key owner (also called the issuer of the certificate).

The trusted third-party entity that issues the certificate is known as a **certificate authority** (**CA**). There are multiple known CAs who issue a certificate and verify identities for businesses and organizations. Most CAs charge fees for their service; some are now free, such as Let's Encrypt (https://letsencrypt.org/). For larger organizations or government bodies, they issue their own certificates; this process is known as self-signing, and hence their certificates are known as **self-signed certificates**. Certificates can have expiry dates by which the certificates will need to be renewed; this is for extra protection in case the entity that owned the certificate in the past has changed.

A web client typically contains a list of CAs that it knows of. So, when the client attempts to connect to a web server, the web server responds with a digital certificate. The web client looks for the issuer of the certificate and compares the issuer with the list of CAs that it knows of. If the web client knows and trusts the certificate issuer, then it will continue with the connection to that server and use the public key in the certificate. The public key that's obtained from the server will then be used to encrypt communications to securely negotiate a shared encryption key (or session key or shared secret) to then be used in symmetrical cryptography communications between the web client and web server.

There are a number of algorithms that can be used to generate this session key, but they are beyond the scope of this chapter. What we need to know is that, once a session key is agreed on, the initial handshake between the web client and web server will conclude, allowing the actual communication session to proceed securely under the protection of the shared session key.

For our web server to support HTTPS, it needs a certificate and a private key to establish the initial HTTPS handshake, as outlined in *step 1* of the *Certificates and private keys* section.

Agreeing on, and using an encryption key

An encryption key is a piece of code that relies on some complex math to encrypt a piece of data. Encrypting a piece of data simply means taking a piece of data in human-readable form and then transforming it into a form that is not readable by humans, and hence protects your data. Another key is then required to decrypt this unreadable data back to a human-readable form.

The type of encryption key used in *steps 2* and *3* in the preceding section is sometimes known as a **symmetric cipher**. This simply means that the same key is utilized by both the client and the server to encrypt and decrypt data between them. This is also known as **symmetrical cryptography**.

Most of the time, this key will be invisible to you during development.

In the next section we will take a look at how to support HTTPS in Gin.

Supporting HTTPS in Gin

In the previous section, we obtained some valuable knowledge about how HTTPS actually works. But how do we support it in our code? It's actually fairly simple. In the previous chapter, we utilized the following piece of code to establish an HTTP web server that's empowered by Gin:

```
//Get gin's default engine
  r := gin.Default()
  /*
    Our code
  */
  //Start listening to incoming HTTP requests...
  r.Run(address)
```

We need to apply a single change in the preceding code to support HTTPS instead of HTTP. Here, we are going to use a method called RunTLS(). This method needs three main arguments:

- The HTTPS address that we would like our backend web service to listen to
- The certificate file (covered in the previous section)
- The private key file (covered in the previous section)

Here is what the code would look like:

```
r.RunTLS(address, "cert.pem", "key.pem")
```

But how do we generate a certificate file and a private key? Obviously, if this is a learning or a weekend project, we wouldn't need to obtain a fully legitimate certificate from a CA.

In this case, we use what is known as a self-signed certificate. When you use such a certificate, it obviously won't be trusted by your web browser, because the certificate won't belong to the list of well-known CAs. For testing purposes, you will either need to configure your browser to trust the certificate or just ignore the warning and proceed.

But how do we generate a self-signed certificate?

There are multiple ways to do this. Most people rely on the OpenSSL (https://www.openssl.org/) tool to generate test self-signed certificates. However, because we are using Go, we can make use of a tool that's provided by the Go language in the standard library instead.

In your project folder, simply run the following command:

```
go run %GOROOT%/src/crypto/tls/generate_cert.go --host=127.0.0.1
```

This is a simple tool that's provided by Go in the `tls` package folder. You can use it to generate certificates. Here, `%GOROOT%` represents your Go root environmental variable. If you were to run this command in Linux, you would need to use `$GOROOT` instead.

The preceding command will generate a certificate for the `127.0.0.1` host (the loopback localhost). This tool has more flags/options that you can configure, such as the following:

```
    -ca
            whether this cert should be its own Certificate Authority
    -duration duration
            Duration that certificate is valid for (default 8760h0m0s)
    -ecdsa-curve string
            ECDSA curve to use to generate a key. Valid values are P224, P256
(recommended), P384, P521
    -host string
            Comma-separated hostnames and IPs to generate a certificate for
    -rsa-bits int
            Size of RSA key to generate. Ignored if --ecdsa-curve is set
(default 2048)
    -start-date string
            Creation date formatted as Jan 1 15:04:05 2011
```

The command will generate the certificate and the private key files and will place them in your current folder. You can then copy them wherever you would like and just reference them from your code.

To get your React application to support HTTPS mode while testing, you will need to run the following command when you start your React application:

```
set HTTPS=true&&npm start
```

Let's take a look at Password hashing in the next section.

Password hashing

Another very important security measure is known as password hashing. Password hashing is an approach that's used to protect the passwords of user accounts that are handled by our application.

Let's take our GoMusic application as an example—we have a `customers` table, which hosts customer's usernames and passwords. So, should we store a customer's passwords in plain text? The answer is a loud and resounding *no*!

What do we do instead? How do we protect our customers' passwords and, at the same time, verify their passwords when they log in? This is where password hashing comes into the picture. It consists of two simple steps:

1. When saving a new customer password, hash the password and then save the hash. Hashing can simply be defined as one-way encryption—you can encrypt the password, but you can never decrypt it back. Hashing functions rely on complex math to achieve that.
2. When it's time to verify an existing customer's password, hash the password provided in the sign-in request, then compare the hash of the new incoming password with the saved hash of the original password.

Password hashing protect your customers' passwords because it ensures that no malicious hacker would be able to access them, even if they hack into your database.

But what about protecting the password while it's en route from the web client to our web server? This is where HTTPS comes in. The password that's sent from the client will be fully encrypted until it reaches our backend web server.

Now, let's start implementing some password hashing in our code. The first step is to go to our database layer and implement the logic to:

- Hash new user's passwords before saving it to the database
- When an existing user signs in, compare the provided password with the saved hashed password

In the next sections we will take a look at how to implement password hashing and verifying incoming passwords

Implementing password hashing

In our database layer, we will define a new type for invalid password errors. In our `dblayer.go` file, we will add the following line:

```
var ErrINVALIDPASSWORD = errors.New("Invalid password")
```

Then, in our `orm.go` file, we'll add the following function:

```
func hashPassword(s *string) error {
  if s == nil {
    return errors.New("Reference provided for hashing password is nil")
  }

  //convert password string to byte slice so that we can use it with the
```

```
bcrypt package
  sBytes := []byte(*s)

  //Obtain hashed password via the GenerateFromPassword() method
  hashedBytes, err := bcrypt.GenerateFromPassword(sBytes,
bcrypt.DefaultCost)
  if err != nil {
    return err
  }

  //update password string with the hashed version
  *s = string(hashedBytes[:])
  return nil
}
```

The preceding code makes use of a package called bcrypt, which is very popular when it comes to hashing passwords. bcrypt stands for a popular password hashing function that was designed in the late 1990s. bcrypt is the default password hashing function in the OpenBSD operating system, and it enjoys support in numerous programming languages.

The package also provides methods to compare hashed passwords with their human-readable counterparts.

If the package is not yet installed in your environment, run the following command:

go get golang.org/x/crypto/bcrypt

We already came across the hashPassword() method in the AddUser() method, which will hash the password and then save it to the database.

Add the following HashPassword () method to your code:

```
func (db *DBORM) AddUser(customer models.Customer) (models.Customer, error)
{
  //pass received password by reference so that we can change it to its
hashed version
  hashPassword(&customer.Pass)
  customer.LoggedIn = true
  err := db.Create(&customer).Error
  customer.Pass = ""
  return customer, err
}
```

The preceding code will perform the password hashing part. Before we return the customer object, we need to set the password to empty because this information doesn't need to be shared again for security purposes.

Comparing the password

Now, let's write the code that will compare the saved hashed passwords with passwords that are provided by users who are attempting to log in.

We just need another method from the `bcrypt` package to compare our saved hash with the incoming password:

```
func checkPassword(existingHash, incomingPass string) bool {
  //this method will return an error if the hash does not match the
provided password string
  return bcrypt.CompareHashAndPassword([]byte(existingHash),
[]byte(incomingPass)) == nil
}
```

Next, we need to add code to the `SignInUser` method so that we can retrieve the hashed passwords of customers who are trying to sign in. Then, we can compare passwords. If the passwords don't match, we return an error. If they do, we continue to log the user in by setting the logged-in flag to `true`:

```
func (db *DBORM) SignInUser(email, pass string) (customer models.Customer,
err error) {
  //Obtain a *gorm.DB object representing our customer's row
  result := db.Table("Customers").Where(&models.Customer{Email: email})
  //Retrieve the data for the customer with the passed email
  err = result.First(&customer).Error
  if err != nil {
    return customer, err
  }
  //Compare the saved hashed password with the password provided by the
user trying to sign in
  if !checkPassword(customer.Pass, pass) {
    //If failed, returns an error
    return customer, ErrINVALIDPASSWORD
  }
  //set customer pass to empty because we don't need to share this
information again
  customer.Pass = ""
  //update the loggedin field
  err = result.Update("loggedin", 1).Error
  if err != nil {
    return customer, err
  }
  //return the new customer row
  return customer, result.Find(&customer).Error
}
```

Finally, there is a tiny change we need to add to our HTTP web handler to handle failed logins.

Let's go back to the `handlers.go` file and edit the `SignIn` method a bit. The edited parts of the code are shown in bold:

```go
func (h *Handler) SignIn(c *gin.Context) {
  if h.db == nil {
    return
  }
  var customer models.Customer
  err := c.ShouldBindJSON(&customer)
  if err != nil {
    c.JSON(http.StatusBadRequest, gin.H{"error": err.Error()})
    return
  }
  customer, err = h.db.SignInUser(customer.Email, customer.Pass)
  if err != nil {
    //if the error is invalid password, return forbidden http error
    if err == dblayer.ErrINVALIDPASSWORD {
      c.JSON(http.StatusForbidden, gin.H{"error": err.Error()})
      return
    }
    c.JSON(http.StatusInternalServerError, gin.H{"error": err.Error()})
    return
  }
  c.JSON(http.StatusOK, customer)
}
```

Let's take a look at credit card handling in the next section.

Credit card handling

We already implemented the credit card logic at the frontend in Chapter 5, *Building a Frontend for GoMusic*. It's now time to implement the backend part of our credit card handling.

For credit card processing at the frontend, we made use of the Stripe API (https://stripe.com/docs/api). In a product environment, you would need to create an account with Stripe and obtain an API key to use for your application. For testing purposes, however, we can make use of testing API keys and test credit card numbers, which Stripe happily provides for developers to build productive apps that are capable of processing credit cards. To learn more about testing credit card numbers and testing tokens that are provided by Stripe, take a look at https://stripe.com/docs/testing.

In our frontend code, we made use of the following Stripe API code to create a token:

```
let { token } = await this.props.stripe.createToken({ name: this.state.name
});
```

We also made use of a very popular framework known as *Stripe elements,* which will collect all of our credit card information and then merge it with the create token request so that we get a token that represents the credit card that we are trying to process.

We then send this token down to the backend so that it can be processed and/or saved.

To process credit card payments, there are some key pieces of information that we need:

- The credit card token that's provided by the Stripe API
- The ID of the customer making the purchase
- The ID of the product the customer is trying to buy
- The selling price of the product
- Whether the card should be remembered for future use
- Whether to use a pre-saved card or not

I changed the frontend code so that it can collect this information and pass it to the HTTP request that's bound to our backend. Here's the part of the frontend code that will create and submit our request. The following code is in the `creditcards.js` file:

```
async handleSubmit(event) {
    event.preventDefault();
    let id = "";
    //If we are not using a pre-saved card, connect with stripe to
obtain a card token
    if (!this.state.useExisting) {
        //Create the token via Stripe's API
        let { token } = await this.props.stripe.createToken({ name:
this.state.name });
        if (token == null) {
            console.log("invalid token");
            this.setState({ status: FAILEDSTATE });
            return;
        }
        id = token.id;
    }
    //Create the request, then send it to the back-end
    let response = await fetch("/users/charge", {
        method: "POST",
        headers: { "Content-Type": "application/json" },
        body: JSON.stringify({
            token: id,
```

```
                customer_id: this.props.user,
                product_id: this.props.productid,
                sell_price: this.props.price,
                rememberCard: this.state.remember !== undefined,
                useExisting: this.state.useExisting
            })
        });
        //If response is ok, consider the operation a success
        if (response.ok) {
            console.log("Purchase Complete!");
            this.setState({ status: SUCCESSSTATE });
        } else {
            this.setState({ status: FAILEDSTATE });
        }
    }
}
```

The preceding code makes use of the fetch() method in order to send a POST request to the backend. The POST request will contain a JSON message which will host all the data that our backend needs to process the request.

In the next section we'll take a look at how the backend of credit card handling works.

Credit card handling at the backend

We can use the Stripe API to process credit card transactions as follows:

1. Create an object of the *stripe.CustomerParams type, which can then take the credit card token that's provided by the frontend. The credit card token is ingested using a method called SetToken().

2. Create an object of the *stripe.Customer type, which takes the object of the stripe.CustomerParams type as input. This is done through the customer.New() function.

3. Create an object of the *stripe.ChargeParams type, which takes information about our transaction, such as the amount, the currency, and the description of the purchase.

4. The *stripe.ChargeParams object must also receive a field, which represents the Stripe customer ID. This is provided by the *stripe.Customer object we covered in *step 2*.

Remember that the Stripe customer ID is different to the actual customer ID that references the customer in our database.

5. If we would like to save this credit card and use it later, we can simply store the Stripe customer ID string for later use.
6. Finally, we can charge the credit card by calling `charge.New()`, which takes the `*stripe.ChargeParams` object as an input.

If the preceding steps sound too difficult to follow, don't worry. Once we start looking at the code, it will become clearer.

Most of our code will live inside the `charge` handler method, which is inside the `handler.go` file. Here is the current state of the method:

```
func (h *Handler) Charge(c *gin.Context) {
  if h.db == nil {
    c.JSON(http.StatusInternalServerError, gin.H{"error": "server database
error"})
    return
  }
}
```

The method doesn't do anything yet. Here is what we need it to do:

1. Obtain the transaction information using the incoming HTTP request.
2. If the request requires that we use an existing saved card, then we need to retrieve the saved customer Stripe ID and charge the card.
3. If the request requires that we remember the currently provided credit card information, then we save it to the database before we charge the card.

First, we need to create a type that can accept the data we are receiving from the frontend. Here is what this looks like:

```
request := struct {
    models.Order
    Remember bool `json:"rememberCard"`
    UseExisting bool `json:"useExisting"`
    Token string `json:"token"`
}{}
```

In the preceding code, we declared the Go struct and initialized it in the same piece of code. This is a quick way to create and use `struct` types on the fly in Go.

Next, we need to parse the incoming JSON payload into the `request` variable:

```
err := c.ShouldBindJSON(&request)
  //If an error occurred during parsing, report it then return
  if err != nil {
    c.JSON(http.StatusBadRequest, request)
    return
  }
```

Now, it's time to start writing some Stripe code. The first thing we need to do is declare the stripe API key—we'll just use a test API key in this case. However, in a production environment, you'll need to use your own Stripe key and protect it very well:

```
stripe.Key = "sk_test_4eC39HqLyjWDarjtT1zdp7dc"
```

Next, we need to create a `*stripe.ChargeParams` object, which we covered in *step 3* at the beginning of this section. Here is what it looks like:

```
chargeP := &stripe.ChargeParams{
  //the price we obtained from the incoming request:
  Amount: stripe.Int64(int64(request.Price)),
  //the currency:
  Currency: stripe.String("usd"),
  //the description:
  Description: stripe.String("GoMusic charge..."),
}
```

Next, we initialize the stripe customer ID string. This is the important field, which was covered in *step 4* at the beginning of this section:

```
stripeCustomerID:=""
```

Now, if the incoming request expects us to use an existing card, we would retrieve the saved Stripe customer ID from the database and then use it. The following code uses a new database method that retrieves the Stripe customer ID from the database. We will implement this method later in this section:

```
if request.UseExisting {
    //use existing
    log.Println("Getting credit card id...")
    //This is a new method which retrieve the stripe customer id from the
database
    stripeCustomerID, err = h.db.GetCreditCardCID(request.CustomerID)
    if err != nil {
```

```
        log.Println(err)
        c.JSON(http.StatusInternalServerError, gin.H{"error": err.Error()})
        return
    }
}
```

Otherwise, we can create a *stripe.CustomerParams object, which is used to create a *stripe.Customer object. This provides us with the Stripe customer ID:

```
...else {
        cp := &stripe.CustomerParams{}
        cp.SetSource(request.Token)
        customer, err := customer.New(cp)
        if err != nil {
            c.JSON(http.StatusInternalServerError, gin.H{"error":
err.Error()})
            return
        }
        stripeCustomerID = customer.ID
```

If we are asked to remember the card, we simply store the Stripe customer ID in the database:

```
if request.Remember {
        //save the stripe customer id, and link it to the actual customer id
in our database
        err = h.db.SaveCreditCardForCustomer(request.CustomerID,
stripeCustomerID)
        if err != nil {
            c.JSON(http.StatusInternalServerError, gin.H{"error": err.Error()})
            return
        }
    }
```

Next, we attempt to charge the credit card:

```
    /*
        we should check if the customer already ordered the same item or not
but for simplicity, let's assume it's a new order
    */

    //Assign the stipe customer id to the *stripe.ChargeParams object:
    chargeP.Customer = stripe.String(stripeCustomerID)

    //Charge the credit card
    _, err = charge.New(chargeP)
    if err != nil {
        c.JSON(http.StatusInternalServerError, gin.H{"error": err.Error()})
```

```
    return
  }
```

Finally, we add the order to our database:

```
err = h.db.AddOrder(request.Order)
if err != nil {
  c.JSON(http.StatusInternalServerError, gin.H{"error": err.Error()})
}
```

And that's it for the charge() method.

There is still some work remaining. The newly added code to the charge() handler made use of several database methods, which we have not created yet:

- GetCreditCardCID(): Retrieves a saved Stripe customer ID from the database
- SaveCreditCardForCustomer(): Saves the stripe customer ID to our database
- AddOrder(): Adds an order to the database

We need to add these three methods to the database layer interface in our dblayer.go file:

```
type DBLayer interface {
  GetAllProducts() ([]models.Product, error)
  GetPromos() ([]models.Product, error)
  GetCustomerByName(string, string) (models.Customer, error)
  GetCustomerByID(int) (models.Customer, error)
  GetProduct(int) (models.Product, error)
  AddUser(models.Customer) (models.Customer, error)
  SignInUser(username, password string) (models.Customer, error)
  SignOutUserById(int) error
  GetCustomerOrdersByID(int) ([]models.Order, error)
  AddOrder(models.Order) error
  GetCreditCardCID(int) (string, error)
  SaveCreditCardForCustomer(int, string) error
}
```

We add the three methods to our concrete implementation of the DBLayer interface. This is done in the orm.go file:

```
//Add the order to the orders table
func (db *DBORM) AddOrder(order models.Order) error {
  return db.Create(&order).Error
}

//Get the id representing the credit card from the database
func (db *DBORM) GetCreditCardCID(id int) (string, error) {
  cusomterWithCCID := struct {
```

```
     models.Customer
     CCID string `gorm:"column:cc_customerid"`
   }{}
   return cusomterWithCCID.CCID, db.First(&cusomterWithCCID, id).Error
}

//Save the credit card information for the customer
func (db *DBORM) SaveCreditCardForCustomer(id int, ccid string) error {
   result := db.Table("customers").Where("id=?", id)
   return result.Update("cc_customerid", ccid).Error
}
```

We now need to go back to our `handler.go` file, and modify our `handler` constructor, such that it can connect to our database:

```
func NewHandler(db, constring string) (HandlerInterface, error) {
  db, err := dblayer.NewORM(db, constring)
  if err != nil {
    return nil, err
  }
  return &Handler{
    db: db,
  }, nil
}
```

Perfect! And with that, the backend code for our GoMusic app is 99% complete, let's revisit our frontend code in the next section.

Revisiting the frontend code

The last deep dive we did in terms of the frontend code was in Chapter 5, *Building a Frontend for GoMusic*. Chapter 4, *Frontend with React.js*, and Chapter 5, *Building a Frontend for GoMusic*, served to build solid and practical foundational knowledge about how to construct a working React app, which can be used as the frontend to our backend Go application.

These two chapters covered about 85% of GoMusic's frontend. However, they did not cover all of the JavaScript code that's needed to glue together the different React components that we built in Chapter 4, *Frontend with React.js*, and Chapter 5, *Building a Frontend for GoMusic*. In this section, we will provide an overview of the overall frontend architectures and fill some of the gaps.

In the next section, we will take a look at the application structure of the frontend of our application.

The app structure

Our frontend component is divided into the following files:

- `index.js`: The entry point to our React application, which calls the `App` component.
- `App.js`: The main component of our React application. It combines all of the other components to form our app. The `App` component hosted in the `App.js` file takes care of some important central tasks such as the signing in or the signing out of a user.
- `modalwindows.js`: This is responsible for all of the modal windows in our application. This includes the sign in, the new user registration, and the buy modal window.
- `Navigation.js`: This is responsible for the navigational menu in our React application, which is how we move from one screen to another.
- `creditcards.js`: This is responsible for the frontend side processing of credit cards.
- `productcards.js`: This is responsible for showing the list of product cards. This includes normal product cards and promotions.
- `orders.js`: This shows a list of customer's orders when a customer is signed in.
- `about.js`: This shows the **About** page.

We'll see how to interconnect our frontend and backend in the next section.

Interactions between the frontend and the backend

In `Chapter 4`, *Frontend with React.js*, we relied on a JSON file that contained some mock data to empower and run our frontend app without needing an actual working backend to be present. Now, we need to replace all of the code where we relied on the JSON sample data file and send full HTTP requests to the backend instead.

For our React app to route the requests to our backend, we first need to add a field called `proxy` to the `package.json` file of our React application. The proxy field needs to point to the backend API address. In our case, the backend component of our application listens on local port `8000`:

```
"proxy": "http://127.0.0.1:8000/",
```

The `package.json` file will exist in the main folder of your React app. This file is used by `node` package managers to figure our global settings, scripts, and dependencies for your `node` app.

Whenever we send a request to the backend, we make use of the powerful `fetch()` method. This method can send HTTP requests to a relative URL. Here is an example of a request to fetch customer's orders:

```
fetch(this.props.location) //send http request to a location. The location
here is /products
            .then(res => res.json())
            .then((result) => {
                this.setState({
                    orders: result
                });
            });
```

In the next section we will explore how to make use of cookies in our application.

Using cookies

Since our application doesn't rely anymore on a global sample data file to answer important questions such as whether a user is currently signed in or not, what the user's information is, and so on. The frontend application now makes use of browser cookies for this. A simple definition for browser cookies is that they are small pieces of information that get stored in the user's device using the web browser. This information can then be simply retrieved from the cookie when needed.

The frontend code makes use of cookies to easily save and retrieve the user's information to populate different screens and React components that need this information. This is done using the `js-cookie` JavaScript package. This package can be installed with the following command:

```
npm install js-cookie --save
```

Here is an example of setting a cookie:

```
cookie.set("user", userdata);
```

Here is an example of retrieving data from a cookie:

```
const user = cookie.getJSON("user");
```

Cookies are used to also check whether a user is currently signed in or signed out. Sign out handling code has been added to the React application since the code we covered in Chapter 5, *Building a Frontend for GoMusic*, to handle the change of state that occurs when a user signs out. When a user signs out, we remove the information of the existing user from the cookie and just retain the fact that no one is logged in. Here is the code to do this:

```
cookie.set("user",{loggedin:false});
```

For more context on how we use cookies in our React application, and how to handle user sign out, have a look at the App react component of our application at: https://github.com/PacktPublishing/Hands-On-Full-Stack-Development-with-Go/blob/master/Chapter07/Frontend/src/App.js

Now, let's explore how to deploy our frontend application to a production environment.

Deploying the frontend application

Once you are done with the frontend code, it will need to be transformed into a form that can be shared and copied to production server environments, without needing to reinstall all the Node.js tools and dependencies that were needed in the development process.

The React framework comes to the rescue here. When we created our React application in Chapter 4, *Frontend with React.js*, and Chapter 5, *Building a Frontend for GoMusic*, we used a tool called create-react-app to create our application and set up the toolchain. The tool supports some scripts that we can use to run and build our React application. We already mentioned the npm start command, which was used to run our React app in development mode, so that we can run our code and debug in real time as we are developing the application.

There is a script that is vital for getting our React app ready for production use and is called build. To run this script, we simply type the npm run build command from the main folder of our React app. This command will compile our entire application to some static files, which we can then serve directly from our Go app. The output of the build script goes to a folder called build, which gets created in our React app root folder.

Let's call this folder the React `build` folder. We can then copy this `build` folder anywhere and get our Go app to utilize it to serve the GoMusic app frontend.

Here are the steps that we need to follow in our Go code to be able to serve the React output `build` folder.

First, we need to import a Gin middleware called `static`, which we can do by executing the following command:

```
go get github.com/gin-contrib/static
```

We will need to go to our `rest.go` file, which hosted our HTTP route definitions. This file can be found in `backend\src\rest.go`. Inside `rest.go`, we will import the Gin static middleware:

```
import (
  "fmt"
  "github.com/gin-contrib/static"
  "github.com/gin-gonic/gin"
)
```

Inside the `RunAPIWithHandler` function, which includes all of our HTTP route definitions, we will replace the code that's used to serve our `img` folder with code that serves all static files from the `build` folder that was generated by the React app. Here is what this will look like:

```
//remove this line: r.Static("/img", "../public/img")
//This assumes the React app 'build' folder exists in the relative
path '../public'
r.Use(static.ServeRoot("/", "../public/build"))
```

The first argument of the `static.ServeRoot()` function is the relative HTTP root URL for our web application, while the second argument is basically the location of the React build folder.

We will also need to move the `img` folder, which included all of the images of our musical instruments, so that it is inside the `build` folder. Now, the `build` folder has all of the assets for our web application.

That's all we need to do. Now, we can just build our Go app into a single executable file by either using the `go build` or the `go install` command. Then, we can copy our executable web application along with the React build folder to wherever we would like to deploy our web application.

Summary

This chapter covered a lot of ground. In this chapter, we learned how to design and implement database layers for our backend services. We learned about the concept of web API middleware and how to make use of it. We also took a deep dive into some practical security concepts such as TLS and password hashing. We then learned how to process credit cards in our backend services through the powerful Stripe API. With this knowledge under your belt, you now have what it takes to build modern production web applications in Go.

In the next chapter, we will cover how to test our application by writing unit tests, and how to measure it's performance, by running benchmarks.

Questions

1. What is middleware?
2. What is a Stripe customer ID?
3. What is an ORM?
4. What is GORM?
5. How can we write a join query using GORM?
6. What is TLS?
7. What is meant by password hashing?
8. What is `bcrypt`?

Further reading

- **Stripe API**: `https://stripe.com/docs/api`
- **GORM**: `http://gorm.io/`
- **Package** `bcrypt`: `https://godoc.org/golang.org/x/crypto/bcrypt`
- **Transport layer security:** `https://www.cloudflare.com/learning/ssl/transport-layer-security-tls/`

8
Testing and Benchmarking Your Web API

Testing is of vital importance in production software environments. Applications not only need to be tested for functionality, but they also need to be benchmarked and profiled so that we can examine the performance of our applications. This chapter will provide a wide and practical exposure about how to properly test and benchmark your application.

In this chapter, we will cover the following topics:

- Mocking types in Go
- Unit testing in Go
- Benchmarking in Go

The code for this chapter can be found in this book's GitHub repository at `https://github.com/PacktPublishing/Hands-On-Full-Stack-Development-with-Go/tree/master/Chapter08`.

Testing in Go

One of the building blocks of the testing process in any piece of software is known as **unit testing**. Unit testing is a very popular concept in virtually any programming language, and there are numerous software frameworks and language extensions that allow you to perform unit testing as efficiently as possible.

The idea of unit testing is to test each unit or component of your software separately. A unit can simply be defined as the smallest testable piece of your software.

The Go language comes equipped with a testing package, as well as some Go commands to make the process of unit testing easier. The package can be found at `https://golang.org/pkg/testing/`.

In this section, we'll dive a bit deeper into how to build unit tests in the Go language. However, before we start writing unit tests in Go, we first need to cover the concept of mocking.

Mocking

The concept of mocking is very popular in the field of unit testing software. It's best described via an example. Let's say we would like to unit test one of the HTTP handler functions of the GoMusic application. The GetProducts() method is a good method to showcase our example, since the purpose of this method was to return a list of all of the products that are available for sale in our GoMusic store. Here is what the code for GetProducts() looked like:

```go
func (h *Handler) GetProducts(c *gin.Context) {
  if h.db == nil {
    c.JSON(http.StatusInternalServerError, gin.H{"error": "server database
error"})
    return
  }
  products, err := h.db.GetAllProducts()
  if err != nil {
    c.JSON(http.StatusInternalServerError, gin.H{"error": err.Error()})
    return
  }
  fmt.Printf("Found %d products\n", len(products))
  c.JSON(http.StatusOK, products)
}
```

This method simply retrieves all of the products from our database and then returns the results as a HTTP response. This method utilized the h.db.GetAllProducts() method to retrieve the data from our database.

So, when it's time to perform a unit test for GetProducts(), we should be able to test the functionality of the method without needing a real database. Furthermore, we should also be able to inject some error scenarios, where we make h.db.GetAllProducts() fail, and then ensure that GetProducts() reacts as expected.

You might be wondering, why is it important to be able to test a method such as GetProducts() without needing a real database? The answer is simple—unit testing is only concerned with the unit you are currently testing, which is the GetProducts() method, not your database connection.

Mock object types can be defined as object types that you can use to *mock* or fake a certain behavior. In other words, in the case of the h.db.GetAllProducts() method, instead of using an object type that connects to a real database, we can use a mock type that does not connect to a real database but can give us the results we need to perform the unit testing of the GetProducts() method.

Let's go back down memory lane and remember how h.db.GetAllProducts() was built. The database part of this piece of code was simply an interface called DBLayer, which we used to describe all the behavior we would need from a database layer.

Here is what the DBLayer interface looked like:

```
type DBLayer interface {
  GetAllProducts() ([]models.Product, error)
  GetPromos() ([]models.Product, error)
  GetCustomerByName(string, string) (models.Customer, error)
  GetCustomerByID(int) (models.Customer, error)
  GetProduct(int) (models.Product, error)
  AddUser(models.Customer) (models.Customer, error)
  SignInUser(username, password string) (models.Customer, error)
  SignOutUserById(int) error
  GetCustomerOrdersByID(int) ([]models.Order, error)
  AddOrder(models.Order) error
  GetCreditCardCID(int) (string, error)
  SaveCreditCardForCustomer(int, string) error
}
```

To create a mock type for our database layer, we just need to create a concrete type that will implement DBLayer but won't connect to a real database.

The mock object will need to return some simulated data, which we use for our testing. We can simply store this data in slices or maps inside our mock object.

Now that we know what mocking is, let's create our mock db type.

Creating a mock db type

Inside our backend/src/dblayer folder, let's add a new file called mockdblayer.go. Inside this new file, let's create a type called MockDBLayer:

```
package dblayer

import (
  "encoding/json"
  "fmt"
```

```
    "strings"

    "github.com/PacktPublishing/Hands-On-Full-Stack-Development-with-
 Go/tree/master/Chapter08/backend/src/models"
 )

 type MockDBLayer struct {
  err error
   products []models.Product
   customers []models.Customer
   orders []models.Order
 }
```

The `MockDBLayer` type hosts four types:

- `err`: This is an error type that we can set at will whenever we need to simulate an error scenario. We'll look at how to use it when it's time to write our unit tests.
- `products`: This is where we store our mock list of products.
- `customers`: This is where we store our mock list of customers.
- `orders`: This is where we store our mock list of orders.

Next, let's write a constructor for our mock type:

```
 func NewMockDBLayer(products []models.Product, customers []models.Customer,
 orders []models.Order) *MockDBLayer {
    return &MockDBLayer{
      products: products,
      customers: customers,
      orders: orders,
    }
 }
```

The constructor takes three arguments: a list of `products`, a list of `customers`, and a list of `orders`. This gives other developers the opportunity to define their own data for testing, which is good for flexibility. However, other developers should be able to initialize the `MockDBLayer` type with some mock data pre-loaded:

```
 func NewMockDBLayerWithData() *MockDBLayer {
    PRODUCTS := `[
      {
        "ID": 1,
        "CreatedAt": "2018-08-14T07:54:19Z",
        "UpdatedAt": "2019-01-11T00:28:40Z",
        "DeletedAt": null,
        "img": "img/strings.png",
        "small_img": "img/img-small/strings.png",
```

```
        "imgalt": "string",
        "price": 100,
        "promotion": 0,
        "productname": "Strings",
        "Description": ""
    },
    {
        "ID": 2,
        "CreatedAt": "2018-08-14T07:54:20Z",
        "UpdatedAt": "2019-01-11T00:29:11Z",
        "DeletedAt": null,
        "img": "img/redguitar.jpeg",
        "small_img": "img/img-small/redguitar.jpeg",
        "imgalt": "redg",
        "price": 299,
        "promotion": 240,
        "productname": "Red Guitar",
        "Description": ""
    },
    {
        "ID": 3,
        "CreatedAt": "2018-08-14T07:54:20Z",
        "UpdatedAt": "2019-01-11T22:05:42Z",
        "DeletedAt": null,
        "img": "img/drums.jpg",
        "small_img": "img/img-small/drums.jpg",
        "imgalt": "drums",
        "price": 17000,
        "promotion": 0,
        "productname": "Drums",
        "Description": ""
    },
    {
        "ID": 4,
        "CreatedAt": "2018-08-14T07:54:20Z",
        "UpdatedAt": "2019-01-11T00:29:53Z",
        "DeletedAt": null,
        "img": "img/flute.jpeg",
        "small_img": "img/img-small/flute.jpeg",
        "imgalt": "flute",
        "price": 210,
        "promotion": 190,
        "productname": "Flute",
        "Description": ""
    },
    {
        "ID": 5,
        "CreatedAt": "2018-08-14T07:54:20Z",
```

```
            "UpdatedAt": "2019-01-11T00:30:12Z",
            "DeletedAt": null,
            "img": "img/blackguitar.jpeg",
            "small_img": "img/img-small/blackguitar.jpeg",
            "imgalt": "Black guitar",
            "price": 200,
            "promotion": 0,
            "productname": "Black Guitar",
            "Description": ""
        },
        {
            "ID": 6,
            "CreatedAt": "2018-08-14T07:54:20Z",
            "UpdatedAt": "2019-01-11T00:30:35Z",
            "DeletedAt": null,
            "img": "img/saxophone.jpeg",
            "small_img": "img/img-small/saxophone.jpeg",
            "imgalt": "Saxophone",
            "price": 1000,
            "promotion": 980,
            "productname": "Saxophone",
            "Description": ""
        }
    ]
`

    ORDERS := `[
    {
        "ID": 1,
        "CreatedAt": "2018-12-29T23:35:36Z",
        "UpdatedAt": "2018-12-29T23:35:36Z",
        "DeletedAt": null,
        "img": "",
        "small_img": "",
        "imgalt": "",
        "price": 0,
        "promotion": 0,
        "productname": "",
        "Description": "",
        "name": "",
        "firstname": "",
        "lastname": "",
        "email": "",
        "password": "",
        "loggedin": false,
        "orders": null,
        "customer_id": 1,
        "product_id": 1,
```

```
        "sell_price": 90,
        "purchase_date": "2018-12-29T23:34:32Z"
    },
    {

        "ID": 2,
        "CreatedAt": "2018-12-29T23:35:48Z",
        "UpdatedAt": "2018-12-29T23:35:48Z",
        "DeletedAt": null,
        "img": "",
        "small_img": "",
        "imgalt": "",
        "price": 0,
        "promotion": 0,
        "productname": "",
        "Description": "",
        "name": "",
        "firstname": "",
        "lastname": "",
        "email": "",
        "password": "",
        "loggedin": false,
        "orders": null,
        "customer_id": 1,
        "product_id": 2,
        "sell_price": 299,
        "purchase_date": "2018-12-29T23:34:53Z"
    },
    {

        "ID": 3,
        "CreatedAt": "2018-12-29T23:35:57Z",
        "UpdatedAt": "2018-12-29T23:35:57Z",
        "DeletedAt": null,
        "img": "",
        "small_img": "",
        "imgalt": "",
        "price": 0,
        "promotion": 0,
        "productname": "",
        "Description": "",
        "name": "",
        "firstname": "",
        "lastname": "",
        "email": "",
        "password": "",
        "loggedin": false,
        "orders": null,
        "customer_id": 1,
        "product_id": 3,
```

```
        "sell_price": 16000,
        "purchase_date": "2018-12-29T23:35:05Z"
    },
    {

        "ID": 4,
        "CreatedAt": "2018-12-29T23:36:18Z",
        "UpdatedAt": "2018-12-29T23:36:18Z",
        "DeletedAt": null,
        "img": "",
        "small_img": "",
        "imgalt": "",
        "price": 0,
        "promotion": 0,
        "productname": "",
        "Description": "",
        "name": "",
        "firstname": "",
        "lastname": "",
        "email": "",
        "password": "",
        "loggedin": false,
        "orders": null,
        "customer_id": 2,
        "product_id": 1,
        "sell_price": 95,
        "purchase_date": "2018-12-29T23:36:18Z"
    },
    {

        "ID": 5,
        "CreatedAt": "2018-12-29T23:36:39Z",
        "UpdatedAt": "2018-12-29T23:36:39Z",
        "DeletedAt": null,
        "img": "",
        "small_img": "",
        "imgalt": "",
        "price": 0,
        "promotion": 0,
        "productname": "",
        "Description": "",
        "name": "",
        "firstname": "",
        "lastname": "",
        "email": "",
        "password": "",
        "loggedin": false,
        "orders": null,
        "customer_id": 2,
        "product_id": 2,
```

```
        "sell_price": 299,
        "purchase_date": "2018-12-29T23:36:39Z"
    },
    {

        "ID": 6,
        "CreatedAt": "2018-12-29T23:38:13Z",
        "UpdatedAt": "2018-12-29T23:38:13Z",
        "DeletedAt": null,
        "img": "",
        "small_img": "",
        "imgalt": "",
        "price": 0,
        "promotion": 0,
        "productname": "",
        "Description": "",
        "name": "",
        "firstname": "",
        "lastname": "",
        "email": "",
        "password": "",
        "loggedin": false,
        "orders": null,
        "customer_id": 2,
        "product_id": 4,
        "sell_price": 205,
        "purchase_date": "2018-12-29T23:37:01Z"
    },
    {

        "ID": 7,
        "CreatedAt": "2018-12-29T23:38:19Z",
        "UpdatedAt": "2018-12-29T23:38:19Z",
        "DeletedAt": null,
        "img": "",
        "small_img": "",
        "imgalt": "",
        "price": 0,
        "promotion": 0,
        "productname": "",
        "Description": "",
        "name": "",
        "firstname": "",
        "lastname": "",
        "email": "",
        "password": "",
        "loggedin": false,
        "orders": null,
        "customer_id": 3,
        "product_id": 4,
```

```
        "sell_price": 210,
        "purchase_date": "2018-12-29T23:37:28Z"
    },
    {
        "ID": 8,
        "CreatedAt": "2018-12-29T23:38:28Z",
        "UpdatedAt": "2018-12-29T23:38:28Z",
        "DeletedAt": null,
        "img": "",
        "small_img": "",
        "imgalt": "",
        "price": 0,
        "promotion": 0,
        "productname": "",
        "Description": "",
        "name": "",
        "firstname": "",
        "lastname": "",
        "email": "",
        "password": "",
        "loggedin": false,
        "orders": null,
        "customer_id": 3,
        "product_id": 5,
        "sell_price": 200,
        "purchase_date": "2018-12-29T23:37:41Z"
    },
    {
        "ID": 9,
        "CreatedAt": "2018-12-29T23:38:32Z",
        "UpdatedAt": "2018-12-29T23:38:32Z",
        "DeletedAt": null,
        "img": "",
        "small_img": "",
        "imgalt": "",
        "price": 0,
        "promotion": 0,
        "productname": "",
        "Description": "",
        "name": "",
        "firstname": "",
        "lastname": "",
        "email": "",
        "password": "",
        "loggedin": false,
        "orders": null,
        "customer_id": 3,
        "product_id": 6,
```

```
        "sell_price": 1000,
        "purchase_date": "2018-12-29T23:37:54Z"
    },
    {
        "ID": 10,
        "CreatedAt": "2019-01-13T00:44:55Z",
        "UpdatedAt": "2019-01-13T00:44:55Z",
        "DeletedAt": null,
        "img": "",
        "small_img": "",
        "imgalt": "",
        "price": 0,
        "promotion": 0,
        "productname": "",
        "Description": "",
        "name": "",
        "firstname": "",
        "lastname": "",
        "email": "",
        "password": "",
        "loggedin": false,
        "orders": null,
        "customer_id": 19,
        "product_id": 6,
        "sell_price": 1000,
        "purchase_date": "2018-12-29T23:37:54Z"
    },
    {
        "ID": 11,
        "CreatedAt": "2019-01-14T06:03:08Z",
        "UpdatedAt": "2019-01-14T06:03:08Z",
        "DeletedAt": null,
        "img": "",
        "small_img": "",
        "imgalt": "",
        "price": 0,
        "promotion": 0,
        "productname": "",
        "Description": "",
        "name": "",
        "firstname": "",
        "lastname": "",
        "email": "",
        "password": "",
        "loggedin": false,
        "orders": null,
        "customer_id": 1,
        "product_id": 3,
```

```
        "sell_price": 17000,
        "purchase_date": "0001-01-01T00:00:00Z"
    }
]
`

    CUSTOMERS := `[
    {
        "ID": 1,
        "CreatedAt": "2018-08-14T07:52:54Z",
        "UpdatedAt": "2019-01-13T22:00:45Z",
        "DeletedAt": null,
        "name": "",
        "firstname": "Mal",
        "lastname": "Zein",
        "email": "mal.zein@email.com",
        "password":
"$2a$10$ZeZI4pPPlQg89zfOOyQmiuKW9Z7pO9/KvG7OfdgjPAZF0Vz9D8fhC",
        "loggedin": true,
        "orders": null
    },
    {

        "ID": 2,
        "CreatedAt": "2018-08-14T07:52:55Z",
        "UpdatedAt": "2019-01-12T22:39:01Z",
        "DeletedAt": null,
        "name": "",
        "firstname": "River",
        "lastname": "Sam",
        "email": "river.sam@email.com",
        "password":
"$2a$10$mNbCLmfCAc0.4crDg3V3fe0iO1yr03aRfE7Rr3vdfKMGVnnzovCZq",
        "loggedin": false,
        "orders": null
    },
    {

        "ID": 3,
        "CreatedAt": "2018-08-14T07:52:55Z",
        "UpdatedAt": "2019-01-13T21:56:05Z",
        "DeletedAt": null,
        "name": "",
        "firstname": "Jayne",
        "lastname": "Ra",
        "email": "jayne.ra@email.com",
        "password":
"$2a$10$ZeZI4pPPlQg89zfOOyQmiuKW9Z7pO9/KvG7OfdgjPAZF0Vz9D8fhC",
        "loggedin": false,
        "orders": null
    },
```

```
    {
        "ID": 19,
        "CreatedAt": "2019-01-13T08:43:44Z",
        "UpdatedAt": "2019-01-13T15:12:25Z",
        "DeletedAt": null,
        "name": "",
        "firstname": "John",
        "lastname": "Doe",
        "email": "john.doe@bla.com",
        "password":
"$2a$10$T4c8rmpbgKrUA0sIqtHCaO0g2XGWWxFY4IGWkkpVQOD/iuBrwKrZu",
        "loggedin": false,
        "orders": null
    }
]
`

    var products []models.Product
    var customers []models.Customer
    var orders []models.Order
    json.Unmarshal([]byte(PRODUCTS), &products)
    json.Unmarshal([]byte(CUSTOMERS), &customers)
    json.Unmarshal([]byte(ORDERS), &orders)
    return NewMockDBLayer(products, customers, orders)
}
```

The preceding function has some data hardcoded inside it, which then gets fed to the MockDBLayer constructor. This allows developers to make use of the MockDBLayer type so that they can use it right away without first needing to come up with data.

Next, we need to offer methods to expose the data that's being used by the MockDBLayer type:

```
func (mock *MockDBLayer) GetMockProductData() []models.Product {
   return mock.products
}

func (mock *MockDBLayer) GetMockCustomersData() []models.Customer {
   return mock.customers
}

func (mock *MockDBLayer) GetMockOrdersData() []models.Order {
   return mock.orders
}
```

Now, we need a method that will allow us to be in full control of the errors that are returned by the methods of `MockDBLayer`. This is important because during our unit tests, it's likely we'll need to test how the code will behave if an error occurs. We'll revisit this concept when we work on our unit test. For now, let's write a method that allows us to set errors that are returned by our mock type:

```
func (mock *MockDBLayer) SetError(err error) {
  mock.err = err
}
```

Now, it's time to implement the `DBLayer` interface methods. Let's start with the `GetAllProducts()` method. This is what it will look like:

```
func (mock *MockDBLayer) GetAllProducts() ([]models.Product, error) {
  //Should we return an error?
  if mock.err != nil {
    return nil, mock.err
  }
  //return products list
  return mock.products, nil
}
```

The first thing we need to check is whether the `MockDBLayer` type returns an error or not. If it needs to return an error, then we just return the error. Otherwise, we return the list of products we saved in our mock type.

Next, let's take a look at the `GetPromos()` method:

```
func (mock *MockDBLayer) GetPromos() ([]models.Product, error) {
  if mock.err != nil {
    return nil, mock.err
  }
  promos := []models.Product{}
  for _, product := range mock.products {
    if product.Promotion > 0 {
      promos = append(promos, product)
    }
  }
  return promos, nil
}
```

In the preceding code, we first checked whether we should return an error, like we did previously. We then looped through the list of products and picked the products that have promotions.

Next, let's explore the `GetProduct(id)` method. This method should be able to retrieve a product based on the `id` that's provided. This is what it looks like:

```
func (mock *MockDBLayer) GetProduct(id int) (models.Product, error) {
  result := models.Product{}
  if mock.err != nil {
    return result, mock.err
  }
  for _, product := range mock.products {
    if product.ID == uint(id) {
      return product, nil
    }
  }
  return result, fmt.Errorf("Could not find product with id %d", id)
}
```

As with the other methods, we first need to check whether we need to return an error, and if so, we return the error and exit the method. Otherwise, we retrieve the piece of data that's being queried by this method. In the case of `GetProduct(id)`, we loop through the products list and then return the product with the requested `id`. This loop could have been replaced by a simple map retrieval if we were to store our products in a map instead of a list. In a production environment, you will need to decide how you would like your data to be represented in your mock objects (maps and/or slices). In this case, I decided to go with a slice for simplicity. In a more complex mock object, you might want to store data in slices for methods that return all the data, as well as in maps for methods that return specific items.

The rest of the code for the mock object will continue to implement the `DBLayer` interface methods.

Here is the method to get a customer by name:

```
func (mock *MockDBLayer) GetCustomerByName(first, last string)
(models.Customer, error) {
  result := models.Customer{}
  if mock.err != nil {
    return result, mock.err
  }
  for _, customer := range mock.customers {
    if strings.EqualFold(customer.FirstName, first) &&
strings.EqualFold(customer.LastName, last) {
      return customer, nil
    }
  }
  return result, fmt.Errorf("Could not find user %s %s", first, last)
}
```

Here is the method to get a customer by their ID:

```
func (mock *MockDBLayer) GetCustomerByID(id int) (models.Customer, error) {
  result := models.Customer{}
  if mock.err != nil {
    return result, mock.err
  }

  for _, customer := range mock.customers {
    if customer.ID == uint(id) {
      return customer, nil
    }
  }
  return result, fmt.Errorf("Could not find user with id %d", id)
}
```

Here is the code to add a user:

```
func(mock *MockDBLayer) AddUser(customer models.Customer) (models.Customer,
error){
  if mock.err != nil {
    return models.Customer{}, mock.err
  }
  mock.customers = append(mock.customers, customer)
  return customer, nil
}
```

Here is the code to sign in a user:

```
func (mock *MockDBLayer) SignInUser(email, password string)
(models.Customer, error) {
  if mock.err != nil {
    return models.Customer{}, mock.err
  }
  for _, customer := range mock.customers {
    if strings.EqualFold(email, customer.Email) && customer.Pass ==
password {
      customer.LoggedIn = true
      return customer, nil
    }
  }
  return models.Customer{}, fmt.Errorf("Could not sign in user %s", email)
}
```

Here is the code to sign out a user by ID:

```
func (mock *MockDBLayer) SignOutUserById(id int) error {
  if mock.err != nil {
    return mock.err
```

```
  }
  for _, customer := range mock.customers {
    if customer.ID == uint(id) {
      customer.LoggedIn = false
      return nil
    }
  }
  return fmt.Errorf("Could not sign out user %d", id)
}
```

Here is the code to get customer orders by ID:

```
func (mock *MockDBLayer) GetCustomerOrdersByID(id int) ([]models.Order,
error) {
  if mock.err != nil {
    return nil, mock.err
  }
  for _, customer := range mock.customers {
    if customer.ID == uint(id) {
      return customer.Orders, nil
    }
  }
  return nil, fmt.Errorf("Could not find customer id %d", id)
}
```

Here is the code to add an order:

```
func (mock *MockDBLayer) AddOrder(order models.Order) error {
  if mock.err != nil {
    return mock.err
  }
  mock.orders = append(mock.orders, order)
  for _, customer := range mock.customers {
    if customer.ID == uint(order.CustomerID) {
      customer.Orders = append(customer.Orders, order)
      return nil
    }
  }
  return fmt.Errorf("Could not find customer id %d for order",
order.CustomerID)
}
```

Finally, the following methods are just place holders for the credit card handling logic. The unit tests that we'll explore in this chapter won't cover credit card handling, so to simplify things; let's just leave them as place holders for now:

```
//The credit card related mock methods will need more work. They are out of
scope of this chapter.
```

```
func (mock *MockDBLayer) GetCreditCardCID(id int) (string, error) {
  if mock.err != nil {
    return "", mock.err
  }
  return "", nil
}

func (mock *MockDBLayer) SaveCreditCardForCustomer(int, string) error {
  if mock.err != nil {
    return mock.err
  }
  return nil
}
```

It is worth mentioning that there are some third-party open source projects in the Go language that can help with the creation and utilization of mock objects. However, in this chapter, we have built our own.

Now that we have created a mock db type, let's cover unit testing in Go.

Unit testing in Go

It's now time to explore unit testing in Go and make use of the MockDBLayer type that we built in the previous section.

The first step for writing unit tests in Go is to create a new file in the same folder as the package you would like to test. The filename has to end with _test.go. In our case, since we seek to test the GetProducts() method in the rest package, we'll create a new file in the same folder and call it handler_test.go.

This file will only build and execute when you run unit tests, but not during regular builds. You may be wondering, how would I run unit tests in Go? The answer is simple—you utilize the go test command! Whenever you run go test, only the files that end with _test.go will build and run.

If you are running the go test command from a different folder than the folder of the package that you would like to test, then you can just point to the package that you would like to test:

```
go test <Your_Package_Path>
```

For example, if we want to run the unit tests for our `rest` package, the command will look like this:

```
go test github.com/PacktPublishing/Hands-On-Full-Stack-Development-with-
Go/tree/master/Chapter08/backend/src/rest
```

Now, let's dive further into the `handler_test.go` file. The first thing we need to do is declare the package:

```
package rest
```

Next, we need to write a function that will represent our unit test. In Go, you need to follow some specific rules to ensure that your function gets executed as part of the unit testing that's produced by the `go test` command:

- Your function has to start with the word `Test`
- The first letter after `Test` has to be in upper case
- The function needs to take the `*testing.T` type as an argument

The `*testing.T` type provides some important methods that will help us signify whether a test has failed or passed. The type also provides some logging features that we can use. We'll see the `*testing.T` type in action shortly, when we start writing our test code.

So, by following the preceding three rules, we'll create a new function called `TestHandler_GetProducts` to host the unit testing code for the `GetProducts()` method in our HTTP handler. Here is what the function will look like:

```
func TestHandler_GetProducts(t *testing.T) {
}
```

The first thing we need to do is enable the test mode of the Gin framework. The testing mode of the Gin framework prevents too much logging:

```
func TestHandler_GetProducts(t *testing.T) {
  // Switch to test mode so you don't get such noisy output
  gin.SetMode(gin.TestMode)
}
```

Next, let's initialize our `mockdbLayer` type. We will use the constructor that included some hardcoded data:

```
func TestHandler_GetProducts(t *testing.T) {
  // Switch to test mode so you don't get such noisy output
  gin.SetMode(gin.TestMode)
  mockdbLayer := dblayer.NewMockDBLayerWithData()
}
```

The GetProducts() method we are seeking to test in this section is an HTTP handler function, which is expected to return a list of products that are available from the GoMusic store. As we covered in the previous chapters, an HTTP handler function can be defined as an action that gets executed when an HTTP request is sent to a specific relative URL. The HTTP handler will process the HTTP request and return a response via HTTP as well.

In our unit test, we'll need to test not only the functionality of GetProducts() as a method, but also how it reacts to HTTP requests.

We'll need to define the relative URL that will activate the HTTP handler function for that. Let's call it /products and make it a constant:

```
func TestHandler_GetProducts(t *testing.T) {
    // Switch to test mode so you don't get such noisy output
    gin.SetMode(gin.TestMode)
    mockdbLayer := dblayer.NewMockDBLayerWithData()
    h := NewHandlerWithDB(mockdbLayer)
    const productsURL string = "/products"
}
```

We'll see how we can make use of that constant in the next chapter.

In the next section we'll cover an important concept known as table-drive development.

Table-driven development

In a typical practical unit test, we seek to test a certain function or method to see how it will react to certain inputs and error conditions. This means that the code of the unit test would need to call the function or method we are trying to test multiple times, and with different inputs and error conditions. Instead of writing large interconnection if statements to make the calls with different inputs, we can instead follow a very popular design pattern known as **table-driven development**.

The idea behind test-driven development is simple—we will use an array of Go structs or a map to represent our tests. The struct array or map will contain information about the inputs and error conditions that we want to pass to the function/method being tested. We will then loop through the array of Go structs and call the method/function to be tested with the current inputs and error conditions. This approach will produce a number of sub-tests under the main unit test.

In our unit test, we'll use an array of Go structs to represent our different subtests. Here is what the array will look like:

```
tests := []struct {
    name string
    inErr error
    outStatusCode int
    expectedRespBody interface{}
}{
    }
```

Let's call the preceding code our `test` table. Here is what the Go struct fields will represent:

- `name`: This is the name of the subtest.
- `inErr`: This is the input error. We will inject this error into the mock db layer type and monitor how the `GetProducts()` method will behave.
- `outStatusCode`: This is the expected HTTP status code that is produced from calling the `GetProducts()` HTTP handler. If the HTTP status code that's returned from calling `GetProducts()` as an HTTP handler does not match this value, then the unit test fails.
- `expectedRespBody`: This is the expected HTTP response body that's returned from calling the `GetProducts()` HTTP handler. If the returned HTTP body does not match this value, then the unit test fails. This field is of the `interface{}` type because it can either be a slice of products or an error message. The `interface{}` type in Go can represent any other data type.

The beauty of the table-driven testing design pattern is the fact that it's very flexible; you can simply add more fields to test more conditions.

There are two expected HTTP response bodies that can be produced from the `GetProducts()` HTTP handler—we either get some list of products, or we get an error message. The error message takes the following format: `{error:"the error message"}`.

Before we start running our subtests from our test table, let's define a `struct` type to represent the error message so that we can use it in our testing:

```
type errMSG struct {
    Error string `json:"error"`
}
```

Next, we need to define our list of subtests. For simplicity, we'll pick two different scenarios to test:

```
tests := []struct {
    name string
    inErr error
    outStatusCode int
    expectedRespBody interface{}
}{
    {
      "getproductsnoerrors",
      nil,
      http.StatusOK,
      mockdbLayer.GetMockProductData(),
    },
    {
      "getproductswitherror",
      errors.New("get products error"),
      http.StatusInternalServerError,
      errMSG{Error: "get products error"},
    },
}
```

In the preceding code, we defined two different subtests:

- The first one is called `getproductsnoerrors`. It represents a straight execution scenario where no errors occurred and everything worked fine. We inject no errors to the mock db layer type, so we expect no errors to return from the `GetProducts()` method. We expect an HTTP response status of `OK`, and we expect to get a list of the product data that's stored in mock db layer as the HTTP response body. The reason why we expect to get a list of the product data stored in the mock db layer as our output is because of the fact that the mock db type will be the database layer for our `GetProducts()` method.
- The second one is called `getproductswitherror`. It represents an execution scenario where an error has occurred. We inject an error called "`get products error`" into the mock db layer type. This error will be expected to be returned as the HTTP response body of the `GetProducts()` handler function call. The HTTP status code that's expected will be `StatusInternalServerError`.

The remainder of our unit test code will loop through the test table and execute our tests. The `*testing.T` type, which got passed as an argument to our unit test function, provides methods that we can use to define subtests within our unit test, which we can then run in parallel.

First, to define a subtest within our unit test, we must utilize the following method:

```
t.Run(name string,f func(t *T))bool
```

The first argument is the name of the subtest, whereas the second argument is a function that represents the subtest we would like to run. In our case, we'll need to loop through our `test` table and call `t.Run()` for each subtest. Here is what this will look like:

```
for _, tt := range tests {
    t.Run(tt.name, func(t *testing.T) {
        //run our sub-test
    }
}
```

Now, let's focus on the code to run for our subtests. The first thing we need to do is inject an error into the mock type:

```
for _, tt := range tests {
    t.Run(tt.name, func(t *testing.T) {
      //set the input error
      mockdbLayer.SetError(tt.inErr)
    }
}
```

Next, we need to create a test HTTP request to represent the HTTP request which will be received by our `GetProducts()` HTTP handler. Again, Go comes to the rescue with a standard package called `httptest`. This package empowers you to create special data types that allow you to test HTTP-related functionality. One of the functions provided by `httptest` is a function called `NewRequest()`, which returns an HTTP request type that we can use for our testing:

```
//Create a test request
req := httptest.NewRequest(http.MethodGet, productsURL, nil)
```

The function takes three arguments: the type of HTTP method, the relative URL where the HTTP request is expected to get sent, and the body of the request, if any.

In the case of the `GetProducts()` HTTP `handler` method, it's expecting an HTTP GET request that targets the `/products` relative URL. We have already stored the `/products` value in the `productsURL` constant.

The `httptest` package also provides a data type called `ResponseRecorder`, which can be used to capture the HTTP response of an HTTP handler function call. The `ResponseRecorder` data type implements Go's `http.ResponseWriter` interface, which enables the `ResponseRecorder` to be injected in any code that makes use of `http.ResponseWriter`. We'll need to obtain a value of this data type so that we can use it in our testing:

```
//create an http response recorder
w := httptest.NewRecorder()
```

Next, we'll need to create an instance of the Gin framework engine to use it in our test. This is because the `GetProducts()` method that we are trying to test is an HTTP handler function for a Gin engine router, so it needs a `*gin.Context` type as its input. Here is what the function signature looks like:

```
GetProducts(c *gin.Context)
```

Luckily, the Gin framework comes prepared with a function called `CreateTestContext()` for the exact purpose of creating an instance of a Gin context and an instance of a Gin engine to use for testing. The `CreateTestContext()` function takes an `http.ResponseWriter` interface as input, which means that we can pass our `httptest.ResponseRecorder` as the input, since it implements the `http.ResponseWriter` interface as input. Here is what the code will look like:

```
//create an http response recorder
w := httptest.NewRecorder()
//create a fresh gin engine object from the response recorder, we will
ignore the context value
_, engine := gin.CreateTestContext(w)
```

As we mentioned earlier, the `CreateTestContext()` function returns two values: a Gin context instance and a Gin engine instance. In our case, we will not make use of the Gin context instance, which is why we didn't receive the value for it in the preceding code. The reason why we won't make use of the Gin context instance is because I prefer to use the Gin engine instance for my testing, as it allows me to test the full workflow of an HTTP request being served.

Next, we'll make use of the Gin engine instance to map our `GetProducts()` method to the `productsURL` relative URL address via an HTTP `GET` request. Here is what this looks like:

```
//configure the get request
engine.GET(productsURL, h.GetProducts)
```

Now, it's time to get our Gin engine to serve the HTTP request, and then pass the HTTP response to our `ResponseRecorder`:

```
//serve the request
  engine.ServeHTTP(w, req)
```

This will, in effect, send our test HTTP request to the `GetProducts()` handler method, since the test request targets `productsURL`. The `GetProducts()` handler method will then process the request and send an HTTP response via `w`, which is our `ResponseRecorder`.

It's now time to test how `GetProducts()` processed the HTTP request. The first thing we need to do is extract the HTTP response from `w`. This is done via the `Result()` method in the `ResponseRecorder` object type:

```
//test the output
response := w.Result()
```

Then, we need to test the HTTP status code of the result. If it's not equal to the expected HTTP status code, then we fail the test case and we log why:

```
if response.StatusCode != tt.outStatusCode {
        t.Errorf("Received Status code %d does not match expected status
code %d", response.StatusCode, tt.outStatusCode)
  }
```

As shown in the preceding code, the `*testing.T` type comes equipped with a method called `Errorf`, which can be used to log a message and then fail the test. If we wanted to log a message without failing the test, we can use a method called `Logf`. If we want to fail a test right away, we can call a method called `Fail`. The `t.Errorf` method is the combination of `t.Logf`, followed by `t.Fail`.

Next, we need to capture the HTTP body of the response so that we're able to compare it to the expected HTTP response body for this subtest. There are two scenarios to consider: either an error was injected into our subtest, which means an error message is expected as the result, or there was no error injected, which means a list of products is the expected HTTP response body:

```
/*
Since we don't know the data type to expect from the http response, we'll
use interface{} as the type
*/
var respBody interface{}
//If an error was injected, then the response should decode to an error
message type
  if tt.inErr != nil {
```

```
            var errmsg errMSG
            json.NewDecoder(response.Body).Decode(&errmsg)
            //Assign decoded error message to respBody
            respBody = errmsg
    } else {
            //If an error was not injected, the response should decode to a
    slice of products data types
            products := []models.Product{}
            json.NewDecoder(response.Body).Decode(&products)
            //Assign decoded products list to respBody
            respBody = products
    }
```

The last thing we need to do is compare the expected HTTP response body with the actual HTTP response body that we received. To do the comparison, we need to make use of a very handy function that is present in Go's `reflect` package. This function is called `reflect.DeepEqual()`, and it helps us to fully compare two values and identify whether they are clones of each other. If the two values are not equal, then we log an error and fail the test. Here is what the code will look like:

```
if !reflect.DeepEqual(respBody, tt.expectedRespBody) {
        t.Errorf("Received HTTP response body %+v does not match expected
HTTP response Body %+v", respBody, tt.expectedRespBody)
    }
```

With this, our unit test is completed! Let's have a look at what the overall testing code will look like:

```
func TestHandler_GetProducts(t *testing.T) {
    // Switch to test mode so you don't get such noisy output
    gin.SetMode(gin.TestMode)
    mockdbLayer := dblayer.NewMockDBLayerWithData()
    h := NewHandlerWithDB(mockdbLayer)
    const productsURL string = "/products"
    type errMSG struct {
        Error string `json:"error"`
    }
    // Use table driven testing
    tests := []struct {
        name string
        inErr error
        outStatusCode int
        expectedRespBody interface{}
    }{
        {
            "getproductsnoerrors",
            nil,
```

```
          http.StatusOK,
          mockdbLayer.GetMockProductData(),
      },
      {
          "getproductswitherror",
          errors.New("get products error"),
          http.StatusInternalServerError,
          errMSG{Error: "get products error"},
      },
  }
  for _, tt := range tests {
    t.Run(tt.name, func(t *testing.T) {
      //set the input error
      mockdbLayer.SetError(tt.inErr)
      //Create a test request
      req := httptest.NewRequest(http.MethodGet, productsURL, nil)
      //create an http response recorder
      w := httptest.NewRecorder()
      //create a fresh gin context and gin engine object from the response
recorder
      _, engine := gin.CreateTestContext(w)

      //configure the get request
      engine.GET(productsURL, h.GetProducts)
      //serve the request
      engine.ServeHTTP(w, req)

      //test the output
      response := w.Result()
      if response.StatusCode != tt.outStatusCode {
        t.Errorf("Received Status code %d does not match expected status
code %d", response.StatusCode, tt.outStatusCode)
      }
      //Since we don't know the data type to expect from the http response,
we'll use interface{} as the type
      var respBody interface{}
      //If an error was injected, then the response should decode to an
error message type
      if tt.inErr != nil {
        var errmsg errMSG
        json.NewDecoder(response.Body).Decode(&errmsg)
        respBody = errmsg
      } else {
        //If an error was not injected, the response should decode to a
slice of products data types
        products := []models.Product{}
        json.NewDecoder(response.Body).Decode(&products)
        respBody = products
```

```
        }

        if !reflect.DeepEqual(respBody, tt.expectedRespBody) {
            t.Errorf("Received HTTP response body %+v does not match expected
HTTP response Body %+v", respBody, tt.expectedRespBody)
        }
    })
  }
}
```

It's worth mentioning that Go gives you the power to run your subtests in parallel to each other. You can invoke this behavior by calling `t.Parallel()` inside your subtests. Here is what this will look like:

```
for _, tt := range tests {
    t.Run(tt.name, func(t *testing.T) {
            t.Parallel()
            //your concurrent code
    }
}
```

However, when you run concurrent subtests, you must make sure that any data types they share won't change state or behavior in parallel, otherwise your test results will not be reliable. For example, in our code, we use a single mock db layer type object, which was initialized outside of the subtests. This means that whenever we change the error state of the mock db layer inside a subtest, it might have affected other subtests running in parallel and made use of the mock db layer object at the same time.

What remains in this section is to run our unit test and witness the results. As we mentioned earlier, you can either run the `go test` command from inside the folder that hosts the package you seek to test, or you can use the `go test <your_package_path>` command from outside your package folder. If the unit test passes, you will see an output that looks like this:

```
PASS
ok github.com/PacktPublishing/Hands-On-Full-Stack-Development-with-
Go/tree/master/Chapter08/backend/src/rest 0.891s
```

The default output shows you the full name of the package that was tested and the time it took to run the test(s).

If you want to see more information, you can run `go test -v`. This is what this command will return:

```
c:\Programming_Projects\GoProjects\src\github.com\PacktPublishing\Hands-On-
Full-Stack-Development-with-Go\8-Testing-and-
benchmarking\backend\src\rest>go test -v
=== RUN   TestHandler_GetProducts
=== RUN   TestHandler_GetProducts/getproductsnoerrors
=== RUN   TestHandler_GetProducts/getproductswitherror
--- PASS: TestHandler_GetProducts (0.00s)
    --- PASS: TestHandler_GetProducts/getproductsnoerrors (0.00s)
    --- PASS: TestHandler_GetProducts/getproductswitherror (0.00s)
PASS
ok github.com/PacktPublishing/Hands-On-Full-Stack-Development-with-Go/8-
Testing-and-benchmarking/backend/src/rest 1.083s
```

The `-v` flag shows verbose output—it will show you the name of the unit test being run, as well as the names of the subtests within the unit test as they run.

Let's take a look at benchmarking in the next section

Benchmarking

Another key topic in the world of testing software is benchmarking. **Benchmarking** is the practice of measuring the performance of your code. The Go `testing` package offers you the ability to perform strong benchmarking on your code.

Let's start by targeting a piece of code and showcase how to benchmark it using Go. A good function to benchmark is the `hashpassword()` function, which is utilized by our database layer. This function can be found in the `backend/src/dblayer/orm.go` file. It takes a reference to a string as an argument, and then it uses a `bcrypt` hash to hash the string. Here is the code:

```go
func hashPassword(s *string) error {
  if s == nil {
    return errors.New("Reference provided for hashing password is nil")
  }
  //converd password string to byte slice
  sBytes := []byte(*s)
  //Obtain hashed password
  hashedBytes, err := bcrypt.GenerateFromPassword(sBytes,
bcrypt.DefaultCost)
  if err != nil {
    return err
```

```
    }
    //update password string with the hashed version
    *s = string(hashedBytes[:])
    return nil
}
```

Let's say that we would like to test the performance of this function. How do we begin?

The first step is to create a new file. The filename should end with _test.go. The file needs to exist in the same folder as the dblayer package, which hosts the function we seek to test. Let's call the file orm_test.go.

As we mentioned earlier, files whose names end with _test.go will not be part of the regular build process. Instead, they activate when we run tests via the go test command.

Next, inside the file, we'll start by declaring the Go package that the file belongs to, which is dblayer. Then, we need to import the testing package that we will use in our code:

```
package dblayer

import "testing"
```

Now, it's time to write the code to benchmark the hashpassword() function. To write benchmark functions in Go, we need to follow these rules:

- The function name has to start with the word Benchmark.
- The first letter after the word Benchmark needs to be in upper case.
- The function takes *testing.B as an argument. The *testing.B type provides methods that facilitate benchmarking our code.

As we follow those three rules, we'll build our benchmark function with the following signature:

```
func BenchmarkHashPassword(b *testing.B) {
}
```

Next, we'll initialize a string to be hashed:

```
func BenchmarkHashPassword(b *testing.B) {
  text := "A String to be Hashed"
}
```

To utilize an object of type `*testing.B` to benchmark a piece of code, we need to run the targeted piece of code `b.N` times. `N` is simply a field in the `*testing.B` type, which adjusts its value until the targeted code can be reliably measured. This is what the code will look like:

```
func BenchmarkHashPassword(b *testing.B) {
 text := "A String to be Hashed"
 for i := 0; i < b.N; i++ {
 hashPassword(&text)
 }
}
```

The preceding code will run `hashPassword()` as many times as it takes to benchmark it. To run the benchmark, we can use the `go test` command in combination with a `-bench` flag:

go test -bench .

The `-bench` flag needs to be provided as a regex expression to indicate the benchmark functions that we would like to run. If we would like to run everything that's available, we can use `.` to indicate all. Otherwise, if we only want to run benchmarks that include the term `HashPassword`, we can modify the command, as follows:

go test -bench HashPassword

The output will look like this:

```
goos: windows
goarch: amd64
pkg: github.com/PacktPublishing/Hands-On-Full-Stack-Development-with-Go/8-
Testing-and-benchmarking/backend/src/dblayer
BenchmarkHashPassword-8 20 69609530 ns/op
PASS
ok github.com/PacktPublishing/Hands-On-Full-Stack-Development-with-Go/8-
Testing-and-benchmarking/backend/src/dblayer 1.797s
```

The output simply states that the `hashPassword` function was run 20 times, and that it had a speed of about 69,609,530 nanoseconds per loop.

In our case, we only initialized a string right before running our benchmark, which is a very straightforward and easy operation:

```
func BenchmarkHashPassword(b *testing.B) {
 text := "A String to be Hashed"
 for i := 0; i < b.N; i++ {
```

```
        hashPassword(&text)
    }
}
```

However, if your initialization is much more complex and takes some time to complete, it's advised that you run `b.ResetTimer()` after you finish your initialization and before you perform your benchmarking. Here is an example:

```
func BenchMarkSomeFunction(b *testing.B){
    someHeavyInitialization()
    b.ResetTimer()
    for i:=0;i<b.N;b++{
        SomeFunction()
    }
}

b.Run(name string, f func(b *testing.B))
```

The `*testing.B` type also comes with an extra method called `RunParallel()`, which can test performance in a parallel setting. This works in concert with a flag known as `go test -cpu`:

```
b.RunParallel(func(pb *testing.PB){
    for pb.Next(){
        //your code
    }
})
```

Summary

This chapter covered a key skill that any software developer should have, which is proper software testing in production. We focused on the features that are offered by the Go language to enable the testing of Go code.

We started by covering how to build mock types and why they are important when it comes to software testing. We then covered how to perform unit testing in Go and how to benchmark your software.

In the next chapter, we'll explore the concept of Isomorphic Go programming, by covering the GopherJS framework.

Questions

1. What is the definition of a mock type? Why is it useful?
2. What is the testing package in Go?
3. What is the `*testing.T` type used for?
4. What is the `*testing.B` type used for?
5. What is the `*testing.T.Run()` method used for?
6. What is the `*testing.T.Parallel()` method used for?
7. What is meant by benchmarking?
8. What is the `*testing.B.ResetTimer()` method used for?

Further reading

For more information, you can go through the following links:

- **The Go testing package**: `https://golang.org/pkg/testing/`

Introduction to Isomorphic Go with GopherJS

9

So far, we have covered how to write our frontend using JavaScript. However, if you prefer to use Go in the frontend, there is an option for that. This option is known as GopherJS, which is a popular Go package combined with a set of commands with only one purpose: to compile (also known as **transpiling**) Go code to JavaScript. Once Go code is compiled to JavaScript, the code could be utilized in the frontend component similarly to JavaScript. An application that relies on the same programming language for the frontend and the backend is known as an **isomorphic application**.

Like any other software-design approach, writing isomorphic applications has its own pros and cons. The chief advantage is the convenience and speed of development that comes with using a single programming language that you are really good at for most of your code. The main disadvantage is the difficulty of troubleshooting non-trivial issues, since you will have to dive into the generated JavaScript code.

This chapter is an introduction to isomorphic web development. We will cover some of the key building blocks of GopherJS, and how you can make use of it to write code that can interact with both web browsers and Node.js modules. We will also cover how to write a simple React application powered by GopherJS, and some open source projects.

In this chapter, we will cover the following topics:

- GopherJS fundamentals
- GopherJS with React

Technical requirements

To follow along with this chapter, you will need the following tools:

- The Go language installed (https://golang.org/doc/install)
- Node.js and npm (https://nodejs.org/en/)
- A code editor, such as VS Code (https://code.visualstudio.com/)

The chapter assumes familiarity with JavaScript, HTML, React, and Go.

If you are not yet familiar with React, please have a look at Chapter 3, *Go Concurrency*, and Chapter 4, *Frontend with React.js*.

The code for this chapter can be found at https://github.com/PacktPublishing/Hands-On-Full-Stack-Development-with-Go.

GopherJS fundamentals

GopherJS is a set of tools, data types, and Go packages that allows you to compile Go code to JavaScript. Compiling the code of one programming language to another is also known as **transpiling**. GopherJS is very useful for Go developers who are not very proficient in JavaScript, because it allows you to write code in Go that can be integrated with JavaScript modules. This means that you can write code in Go that empowers the frontend of your application, or can be integrated with Node.js modules, offering you the flexibility of JavaScript combined with the power of Go.

GopherJS is a very a powerful piece of software that is used in numerous applications. However, in order to effectively utilize GopherJS, you need to understand its building blocks. The first step is to retrieve the package using the go get command:

```
go get -u github.com/gopherjs/gopherjs
```

Also, to be able to run some of GopherJS commands, we need to install the source-map-support node module:

```
npm install --global source-map-support
```

This allows you to debug your code from Go when the need arises. This is very useful when writing non-trivial applications in GopherJS.

Great, now we are ready to explore the package a bit more. GopherJS provides a playground where you can test your GopherJS code at `https://gopherjs.github.io/playground/`.

Now that our GopherJS is set up, let's take a look at the GopherJS types.

GopherJS types

GopherJS includes a sub-package called `js`. This package provides the functionalities needed to bridge between Go and JavaScript. The package can be found at `https://godoc.org/github.com/gopherjs/gopherjs/js`.

The key feature provided by the `js` package is the ability to transform Go types into JavaScript types, and vice versa.

When we consider data types, there are two main categories that need to be supported: basic types (`int`, `float`, and `string`) and constructed types (structs and interfaces). The following table shows the type mappings between Go basic types and JavaScript types, as supported by GopherJS:

Go type	JavaScript type
`bool`	`Boolean`
`int` and `float`	`Number`
`string`	`String`
`[]int8`	`Int8Array`
`[]int16`	`Int16Array`
`[]int32, []int`	`Int32Array`
`[]uint8`	`Uint8Array`
`[]uint16`	`Uint16Array`
`[]uint32, []uint`	`Uint32Array`
`[]float32`	`Float32Array`
`[]float64`	`Float64Array`

For example, if you utilize GopherJS to compile a piece of code that includes a Go `int` type into JavaScript, the `int` type will become a JavaScript `Number` type. It is recommended that you stick with the `int` type, instead of the `uint8`/`uint16`/`uint32`/`uint64` types, to improve performance of your transpiled code. It is also recommended to use `float64` over `float32`.

Now that we know the different GopherJS types, let's move on to object types.

Object types

Basic types are good; however, they are just a simple component of any real piece of code. What about Go structs, interfaces, methods, functions, and goroutines? The `js` package gives you the power to convert those types to JavaScript.

One of the key building blocks provided by the `js` package is the `*js.Object` type. This type is simply a container for a native JavaScript object. Most of GopherJS's code involves converting Go objects to `*js.Object` or vice versa. JavaScript modules are exposed as `*js.Object` in our Go code.

Now, let's explore how to call JavaScript functions from our Go code in the next section.

Calling JavaScript functions from your Go code

Typically, JavaScript code runs either on Node.js or in the browser. Any code that runs on Node.js should have access to what is known as *Node.js global objects* (`https://nodejs.org/api/globals.html`). If your code ends up running on a Node.js environment, GopherJS gives you access to the global objects using the `js.Global` variable, which returns a `*js.Object` that hosts your global variables. You can then access a specific object using a method called `Get`, then call the object methods using a method called `Call`. Let's see an example to better explain this paragraph.

Run the following code:

```
package main

import (
  "github.com/gopherjs/gopherjs/js"
)

func main() {
  //the console variable is of type *js.Object
  console := js.Global.Get("console")
  /*
    the *js.Object support a method called Call which     can access the
  methods of console.
  */
  console.Call("log", "Hello world!!")
}
```

This will be the equivalent of writing a piece of Node.js JavaScript code that looks like this:

```
console.log("Hello World!!");
```

The js.Global object opens up very interesting possibilities, as it allows you to access Node.js modules and use them in your Go code. For example, let's assume we imported a Node.js module called prettyjson to our node project, and we would like to use it in our Go code. prettyjson is a real package, it has a method called render(), which converts objects to beautiful-looking JSON. This is shown in the following code:

```
package main

import (
  "fmt"

  "github.com/gopherjs/gopherjs/js"
)

func main() {
  //Some data type
  type MyType struct {
    Name string
    Projects []string
  }
  //A value from our data type
  value := MyType{Name: "mina", Projects: []string{"GopherJS", "ReactJS"}}
  /*
    Call the prettyjson module, this is equivalent to the following code in
JavaScript:
        var prettyjson = require("prettyjson");
  */
  prettyjson := js.Global.Call("require", "prettyjson")

  // The line below is equivalent to 'prettyjson.render(value);' in
JavaScript
  result := prettyjson.Call("render", value)
  /*
    Do something with result
    */
}
```

As mentioned, JavaScript code can also run on a browser. The globals available to the browser are different. For example, the following piece of code will run fine on a browser, but won't be happy if you try to run it with Node.js:

```
package main

import (
  "github.com/gopherjs/gopherjs/js"
)
```

```
func main() {
  document := js.Global.Get("document")
  document.Call("write", "Hello world!!")
}
```

That is because `"document"` is a global object available for almost all browsers.

In the next section, we will take a look at the GopherJS commands.

GopherJS commands

We now have enough knowledge to start exploring the commands provided by GopherJS in order to compile Go code into JavaScript. For any GopherJS command you run, make sure the GOOS flag is set to either `darwin` or `linux`. If you are running on Windows, you'll need to run the following command from the Terminal session expected to run GopherJS's commands:

set GOOS=linux

Here is what we need to do next—let's start by getting an environment ready. After installing GopherJS and the `source-map-support` module, as covered earlier in *GopherJS fundamentals* section, create a new folder inside your Go `src` folder that is in your GOPATH. Let's name the new folder 9-Isomorphic-GO. Inside the new folder, create another folder called `node`. This is where we'll write our code that is expecting to interface with node packages.

Now create a file called `main.go` inside the `node` folder. Then type the following code into the file:

```
package main

import (
  "github.com/gopherjs/gopherjs/js"
)

func main() {
  console := js.Global.Get("console")
  console.Call("log", "Hello world!!")
}
```

The next step is to use the power of GopherJS to convert the preceding code into JavaScript. This can simply be done using the `gopherjs build` command. So in the console, navigate to the `node` folder, then type the following:

```
gopherjs build main.go
```

This will create a new file called `main.js`, which will host your converted JavaScript code. You will notice that the `main.js` file has a lot of JavaScript code. This is because GopherJS re-implements key pieces of Go runtime in the generated JavaScript file, in order to be able to support a large number of Go apps and packages.

Like any other Node.js file, you can simply run JavaScript code in the new file by typing the following:

```
node main.js
```

GopherJS also supports the `install` command. Run the following command:

```
gopherjs install
```

Doing so will produce a JavaScript file in your `bin` folder. This is similar to what the `go install` command would do, except that the result in this case is a JavaScript file, not an executable file.

The GopherJS commands support a flag that allows us to output minified JavaScript, this flag is `-m`. Minifying JavaScript involves removing all unnecessary characters, such as white spaces, new line characters, and comments.

If you would like to run the code directly, and you already have Node.js's `source-map-support` module installed, you can simply use the `gopherjs run` command, so it would look like this:

```
gopherjs run main.go
```

What if we want to try some browser code?

Let's go back to the parent folder we created, it was called `9-Isomorphic-GO`. Under that folder, create a new folder called `browser`, then underneath, create a new file called `main.go`. Inside the `main.go` file, write the following code:

```
package main

import (
  "github.com/gopherjs/gopherjs/js"
```

```
)

func main() {
  document := js.Global.Get("document")
  document.Call("write", "Hello world!!")
}
```

The preceding code is obviously expected to run on the browser, since it makes use of the document object. We can still utilize gopherjs build here in order to convert it into JavaScript. However, we have another option.

Run the following command at the browser folder:

gopherjs serve

A web server will be started, which, by default, will serve your generated files at the localhost:8080 address. Any changes you make to the main.go file will be reflected in the web-served page; however, you will probably need to refresh the web page to see changes.

If your Go code exists in a subfolder from where you run the gopherjs serve command, your page will get served at localhost:8080/your/sub/folder, where your/sub/folder refers to the folder path to your main.go file. So for example, if your code is at /test/main.go, your page will get served at localhost:8080/test.

Now, let's discover the bindings between Go and JavaScript that GopherJS provides to us.

Go bindings

So far, we've looked at how to embed JavaScript packages into our Go code through GopherJS. However, that can get tedious, especially since there are lots of shared functionalities between JavaScript and Go packages. Luckily, GopherJS supports the conversion of most of Go's standard packages into JavaScript. The list of compatible Go packages can be found at https://github.com/gopherjs/gopherjs/blob/master/doc/packages.md.

Some of the packages, such as the os package, are only supported in Node.js environments. This is because most of the package operations are not meant for the browser.

For example, if you look at the list of compatible Go packages, you'll find the `encoding/csv`, `fmt`, and `string` packages as some of the supported packages. Let's write the following program in Go:

```go
package main

import (
  "encoding/csv"
  "fmt"
  "strings"
)

func main() {
  //sample csv data
  data :=
"item11,item12,item13\nitem21,item22,item23\nitem31,item32,item33\n"
  //create a new csv reader
  csvReader := csv.NewReader(strings.NewReader(data))
  i := 0
  for {
    row, err := csvReader.Read()
    if err != nil {
      break
    }
    i++
    fmt.Println("Line", i, "of CSV data:", row)
  }
}
```

The preceding code will produce the following output:

```
Line 1 of CSV data: [item11 item12 item13]
Line 2 of CSV data: [item21 item22 item23]
Line 3 of CSV data: [item31 item32 item33]
```

If the code is compiled with GopherJS, it will generate a JavaScript file that will produce the same result. This is a very powerful feature in GopherJS, as we didn't even need to import GopherJS packages in this project to make it compatible with JavaScript.

Let's see how to export JavaScript modules from Go code in the next section.

Exporting code

When working with GopherJS, an interesting use case is writing code modules in Go that are then expected to be used by JavaScript module.

Before we explore how to export JavaScript modules that originated from Go code, let's go through some vanilla JavaScript code in order to gain a simple understanding of how module exporting works in the language.

Inside our `node` folder, create a new folder called `calc`. In that folder, we'll write a simple JavaScript module that will allow us to add and/or subtract some numbers.

Inside the `calc` folder, create a file called `addsub.js`. There, we'll create two functions, `add()` and `sub()`:

```
function add(i,j){
    return i+j;
}

function sub(i,j){
    return i-j;
}
```

The next step needed is to export these two functions so that other JavaScript modules can make calls to them. This is done by assigning the two functions to `modules.exports`:

```
module.exports={
    Add: add,
    Sub: sub
}
```

The preceding code will expose the two functions as `Add()` and `Sub()`, so that they can be imported and called by other JavaScript files.

Let's create a new file called `calc.js`. This is where we'll call the exported functions from the `addsub.js` file. To access the exported functions from `addsub.js`, we just need to execute the following code:

```
var calc = require('./addsub.js');
```

We can then very simply execute our exported functions like this:

```
//Call Add() then save result in the add variable
var add = calc.Add(2,3);

//Call Sub() then save result in the sub variable
var sub = calc.Sub(5,2);
```

We can then print the output like this:

```
console.log(add);
console.log(sub);
```

Now, how can we write an equivalent code to the `addsub.js` module in Go?

It's simple—we start by writing our functions in Go. Let's create a new file called `addsubgo.go`, and in there, write the following code:

```
package main

import (
  "github.com/gopherjs/gopherjs/js"
)

//The Add function
func Add(i, j int) int {
 return i + j
}

//The Sub function
func Sub(i, j int) int {
 return i - j
}
```

Now, in Go's main function, we'll utilize a variable provided by GopherJS, which is called `js.Module`. This variable gives you access to the `module` variable set by Node.js. Let's type the following code:

```
js.Module.Get("exports")
```

It will be equivalent to `module.exports` in the JavaScript code.

As with most of GopherJS's variables, `js.Module` is of the `*js.Object` type, which basically means that we can call `Get` or `Set` on it to get or set objects. Consider the following code in Go:

```
exports := js.Module.Get("exports")
exports.Set("Add", Add)
exports.Set("Sub", Sub)
```

It is equivalent to the following code in JavaScript:

```
module.exports={
    Add: add,
    Sub: sub
}
```

And that is the key piece of knowledge you need to write exportable JavaScript code in Go through GopherJS. Here is how the whole Go file would look:

```
package main

import (
 "github.com/gopherjs/gopherjs/js"
)

func main() {
 exports := js.Module.Get("exports")
 exports.Set("Add", Add)
 exports.Set("Sub", Sub)
}

func Add(i, j int) int {
 return i + j
}

func Sub(i, j int) int {
 return i - j
}
```

We then need to build the preceding code through GopherJS in order to compile it into JavaScript:

```
gopherjs build addsubgo.go
```

This will generate a new file called addsubgo.js, which we can now import or use with other JavaScript files. If we go back to calc.js, we can change it a bit to look like this:

```
//We import the compiled JavaScript file here
var calc = require('./addsubgo.js');

//Call Add() then save result in the add variable
var add = calc.Add(2,3);

//Call Sub() then save result in the sub variable
var sub = calc.Sub(5,2);

console.log(add);
console.log(sub);
```

The preceding code will produce the same result we expect.

What if we want to write a function that expects an object or a number of objects as arguments? Take this one, for example:

```
function formatnumbers(Obj){
    return "First number: " + Obj.first + " second number: " + Obj.second;
}
```

This is a very simple function that takes an object as an argument. It then returns a `string`, which includes the object fields. The object expects to contain two fields: `first` and `second`. When this function gets called, we will need to pass an object as an argument to it. Here is how calling the function looks:

```
//Call FormatWords then save the result in the fw variable
var fw = calc.FormatNumbers({
    first: 10,
    second: 20,
});
```

Writing the equivalent code in Go is very easy, thanks to GopherJS.

Since Go is a statically-typed programming language, first we need to define the data type of our object argument. Let's continue to write code in the `addsubgo.go` file. Here is how this looks in Go:

```
type Obj struct {
  /*
For any struct type expected to be processed by GopherJS, we need to embed
the *js.Object type to it, like below:
*/

  *js.Object

/*
  We then define the fields of our object
*/
  First int `js:"first"` //struct tag represents the field name in
JavaScript
  Second int `js:"second"` //struct tag represents the field name in
JavaScript
}
```

The `struct` type was built with two rules in mind:

- Embed the `*js.Object` type in the Go struct
- Assign the `js` struct tag for any field name expected to be converted to JavaScript

Perfect—the next step is to write our function in Go:

```go
func FormatNumbers(o Obj) string {
    return fmt.Sprintf("First number: %d second number: %d", o.First,
o.Second)
}
```

This function will be capable of translating to JavaScript using GopherJS, thanks to the fact that we followed the two rules when creating the `Obj` type.

Next, we export the `FormatNumbers()` function:

```go
func main() {
    exports := js.Module.Get("exports")
    exports.Set("Add", Add)
    exports.Set("Sub", Sub)
    //Make the FormatNumbers function exportable as a JavaScript module
    exports.Set("FormatNumbers", FormatNumbers)
}
```

Once we build this code using the `gopherjs build addsubgo.go` command, our new function will callable from JavaScript modules.

Now that we know how to export our code, let's take a look at Go methods and goroutines in the next section.

Go Methods

What if we want to expose a Go type with methods to JavaScript?

Let's explore a Go type. The following code has a `struct` type that represents a musical instrument, and has some `getter` and `setter` methods:

```go
type MI struct {
    MIType string
    Price float64
    Color string
    Age int
}

func (mi *MI) SetMIType(s string) {
    mi.MIType = s
}

func (mi *MI) GetMIType() string {
    return mi.MIType
```

```
}

func (mi *MI) SetPrice(f float64) {
  mi.Price = f
}

func (mi *MI) GetPrice() float64 {
  return mi.Price
}

func (mi *MI) SetColor(c string) {
  mi.Color = c
}

func (mi *MI) GetColor() string {
  return mi.Color
}

func (mi *MI) SetAge(a int) {
  mi.Age = a
}

func (mi *MI) GetAge() int {
  return mi.Age
}
```

Let's say we want this type to be accessible to JavaScript code. GopherJS comes to the rescue with a function called `js.MakeWrapper()`. This function can take a Go type as an argument, and it then returns a `*js.Object` that represents the Go type with all its exportable methods.

Create a constructor for our `MI` `struct` type. It will look like this:

```
func New() *js.Object {
  return js.MakeWrapper(&MI{})
}
```

In our `main` function, we can make this constructor available to JavaScript by adding it to the `Global` object:

```
func main() {
  //musicalInstruments is the namespace, 'New' is the available function
  js.Global.Set("musicalInstruments", map[string]interface{}{
    "New": New,
  })
}
```

The preceding code will create a JavaScript function called `New()`, under a namespace called `musicalInstruments`.

We could have made the `New()` constructor available through a module export, through the `js.Module` variable. But for simplicity, it's added to the `Global` object for now.

Let's assume that the filename where this code is hosted is called `mi.go`. The GopherJS command to compile this code to JavaScript will look like this:

```
gopherjs build mi.go
```

A new file called `mi.js` will get generated, JavaScript can simply access the `MI struct` type by importing the file, then call the `New()` function from the `musicalinstruments` namespace:

```
require("./mi.js");

var mi = musicalInstruments.New();

mi.SetAge(20);

console.log(mi.GetAge());
```

This will create a new musical instrument object. We can then set its age. Finally, we get the age and log it to the standard output.

Goroutines

GopherJS supports goroutines, so you can use goroutines in your Go code, and GopherJS will take care of the rest.

One important requirement is that goroutines must be used if you need to call some blocking code from an external JavaScript.

For example, consider the following JavaScript code running in the browser:

```
document.getElementById("myBtn").addEventListener("click", function(){
    /*SOME BLOCKING CODE*/
});
```

The preceding code defines a callback function that is expected to execute when a button is clicked.

Here is how this should be handled in Go with the help of GopherJS:

```
js.Global.Get("document").Call("getElementById",
"mybtn").Call("addEventListener","call", func() {
  go func() {
        /*SOME BLOCKING CODE*/
  }()
})
```

As shown in the preceding code snippet, we had to use a goroutine inside the event listener callback code, because it was expected to run some blocking code.

Now that we know the fundamentals of GopherJS, let's use GopherJS with React.

GopherJS with React

Previously in `Chapter 4`, *Frontend with React.js*, we covered the powerful and popular React.js framework. Due to the power of GopherJS, there are now several open source projects that allow you to write React applications in Go. In this chapter, we'll cover one of these open source projects with the aid of an example, to offer us an idea about how to build a practical React application using Go.

The project

In this chapter, we'll build a very simple interactive web app using React. The app contains an input text and a button:

Whenever we type a name and then hit **Submit**, it gets added to a list on the screen, with the word **Hello** next to it:

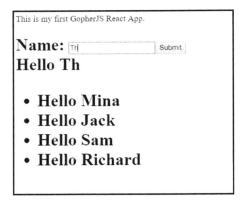

The text input is interactive. So, as you type text, it will display on the screen in real time. This is the kind of reactivity that React is known for.

Let's take a look at the project architecture in the next section.

The project application's architecture

The React application we are about to implement is simple, so we will not need more than one component. Our single component will include the input text, the **Submit** button, the interactive text, and the list of names. Here is our component:

In order to cover all the key React concepts in this section, our component will make use of React elements, state, props, and forms.

The form will consist of the input text and the **Submit** button:

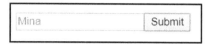

Our React `state` object will host two values:

- The current name being written
- The list of names:

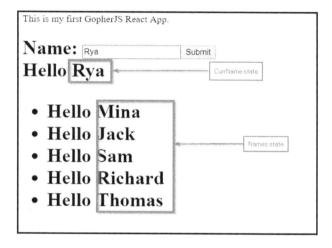

The prop value for our component will be the generic message that shows up next to the displayed name. In other words, our prop is the word **Hello**:

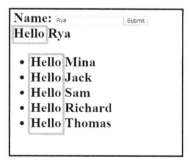

Let's go ahead and build this React application in Go in the next section.

Building the React application in Go

Now it's time to start writing our React application in Go. We will make use of a popular package known as myitcv.io/react. This package offers some GopherJS bindings for the React framework. The package documentation can be found at https://github.com/myitcv/x/tree/master/react.

The first thing we need to do is retrieve the myitcv.io/react package, in order to use it in our code:

```
go get -u myitcv.io/react
```

Retrieve a tool called reactGen, this tool facilitates building React applications in Go. It can be used to auto-build skeleton applications that act as building blocks for more complex applications:

```
go get -u myitcv.io/react myitcv.io/react/cmd/reactGen
```

Open a Terminal window, then navigate to the reactGen folder:

```
//In windows:
cd %GOPATH%\src\myitcv.io\react\cmd\reactGen

//or in other operating systems:
cd $GOPATH\src\myitcv.io\react\cmd\reactGen
```

Type the go install command. This should compile and deploy the reactGen tool to the %GOPATH%\bin folder. Make sure that path is present in your PATH environmental variable.

Type the following command to inspect whether reactGen is installed yet:

```
reactGen -help
```

Once reactGen is installed, we are ready to write our application. Go to the 9-Isomorphic-Go folder. Inside, we'll create a new folder called reactproject. In the Terminal, navigate to the reactproject folder, then type the following command:

```
reactGen -init minimal
```

This will create a skeleton for our React application. Let's explore the generated app—there are four files inside:

- `main.go`: The entry point for our app.
- `index.html`: The entry HTML file for our app.
- `app.go`: The App component of our React application—this will be the first component to get rendered in our application.
- `gen_App_reactGen.go`: This file is auto-generated from `app.go`. For any component we write, some auto-generated code will get created afterward, which will contain all the plumbing code needed to make our component work. This code generation allows us to focus only on building the important pieces in our React components, such as props, states, and elements.

Before we start writing our React component, let's explore the App component that we created in the `app.go` file, with the `reactGen` tool:

```
// Template generated by reactGen

package main

import (
  "myitcv.io/react"
)

type AppDef struct {
  react.ComponentDef
}

func App() *AppElem {
  return buildAppElem()
}

func (a AppDef) Render() react.Element {
  return react.Div(nil,
    react.H1(nil,
      react.S("Hello World"),
    ),
    react.P(nil,
      react.S("This is my first GopherJS React App."),
    ),
  )
}
```

The preceding code creates a Go struct called `AppDef`, which acts as a React component. In order for a Go `struct` type to qualify as a React component, it needs to satisfy three requirements:

- The Go struct name must have the `Def` suffix.
- The Go struct has to embed the `react.ComponentDef` type.
- The `struct` type must implement the `Render()` method, which acts as the equivalent of the React's `render()` method.

Similar to React.js, the `Render()` method has to return React elements. The `myitcv.io/react` framework offers methods that correspond to React elements. From the preceding code, we see that `Render()` returns the following:

```
react.Div(nil,
    react.H1(nil,
      react.S("Hello World"),
    ),
    react.P(nil,
      react.S("This is my first GopherJS React App."),
    ),
  )
```

The preceding code corresponds to the following React JSX:

```
<div>
    <h1>Hello World</h1>
    <p>This is my first GopherJS React App.</p>
</div>
```

Each one of the JSX elements corresponds to a `react.<element type>` function in Go. There were a total of three elements. The first is the `<div>` element, which hosted the other two elements. In Go, this translated to `react.Div(nil, ...other_elements)`. The first argument is our element's props. Since we didn't include any props, the first argument ended up being `nil`. If we needed to add a React prop—let's say, the `className` prop—it can simply be done like this:

```
react.Div(&react.DivProps{
    ClassName:"css_class_name"
  },...other_elements)
```

The second element is the h1 element. In Go, we represented it as `react.H1(nil,react.S("Hello World"))`. The first argument represents props passed to the element. The `react.S("")` function simply represents a string.

The third element is the P element. In Go, it looked like this:

```
react.P(nil, react.S("This is my first GopherJS React App."))
```

Now, let's see this code in action. Set the GOOS environmental variable to linux if you're using Windows:

set GOOS=linux

From our reactproject folder, run the following command in the Terminal:

gopherjs serve

This will serve our React application on port 8080. If we open a web browser and visit localhost:8080/<the Go project folder from src>, we'll be greeted with this simple application:

Now, we are ready to build our custom component, which we will do in the next section.

Building a custom component

Under the reactproject folder, create a new folder called hello_message. Inside the folder, we'll create a new file called hello_message.go. In the file, we will call the hellomessage package:

```
package hellomessage
```

We then create a Go struct to represent our React component:

```
import "myitcv.io/react"
type HelloMessageDef struct {
  react.ComponentDef
}
```

Now, it's time to define our props. This can simply be done by a `struct` type that contains our expected props. As mentioned, our prop is the message string:

```
//Naming convention is *props
type HelloMessageProps struct {
  Message string
}
```

Defining a `state` object is very similar to props. A `struct` type needs to be created with the expected React `state` object fields. Our `state` object fields are the current name being written to the text input, as well as the list of names written so far:

```
//Naming convention is *State
type HelloMessageState struct {
  CurrName string
  Names []string
}
```

As mentioned in Chapter 4, *Frontend with React.js*, the React framework makes a decision to re-render your component whenever React detects that the `state` object has changed. Since our `state` object here contains a Go slice, future and current states cannot simply be compared using an == operator. In this case, it's strongly recommended to provide React with a way to decide whether the React object has changed. This is done using the `Equals` method, which is implemented by the `state` Go struct. Here is how this looks:

```
func (c HelloMessageState) Equals(v HelloMessageState) bool {
  //compare CurrName between current and future states
  if c.CurrName != v.CurrName {
    return false
  }
  //compare Names between current and future states
  /*there are other ways to compare slices, below is a very simplistic
approach*/
  if len(c.Names) != len(v.Names) {
    return false
  }

  for i := range v.Names {
    if v.Names[i] != c.Names[i] {
      return false
    }
  }
  return true
}
```

At this point, we need to run the `go generate` command from the Terminal to generate some helper code that we can use to write the rest of our component. After you run the `go generate` command, you will notice that a new file, called `gen_HelloMessage_reactGen.go`, was generated for us. Do not edit this file.

The generated file will provide a new data type for you to use: `*HelloMessageElem`. This type represents our component's React element.

Let's go back to our code inside `hello_message.go`, the next step is to write a constructor for our new React component. The constructor will need to take props as an argument, and returns the React element as a result. Here is how this will look:

```
func HelloMessage(p HelloMessageProps) *HelloMessageElem {
  fmt.Println("Building element...")
  return buildHelloMessageElem(p)
}
```

Since our code gets compiled to JavaScript through GopherJS, the `fmt.Println()` function will get translated to `console.log()`, as covered in the *Go bindings* section.

Next, we need to define the `Render()` method of our component. The `Render()` method needs to be defined in a non-pointer type of our component Go struct. Here is an empty `Render()` method:

```
func (r HelloMessageDef) Render() react.Element {
    return nil
}
```

We now have to fill up the `Render()` method with the following:

- A form that includes an input text box, and a **Submit** button
- A string to host the name currently being written
- A list of strings to represent a history of the names entered

As a refresher, have a look at the following diagram:

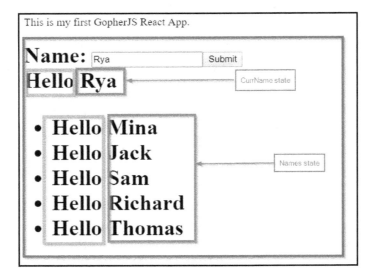

The red rectangles represent our React states, the green rectangles represent our props, and the blue rectangle represents our entire React component.

Going back to our `Render()` method, first, we need to write the text input element. It's an HTML form input element of the `"text"` type. Here is how this looks:

```
InputName := react.Input(&react.InputProps{
    Type: "text",
    Key: "FirstName",
    Placeholder: "Mina",
    Value: r.State().CurrName,
    OnChange: r,
}, nil)
```

The preceding code represents a React `input` element, courtesy of the `myitcv.io/react` package. The first argument is the props for the input element; the second argument is `nil`, because we don't need any children for this element. The input props are the same as the ones we used in the JSX format. There are two notable props that we used here:

```
Value: r.State().CurrName,
OnChange: r,
```

The `Value` prop is the current value of the input text. By assigning the `State` object of the `CurrName` field to the input text `Value` field, we've guaranteed that the input text will change based on the name you enter.

The `OnChange` prop represents the action taken whenever a change happens to our input text. The prop must point to a type that implements the `OnChange(event)` method. Since we assign `r` to it, we must implement `OnChange`. Here is how this will look:

```
func (r HelloMessageDef) OnChange(e *react.SyntheticEvent) {
    //we need to import "honnef.co/go/js/dom" for this to work
    //get target: our input text HTML element
    target := e.Target().(*dom.HTMLInputElement)
    //get current state
    currState := r.State()
    //change state to include new value in our input text component, as well
as the existing history of names
    r.SetState(HelloMessageState{CurrName: target.Value, Names:
currState.Names})
}
```

The preceding code is self-explanatory:

- The Go React framework provides a type called `*react.SyntheticEvent`, which represents the event getting passed to the `OnChange` method.
- We retrieve the value of the text being written to the input text.
- We retrieve our current React state. This is done using the `State()` method.
- We change our React state to represent the new name. This is done using the `SetState()` method.

Now, let's go back to our `Render()` method. The next step is to write the **Submit** button component. It is also an HTML form input element, but it's of the `"Submit"` type. An HTML form input element of the `"Submit"` type is a button. Whenever the **Submit** button gets pressed, the form will get submitted:

```
InputBtn := react.Input(&react.InputProps{
    Type: "Submit",
    Value: "Submit",
}, nil)
```

Next, we need to write our React form. The form element will act as a parent element for both the text and the button elements. Our form element will also host a `"Name:"` string.

As mentioned earlier, whenever the **Submit** button gets pressed, the form will be submitted. Typically, when an HTML form gets submitted, its input data is sent to the server, where the form's input data gets processed. In our case, we want to capture the submission event, and then instead of the form submission's default behavior, we want to change our `state` object to add the new input name to our `state.Names` list.

Before we delve more into how to define the actions taken on form submission, let's go back to the `render` method, and define our form:

```
Form := react.Form(&react.FormProps{
    OnSubmit: r,
},
    react.S("Name: "),
    InputName,
    InputBtn)
```

Notice that we defined an `OnSubmit` React form prop. This is how we define the actions taken on form submission in our Go code. The data type we pass to the `OnSubmit` prop must implement a method with the `OnSubmit(*react.SyntheticEvent)` signature. Let's implement this method in our code:

```
func (r HelloMessageDef) OnSubmit(e *react.SyntheticEvent) {
    //Prevent the default form submission action
    e.PreventDefault()
    //Add the new name to the list of names in the state object
    names := r.State().Names
    names = append(names, r.State().CurrName)
    /*
        Change the state so that the current name is now empty, and the new
    name gets added to the existing list of names
    */
    r.SetState(HelloMessageState{CurrName: "", Names: names})
}
```

Perfect—now we just need to finish the `Render()` method. Here are the remaining tasks for our custom form's `Render()` method:

- Get the list of saved names in our `state` object.
- For each saved name in the list, convert it to an `Li` element. This is a form list element.

- Return a `Div` object, which contains the following:
    - The defined form
    - A string with the prop message, combined with the current name saved in the `state` object
    - The list of existing names

Here is how the rest of the code will look:

```
names := r.State().Names
fmt.Println(names)
entries := make([]react.RendersLi, len(names))
for i, name := range names {
  entries[i] = react.Li(nil, react.S(r.Props().Message+" "+name))
  }
 return react.Div(nil,
    Form,
    react.S(r.Props().Message+" "+r.State().CurrName),
    react.Ul(nil, entries...),
  )
```

And here is the entire `Render()` method:

```
func (r HelloMessageDef) Render() react.Element {
  InputName := react.Input(&react.InputProps{
    Type: "text",
    Key: "FirstName",
    Placeholder: "Mina",
    Value: r.State().CurrName,
    OnChange: r,
  }, nil)
  InputBtn := react.Input(&react.InputProps{
    Type: "Submit",
    Value: "Submit",
  }, nil)
  Form := react.Form(&react.FormProps{
    OnSubmit: r,
  },
    react.S("Name: "),
    InputName,
    InputBtn)
  names := r.State().Names
  fmt.Println(names)
  entries := make([]react.RendersLi, len(names))
  for i, name := range names {
    entries[i] = react.Li(nil, react.S(r.Props().Message+" "+name))
  }
  return react.Div(nil,
```

```
        Form,
        react.S(r.Props().Message+" "+r.State().CurrName),
        react.Ul(nil, entries...),
    )
}
```

Now, we can run `go generate`.

Our component is done; however, there is still some work left. We need to call our newly-created component from the `App` component, located in the `app.go` file. This will be done using the `HelloMessage(p HelloMessageProps) *HelloMessageElem` constructor, which we created before. The constructor takes the props as an argument and returns our custom component React element. The code we need to modify is under the `Render()` method of our `App` component. The prop object contains a field called `Message`. The value of the message we would like to pass is simply `"Hello"`:

```
func (a AppDef) Render() react.Element {
    /*
        Return a react div that hosts a title, as well as our custom hello
    message component
    */
    return react.Div(nil,
        react.P(nil,
            react.S("This is my first GopherJS React App."),
        ),
        react.H1(nil,
            hellomessage.HelloMessage(hellomessage.HelloMessageProps{Message:
    "Hello"}),
        ),
    )
}
```

That's it for our code. If you run the `gopherjs serve` command from your Terminal at the `reactproject` folder, the project will be accessible in the browser at the `localhost:8080/<your project folder from src>` address.

When you are ready to transpile your React project to JavaScript, simply run the `gopherjs build` command from the `reactproject` folder. This will generate a `reactproject.js` file that can be used from the `index.html` file in your project folder. If you look at the `index.html` file in your project folder, you will find that it references a script called `reactproject.js`. If you open `index.html` from a browser after performing the build step, you will find your application working as expected.

Summary

In this chapter, we focused on building isomorphic applications using Go. We covered some key topics regarding converting Go code into JavaScript code. We dove into Go bindings in GopherJS, and considered how it can empower us to bridge the two languages.

We also made use of the GopherJS framework to build Go applications that integrate with JavaScript, whether at the frontend or on the server side. We explored important topics, such as concurrency and methods.

We also covered the Go React framework, and went through the process of building a simple React application in Go.

In the next chapter, we'll cover topics such as cloud-native applications and the React Native framework so that you can further hone your skills.

Questions

1. What does transpling mean?
2. What is GopherJS?
3. What is the `*js.Object` type?
4. What is the `js.Global` variable?
5. What is the `js.Module` variable?
6. What does the `js.MakeWrapper()` function do?
7. What does the `js` Go struct tag do?
8. What are the main steps to build a React component in Go?

Further reading

For more information, check out the following links:

- **GopherJS**: https://github.com/gopherjs/gopherjs
- **GopherJS with React**: https://github.com/myitcv/x/tree/master/react/_doc
- **Creating a GopherJS React app**: https://github.com/myitcv/x/blob/master/react/_doc/creating_app.md
- **GopherJS React examples**: https://blog.myitcv.io/gopherjs_examples_sites/examplesshowcase/

10
Where to Go from Here?

Welcome to the final chapter of our book. In this book, we covered many practical topics on how to develop full stack web software with the powerful Go language. In this chapter, we'll shed some light on topics the reader should explore to in order to enhance their skills and take their knowledge to the next level. We'll focus on two topics:

- Cloud-native applications
- The React Native framework

Cloud-native applications

Cloud-native applications are an important topic for people looking to take their applications to the point of being infinitely scalable to growing user needs and expanding data loads. **Cloud-native applications** can be defined as applications built to run on a distributed and scalable infrastructure. They are expected to always be available, reliable, capable of getting updates in real time, and not crumble under pressure. They typically rely on redundancy, load balancing, and various other techniques to achieve their objectives. The topic is not trivial by any measure. In fact, entire books have been dedicated to how to build cloud-native applications. In this section, we'll cover some key technologies utilized in the construction of cloud-native applications.

Cloud-native applications are not always deployed to a *cloud*, such as AWS or Azure. They could be deployed to an organization's internal infrastructure that supports scalability.

In the next sections. we'll take a look at microservices, container, serverless applications and continuous delivery which are some of the important concepts of cloud-native applications

Microservices

Microservice is a very popular concept in modern software. It's the idea of dividing your application's tasks into small self-contained software services. So, instead of having a large application that covers a wide array of tasks, you utilize a microservice for each task. Microservices allow your application to be very scalable.

The concept of microservice is the opposite of the concept of a monolithic application, which is the kind of application where all the tasks are coded together.

Here is an example of a monolithic application that represents an event booking application:

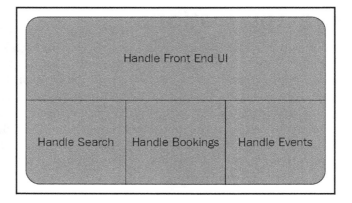

And here is how a microservice application represents the same event booking application:

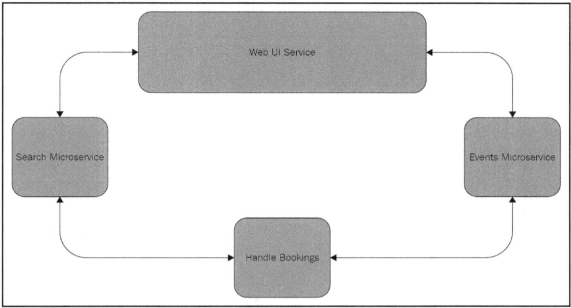

Each block in the preceding diagram represents a microservice that is tasked with one specific task.

You can spread your microservices over multiple server nodes, achieving load balancing on multiple systems. You can make your microservices redundant, so that if one service goes down, another one picks up the work as if nothing happened. This redundancy can also be very useful when deploying patches and updates to your application.

Here is an example diagram of our microservices now supporting redundancy to ensure the application will always be available. If one of the services goes down due to maintenance, or system crashes, the other service will take over:

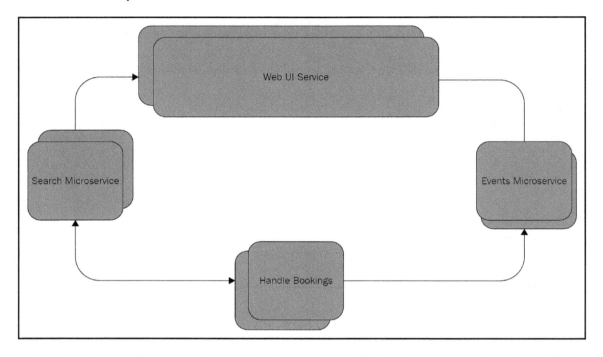

Even though microservices offer tons of scalability and flexibility in an application, they can be challenging to maintain in the long run, especially if your architecture grows to hundreds or thousands of microservices. Some special monitoring tools will be needed to ensure they are properly maintained and looked after.

In the next section, we'll discuss the concept of containers.

Containers

Containers technology is a relatively new technology. However, it has grown in popularity to the point that it has become a key piece of infrastructure software in the world of cloud-native applications. Containers allow you to surround your software with an isolated user space or a *container*.

Containers are very useful in deploying and running scalable microservices because they allow your microservices to run in an isolated space that contains all the microservice configurations, environmental variables, dependencies, runtimes, and any other files or settings needed for the service.

Containers allow software developers to deploy isolated services in the same server nodes, ensuring that your services are run unaffected by any other services on the same node. Containers also allow developers to deploy a microservice with everything the microservice needs to run in one go through a container image. Containers are not only used for microservices; they can also be used in any piece of software that can benefit from being in a container, such as database engines. For example, using a container image to deploy MySQL is a popular approach to deploying and running MySQL with relative ease. One of the most popular container technologies nowadays is Docker (`https://www.docker.com`).

Here is an example of some containers running on a server node:

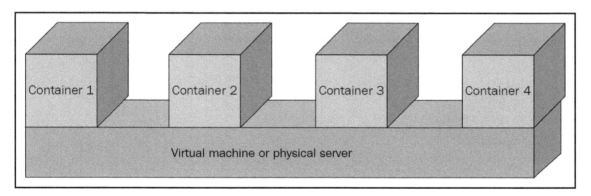

Let's take a look at serverless applications in the next section.

Serverless applications

Serverless applications are another relatively new technology in the world of cloud-native applications. They are mostly used for tasks that don't need to run continuously. To properly understand the concept of serverless applications, let's go through an example.

Consider Amazon's AWS Lambda service (`https://aws.amazon.com/lambda/`), which is utilized by numerous applications worldwide. In order to perform a specific task, the service allows users to request a function to run remotely. So, in other words, you ask AWS Lambda to run some code for you. After the code is executed, the output is returned to you. No stateful data is maintained. The code or function that runs on Lambda is provided by you.

Serverless applications make use of services such as AWS Lambda in order to run intermittent tasks that are not expected to run all the time. This provides scalability for your application, because it relieves the need to maintain software services just to execute temporary tasks. Services such as AWS Lambda are also known as **FaaS** (**function as a service**).

Here is an example application where some services are substituted by functions:

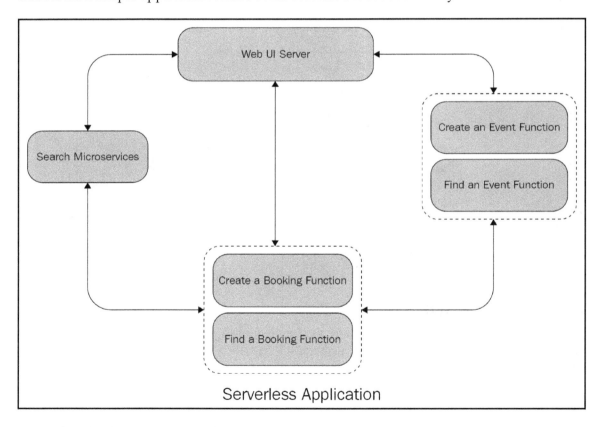

Let's take a look at continuous delivery in the next section.

Continuous delivery

Continuous delivery is the idea that software should be released in fast and short cycles, as opposed to longer and slow ones. Continuous delivery allows organizations to effectively and continuously improve their software by being able to release improvements and fixes all the time.

Continuous delivery is not just about using software tools; it also involves a way of thinking that the entire organization needs to adhere to. There needs to be a process where any additions to the software can be quickly built, tested, and deployed/delivered.

Continuous delivery proved to be very practical and effective for organizations running cloud-native applications because it allows incremental and fast improvements, as opposed to huge step changes that can break the software in production. It is important to automate the process as much as possible in order to gain the most benefits.

Let's take a glimpse at the popular React Native framework for building mobile apps in the next section.

React Native

In this book, we covered how to design and write a React app from the ground up. This is a very powerful skill in modern software. React is currently being used to power some of the most popular websites on the internet. Another powerful advantage of learning React.js is the fact that your skills could be utilized to build cross-platform mobile applications through React Native.

What is React Native?

React Native (`https://facebook.github.io/react-native/`) is an open source project developed by Facebook. It makes use of the features of the React.js framework to build cross-platform mobile applications that can run on Android or iOS. React Native is very popular, and is currently being used by organizations big and small to build practical mobile apps.

One major advantage of React Native is that almost all the code you write would work on both Android and iOS devices. This means that you only have to worry about a single code base for almost your entire application. Another major advantage is that React Native uses native APIs for the targeted platform. This is why mobile applications written in React Native tend to have better performance than applications written by other JavaScript mobile frameworks.

In the next section, we'll take a look at some of the differences between React.js and React Native.

React.js versus React Native

Even though both frameworks are named React, there are some differences between the two. Let's first cover the similarities, and then we'll go over some of the differences

Similarities between React.js and React Native

Here are some of the similarities between React.js and React Native:

- They both use JavaScript ES6
- They both rely on React components, involving the `render()` method
- They both rely on React elements
- They both use JSX to build visual elements

Differences between React.js and React Native

Here are some of the differences between React.js and React Native:

- React Native has its own special JSX syntax to build UI components. By default, it does not make use of CSS and HTML like React.js.
- React Native relies on some special libraries to interface with mobile devices. For example, you need to use React-Native-specific packages to write code around a phone camera or accelerometer.
- Deploying React Native apps is a different experience to deploying React.js, since the deployment into mobile device with all its app rules.

Expo

Expo (`https://expo.io/`) is a very popular free and open source toolchain that allows users to build React Native mobile applications with relative ease. It provides an SDK that exposes important features such as camera access, filesystems, and push notifications. Expo is the best place to start, when you are building React Native applications as a beginner.

Summary

In this chapter, we covered a number of very popular and modern technologies. Cloud-native applications are very popular nowadays, especially with the growing need to build reliable, scalable applications.

React Native is a key framework for building performant, cross-platform mobile applications. It makes use of the principles and architecture of the powerful React framework to achieve that.

We hope you enjoyed the learning journey with us in this book, we wish you all the best in building full stack applications in Go.

Questions

1. What are cloud-native applications?
2. Is it necessary to deploy cloud-native applications to the cloud?
3. What are microservices?
4. What are containers?
5. What is Docker?
6. What are serverless applications?
7. What is React Native?
8. What is Expo?

Other Books You May Enjoy

If you enjoyed this book, you may be interested in these other books by Packt:

Hands-On Software Architecture with Golang
Jyotiswarup Raiturkar

ISBN: 9781788622592

- Understand architectural paradigms and deep dive into Microservices
- Design parallelism/concurrency patterns and learn object-oriented design patterns in Go
- Explore API-driven systems architecture with introduction to REST and GraphQL standards
- Build event-driven architectures and make your architectures anti-fragile
- Engineer scalability and learn how to migrate to Go from other languages
- Get to grips with deployment considerations with CICD pipeline, cloud deployments, and so on
- Build an end-to-end e-commerce (travel) application backend in Go

Hands-On GUI Application Development in Go
Andrew Williams

ISBN: 9781789138412

- Understand the benefits and complexities of building native graphical applications
- Gain insights into how Go makes cross-platform graphical application development simple
- Build platform-native GUI applications using andlabs/ui
- Develop graphical Windows applications using Walk
- Create multiplatform GUI applications using Shiny, Nuklear, and Fyne
- Use Go wrappers for GTK and Qt for GUI application development
- Streamline your requirements to pick the correct toolkit strategy

Leave a review - let other readers know what you think

Please share your thoughts on this book with others by leaving a review on the site that you bought it from. If you purchased the book from Amazon, please leave us an honest review on this book's Amazon page. This is vital so that other potential readers can see and use your unbiased opinion to make purchasing decisions, we can understand what our customers think about our products, and our authors can see your feedback on the title that they have worked with Packt to create. It will only take a few minutes of your time, but is valuable to other potential customers, our authors, and Packt. Thank you!

Index

www.ingramcontent.com/pod-product-compliance
Lightning Source LLC
Chambersburg PA
CBHW080624060326
40690CB00021B/4803